Women and Law in Classical Greece

D1256644

Women and Law in Classical Greece

. . . .

RAPHAEL SEALEY

The University of North Carolina Press

Chapel Hill and London

© 1990 The University of North Carolina Press

All rights reserved

Library of Congress Cataloging-in-Publication Data

Sealey, Raphael.

Women and law in classical Greece / by Raphael Sealey.

p.   cm.

Bibliography: p.

Includes index.

ISBN 0-8078-1872-0 (alk. paper). — ISBN 0-8078-4262-1 (pbk. :
alk. paper)

1. Women—Legal status, laws, etc. (Greek law)   I. Title.

LAW ‹GREECE 7 Seal 1990›

346.3801′34—dc20

[343.806134]   89-16469

                                                          CIP

The paper in this book meets the guidelines for permanence and
durability of the Committee on Production Guidelines for Book
Longevity of the Council on Library Resources.

Design by April Leidig-Higgins

Printed in the United States of America

94 93 92 91 90   5 4 3 2 1

THIS BOOK WAS DIGITALLY MANUFACTURED.

To Dorte-Freyja Sealey

CONTENTS

PREFACE

In 1973 the first visit of the dedicand to California prompted me to pay attention to the women of ancient Greece. Since then my views have changed much. I reached my main conclusion, on the elements of homogeneity in Greek law of the family, only when most of my script had been written.

Discussion with several colleagues has helped me. I am especially indebted to D. Cohen for ideas on the law of adultery, and to J. K. Anderson for information and references on the boar's tusk helmet in Crete, on change in the coastline near Hisarlık, and on the defense of Sinope against Datames. Needless to say, this should not be taken to indicate their view on anything treated in this book. It is a pleasure to thank Lewis Bateman, of the University of North Carolina Press, and his two readers for sympathy and encouragement. They have saved me from several oversights. Translations in this book are my own, and dates are B.C. unless otherwise indicated.

The gentle reader is asked to note that "women and law" is not the same as "women in law." I do not restrict myself to women in law, for I think that I have something to say about law.

Berkeley, California
Advent 1988

Women and Law in Classical Greece

ONE

Introduction: Women in Greek Thought

.   .   .   .

He is a barbarian, and thinks that the customs of his tribe and island are the laws of nature.—Caesar in G. B. Shaw, *Caesar and Cleopatra*

Xerxes, the Great King, led his army and his fleet against European Greece in 480. After he had turned the pass of Thermopylai by a bold maneuver, most of the cities of central Greece yielded to him. They had little choice, for north of the isthmus of Corinth there was no longer any position where the Persian advance could be checked on land. But the Athenians responded differently to the Persian approach. They asked the Hellenic fleet, which was retiring from Artemision, to put in to Salamis, and Herodotos says:

> For the following reason the Athenians asked them to put in to Salamis, in order that they might evacuate their children and their wives from Attica, and also in order that they might deliberate about what they ought to do. (8.40.1)

Herodotos, that is, says that the Athenians wished to save "their children and their wives," although a rightly respected translator (G. Rawlinson) would make him say "their women and children."

Yet perhaps the reader of Herodotos will doubt whether the phrase "their children and their wives" reveals an order of value. If so, one has but to read on. After explaining what the Athenians had to deliberate about, the historian continues:

> The naval contingents of the other Greeks put in to Salamis, but the Athenians put in to their own territory. After their ar-

rival they issued a proclamation, that each of the Athenians should save his children and his slaves as best he could. Then most of the Athenians dispatched them to Troezen but some to Aigina and some to Salamis. (8.41.1)

Here Herodotos makes no explicit reference to the women. They could be understood, since he mentioned the children.

Forty-nine years later the Peloponnesians invaded Attica. The Athenians withdrew within the safety of their fortifications. Thucydides reports this and continues:

After listening [to Perikles] the Athenians were persuaded and brought in from the fields their children and their wives, the furniture which they used at home and even the woodwork of their houses, which they dismantled; they sent their sheep and beasts of burden to Euboia and the neighboring islands. (2.14.1)

Several translators (R. Crawley, J. H. Finley, Jr., R. Warner), among them even a man as sympathetic to Thucydides as Thomas Hobbes of Malmesbury, would make the historian say "their wives and children." B. Jowett is exceptional, for he writes "their children and wives" in his version.

Herodotos and Thucydides speak of women and children in many other passages. Their preferred order is "children and women (or wives)." Occasionally Thucydides writes "women (or wives) and children," but reasons can be conjectured for this variation.[1] Writing some four hundred years later, Dionysios of Halikarnassos offered a significant contrast. In the *Roman Antiquities* he said "women and children" more often than "children and women," even though he tried to imitate Thucydides. Attitudes current in Rome in the time of Augustus were different from those of fifth-century Greeks.

The tasks of the translator and of the historian are much alike. Each has to select from the material provided by his source. The translator selects those features of the original which in the translator's opinion deserve the attention of the reader. Translators of Thucydides have set out to furnish the reader with a Thucydidean account of the political and military events of the Peloponnesian War. Often they have assumed that their readers would not be concerned to ascertain the relative esteem in which Greeks held their wives and their children and that therefore the phrase "their children and their wives" would merely jar. If, on the other hand, students of ancient Greece wish to find out how men of the fifth century regarded women, they will attach importance to the preferred order in the phrase about women and children. They will conjecture that this preference reflects outlooks concerning marriage and the treatment of women. They may conclude that Greek men valued their children for their own sake and valued their wives for supplying them with children. If they have a speculative turn of mind, they will wonder whether this feature of Greek thought reflects assumptions held at a deep level in other societies but not often acknowledged.

Several passages of classical prose reveal an estimation of women which jars the modern reader. Perikles, as portrayed by Thucydides, delivered a funeral oration on the men who had fallen in the first year of the Peloponnesian War. After praising them and consoling the survivors, he added:

> If I need to mention also the merits of women who will now find themselves bereft, I will address them comprehensively with a brief exhortation. High praise is your due, if your behavior is not inferior to your natural endowment and if that endowment is least spoken of among men for laudation or censure. (2.45.2)

Again, about 340 a pleader in court distinguished between the spheres proper for women of different kinds:

> We have prostitutes for the sake of pleasure, concubines for daily care of the body, and wives for the purpose of begetting legitimate children and having a reliable guardian of the contents of the house. ([Dem.] 59.122)

A remark attributed to Sokrates by Xenophon is more telling, since it professes to express a higher estimate of women than it recognizes as customary. Xenophon describes a party where the company were entertained by a female juggler. She contrived to keep twelve hoops in the air at once. Sokrates commented:

> In the performance of this girl, as on many other occasions, it is evident that female nature is not in the least inferior to that of the male. It only lacks intellectual and physical strength. (Xen. *Symp.* 2.9)

Historians, like translators, must present a strange society to people of their own society, whose assumptions they share. They must be on their guard against imposing those assumptions on the distant society. Progress in understanding classical antiquity has often been achieved by challenging modern assumptions which had been imported into the material. Goethe even assumed that Pindar was excited by chariot races.[2] Not the least reason why the position of women in Greek society merits study is that Greek assumptions on this matter jar the modern reader.

The prose texts of which a sample has been reviewed speak as if Greek women were narrowly restricted to the domestic sphere. Other texts offer a different picture. In particular the Attic tragedies present women who are fully developed personalities; they take decisions and make their will felt. Faced with the dilemma between the women of prose and the women of tragedy, some have thought that the latter reflect the real women of Greece and the portrayal in prose is a conventional fiction. Others have argued that both portrayals are products of male imagination and the women of everyday life need not have resembled either.[3] It must be admitted that the real women of everyday Athens are inaccessible to historical research. None of their utterances has survived. The inscriptions on their tombstones were carved by men, and the vases which show their everyday activities were painted by men.[4]

If the women of ancient Greece, their thoughts, and for the most part their deeds remain elusive, one may still hope to discover the attitudes held by men toward women. A sample was given above of statements made by men about women and their proper behavior, and a great deal of Greek imaginative literature, notably the tragedies, portrays women with care. Writings of these two kinds may be consulted for information on male attitudes toward women, but some doubt must remain about the soundness of the conclusions drawn. For writings of both kinds are relatively self-conscious utterances; for example, it is difficult to tell whether the distinctions drawn by Pseudo-Demosthenes between prostitutes, concubines, and wives expressed what all male Athenians thought, or what the speaker wished them to think, or what he professed to think for his immediate purpose in litigation although outside the courtroom he may have held a different view. Unguarded utterances, such as the preferred order of words in the phrase "children and women," are likely to reveal attitudes held at a deep level, but they are not numerous; most Greek literature was highly self-conscious.

The law in relation to women in Greek cities was relatively stable and is therefore likely to reveal attitudes held at a deep level. Indeed the study of this branch of law promises to be fruitful for two further reasons. First, students of comparative law are somewhat immune to the disease of imposing assumptions drawn from their own society on to the material which they study. They are confronted constantly with institutions which are strange to them, and so they learn not to take the beliefs or concepts of their own society for granted. They learn, for example, at an early stage in their investigations that Athenian women were given in marriage by their male relatives and their own choice had no legal bearing on the contract. Inquirers who are accustomed to a society in which marriage comes about by the consent of the man and of the woman discover that this practice, however commendable, cannot be assumed as a universal law of nature but has been brought into existence by thought and effort, something which will call for note in chapter 7. The second reason why the law concerning Greek women is a promising field for study is that it brings the inquirer close in one respect to the real women of antiquity. Admittedly the law was not designed by women and there is no reason to suppose that it reflects their beliefs or their wishes. But it was imposed on them and an attempt was made to make them conform to its institutions. They had to take note of the law, even if they sometimes succeeded in circumventing it.

Social reality may sometimes have differed from what the law envisaged. Occasionally there is evidence for asserting this. In the *Epitrepontes* (Arbitration) of Menander Smikrines has given his daughter in marriage recently to Charisios with a dowry of no less than four talents. He learns that Charisios is wasting the property in riotous living, and so he sets about dissolving the marriage. He exclaims indignantly that a husband who has received so large a dowry ought to consider himself the slave of his wife (ll. 134–35). Athenian law never required a man to be subservient to his wife. Although the dowry had to be refunded if the marriage was dissolved, as long as the marriage lasted the husband's discretionary authority to administer the dowry was unlimited. Yet the remark of Smikrines implies that a bride who brought a large dowry might in fact tyrannize over her husband.

Far more is known about the laws of Athens than about those of other Greek cities. Much of Aristotle's *Constitution of the Athenians*, whether written by him or by a pupil, has been found on papyrus; though mainly concerned with public matters, it throws some light on private institutions. Moreover, the extant speeches of the Athenian orators, especially those of Isaios and the private speeches in the Demosthenic corpus, are an invaluable source, both because the information they provide is extensive and because they reveal the law as actually observed in transactions and litigation. The main deficiency of this source is that usually only one speech is preserved from each lawsuit; the answer of the other party and often the outcome of the case are not known. The Byzantine manuscripts transmitting the speeches include at many points putative texts of laws. A few of these texts have been shown to be forgeries, but the tenor and even the wording of some are guaranteed by the orator's argument and many of the texts have stood up to criticism successfully.[5]

If evidence on Athenian institutions is relatively plentiful, this is due to a fact of major importance to the historian of Greece. Athens was far larger in population and wealthier than the average Greek city. It will not be amiss to note here something about the comparative size of the Athenian population and about its composition. In 322, at the end of the Lamian War, Antipater imposed terms on

the Athenians and restricted active citizenship by a property qualification; the number of citizens who met the qualification was
9,000, and 12,000 were excluded. Thus there were 21,000 adult
male citizens. Demetrios of Phaleron controlled Athens for the
Macedonians from 317 until 307 and held a census; it reported
21,000 citizens and 10,000 metics or resident aliens.[6] The other
data on population, though scanty, conform to the hypothesis that
in the fourth century Athens usually had about 21,000 adult male
citizens. One must allow for a complement of women and children.
The figure of 9,000, those embraced by the property qualification of
322, is suggestive. In 411 a plan was launched to restrict some degree of privilege to those wealthy enough for service as hoplites,
and when these were enrolled, they are said to have numbered
9,000.[7] Within the approximately constant body of 21,000 adult
male citizens there was perhaps an even more approximate number
of 9,000, who were recognizably wealthier than their fellows. It has
been argued plausibly that the 9,000 were those whose property,
usually a small-holding of land, gave them independence; the other
12,000 were landless men, living from hand to mouth at the border
of destitution.[8] Doubtless the total population of citizens and the
proportion who had a viable holding of land for subsistence were
larger shortly before the Peloponnesian War, when Athens reached
its highest point of power; so much is implied by the figures given
by Thucydides (2.13.6–8) for the troops under arms at the beginning
of the war.

Greek cities were numerous and most of them were not nearly
so large as Athens. Xenophon (Memorabilia 3.5.2) says that the
Boiotians were as numerous as the Athenians. That may or may not
be true. Boiotia was a federation of many cities; Athens was a uni-
tary state. A recent estimate puts the total number of Greek cities,
including the islands and the cities on the coast of Asia Minor but
excluding Sicily, South Italy, and Cyrene, at 750 at least. In view of
the amount of arable land available in each place it has been calcu-
lated that the average area of a Greek city varied between 25 and
100 square kilometers. For the Aegean islands totals of population
at intervals since A.D. 1879 are available; these figures embrace the
period when the population was the largest that the islands could

support, before migration to the towns of the mainland began on a large scale. Hence it has been estimated that in the classical period the normal Greek city had between 230 and 910 adult male citizens. That was consequently the number of families, and there was no room for resident aliens or slaves. The "city," the *polis*, was a village whose inhabitants could go out on foot to till their fields. The few ancient data agree.[9] Most of the cities which appear as actors in narrative histories—Corinth, Sparta, Thebes, Chios, Mytilene, Rhodes, and even Megara and Poteidaia—were a good deal larger than the average *polis*. Athens was the largest and richest of the Greek cities in the classical period, and this has a consequence for understanding institutions and the ideas which they embodied. The Athenians could achieve ideals which the inhabitants of most Greek cities could only dream about.

Among the inhabitants of Attica noncitizens require only brief notice. The few ancient figures for slave population are incredibly large; defensible modern estimates vary between 20,000 and 75,000.[10] The only ancient figure for metics is that of 10,000 in the census taken by Demetrios of Phaleron. It is difficult to interpret, since one cannot tell whether it included women. Both male and female metics paid a poll tax, the *metoikion*,[11] and Demetrios may have drawn on the records of payment. Metic status was acquired in two ways. Some metics were free aliens who came to Athens from abroad, and historians have sometimes supposed that these were the typical metics. On the other hand, if an Athenian manumitted a slave, the former slave became not a citizen but a metic.[12] It is impossible to estimate what proportion of metics were former slaves. The metic of whom most is known is Phormion the banker. He spoke Attic with a foreign accent.[13] His wife, Archippe, will call for attention later. A few metics became rich, and some of these, like Phormion, received Athenian citizenship for their services to the state or to its statesmen. The range of wealth and poverty may have been as extensive among metics as among citizens, even though metics could not own immovable property. Private law for metics was probably much the same as for citizens. Aristotle (*Constitution of the Athenians* 58.2–3) says that the polemarch receives lawsuits concerning metics, just as the archon receives those concerning citizens, and he adds that the one officer performs for metics the services which the other performs for citizens.

Two lines of division were recognized among citizens on grounds of wealth. One of them has already been noted. It divided those who had at least enough property for subsistence from those who lacked property. The former numbered about 9,000, and the latter about 12,000. Aristophanes described the distinction well:

> It is the life of a beggar (ptōchos) to stay alive without having anything. But it is the life of a poor man (penēs) to live thriftily and attending to his own tasks, and to have nothing left over but not to be in want. (Ploutos 552–54)

The destitute 12,000 were spoken of as ptōchoi, "beggars." They tried to survive as hired laborers in the employ of rich men or of the state. They had to take orders from other men, a condition resented by Greeks to this day, and they were despised; "harvesters" was a stock metaphor for the hirelings of a tyrant.[14] Most of the more fortunate 9,000 were called aporoi ("lacking resources") or penētes ("poor"), that is, men who engaged in toil (ponos).

The other line of division separated a wealthy minority from the bulk of the 9,000. The former have lately come to be called "the liturgical class," for they bore the fiscal burden of the liturgies or major financial contributions to administration. Two of the liturgies, the trierarchy and after 378/77 the proeisphora, were severe burdens, and in the fourth century compulsion was often applied to make men undertake them. The other liturgies, which provided funds for festivals, were numerous but far less burdensome and volunteers may usually have sufficed. The liturgies had begun as occasions for a wealthy man to display his status, bring benefit to his fellow citizens, and win their gratitude and esteem. This feature of the system was never wholly forgotten, even when compulsion was applied and (from 357) trierarchs were organized in "symmories" or contribution groups.[15] Athenian usage called men of the liturgical class plousioi ("rich") or euporoi ("having resources") in contrast to most of the 9,000.[16] A client of Isaios said in court:

You are all my witnesses that my mother's brothers, Chaireleos
and Makartatos, were not among those who perform liturgies
but among those who own modest property. (11.48; cf. 40)

The epithet *plousios* was associated with the trierarchy and other
liturgies and with large houses.[17] It is likely that in the fourth century men whose property amounted to less than three talents were
exempt from liturgies, but men owning at least four talents were
unlikely to escape the burdens.[18] There is controversy about the
number of men liable in the fourth century for the "military liturgies" (the trierarchy and the *proeisphora*); some estimate them at
about 200 to 400, others at about 1,200 (see Appendix A). No doubt
the class performing the festival liturgies was less precisely limited,
but it was probably not much larger; the festival liturgies were a
relatively inexpensive way of winning prestige.

The institutions of Athens were designed for people who had
the modicum of property needed for independence, that is, for the
men who numbered about 9,000. They and especially the wealthier
among them were more likely to engage in litigation than their
unfortunate fellows, and only men of some property could hire
skillful writers of speeches. Since the surviving speeches are the
main source of information on women and the family, the evidence
is slanted toward telling the inquirer about the rich. That the poor
and the indigent borrowed the norms of the rich is a defensible
conjecture, although it leaves some room for uncertainty. Evidence
on other Greek cities, though not derived from speeches, may also
be slanted toward wealth; one had to have more than enough for
mere subsistence before one set up private inscriptions, and travelers' reports probably drew much from the behavior and utterances
of well-to-do hosts.

In consequence of the preservation of forensic speeches the law of
the Athenians concerning women is better known than that of any
other Greek city. It will be the subject of chapter 2. The only other
Greek city for which there is relatively plentiful information is
Gortyn, the source being a long and well-preserved inscription. It
will be studied in chapter 3. A sample of the scanty information on
other Greek cities will be reviewed in chapter 4, mainly to recog-

nize the narrow limits of understanding. For the purpose of comparison chapter 5 will present the legal condition of women in the Roman Republic. Chapter 6 will deal with the portrayal of women in the Homeric poems, a body of evidence comparable in bulk to the private speeches of the Athenian orators. The question of a Homeric society—the question, that is, whether the poems reflect conditions which actually obtained at a recognizable time—will have to be faced. Some hypotheses and comparisons will remain for chapter 7.

The present essay will thus diverge from the pattern followed in many modern inquiries into the condition of Greek women. Those inquiries have often proceeded in chronological order from early conditions to late conditions and they have assumed that early conditions can be discerned in the *Iliad* and the *Odyssey*. But it is doubtful whether those two poems in their totality present the actual conditions of any age; certainly at least one feature of the marriage customs which they portray, namely the payment of *hedna*, has no counterpart in the historically attested societies of Greece. So here a different order of inquiry will be adopted; the attempt will be made to proceed from what is known or moderately well known (chapters 2 and 3) through what is poorly attested (chapter 4) and past a comparable society (chapter 5) to the imaginary (chapter 6).

TWO

Women in Athenian Law

· · · · · · · · · ·

Wīp muoz iemer sīn der wībe hōhste name
und tiuret baz dan frouwe, als ich 'z erkenne.

("Woman" must always be the highest name of women and honors them better
than "lady," as I understand.)—Walther von der Vogelweide

From Athens alone among Greek cities it is possible through the
study of forensic speeches to gain a sense of the seamless web of the
law, as it is sometimes called. One may discern principles, aims,
and beliefs underlying particular rules, and one may recognize how
the underlying considerations cohere to form a harmonious system.
Consequently study of the fabric may begin almost indifferently at
any point. This chapter will consider in turn the law of citizenship
in relation to women, the festivals in which they took part and the
phratries of which they were probably not members, marriage, the
relation of a woman to her *kyrios* and to property, Aristotle's explanation for the legal disabilities of women, and objections to that
explanation. An alternative explanation for the disabilities will be
proposed in chapter 7.

Women and Citizenship

In 451/50 the Athenians passed a law about citizenship on the proposal of Perikles. It provided that a child should only have citizenship if both its parents were citizens.[1] This law implied that wom-
en, as well as men, could be citizens. Attic Greek had two words for

"citizen," *astos* (feminine *astē*) and *politēs* (feminine *politis*). Both are used of women.[2] But proof of citizenship was not the same for men and for women. This is shown by the questions asked at the examination of men who had been chosen to the nine archonships. Each candidate was asked to state the name of his father, the deme of his father, the name of his father's father, the name of his mother, the name of his mother's father, and the deme of his mother's father.[3] He was not asked to state the deme of his father's father, since it was the same as that of his father, membership in demes being hereditary in the male line. The candidate was not asked to state the deme of his mother, since women were not registered in demes. The lists kept by the demes attested the status of male citizens, but no such lists were kept to attest that of female citizens.

Before 451/50 there may have been no statute nor even any acknowledged rule governing the transmission of citizenship by descent. Certainly some male Athenians of earlier generations took foreign wives and their sons were citizens.[4] In the fourth century the crucial step in recognizing a young man as a citizen came when he was in his eighteenth year and was presented to the assembly of his father's deme; the demesmen voted on oath whether to add him to their list.[5] It can only be conjectured whether this procedure had been observed uniformly ever since Kleisthenes divided Attica into 139 demes towards the end of the sixth century. If there was no law on citizenship before 451/50, the acceptance of a candidate into a deme must have depended on the arguments offered by his relatives to the demesmen and the response of the latter.

To understand why the law of 451/50 was passed one should consider the viewpoint of an Athenian father who sought to marry off his daughter. He wished to find her a good husband. He would prefer a citizen to a metic as a son-in-law. Metics had special fiscal burdens, such as the *metoikion*; moreover, they could not own immovable property or, in the Greek phrase, "land and house."[6] If an unmarried male citizen could take a wife from among citizens and aliens indifferently and be confident that his children would have citizenship, the Athenian father of a daughter had to compete with metic fathers of daughters. The competition became less intense when the law of 451/50 provided that a male citizen must marry a female citizen if he desired citizenship for his children.[7] Further-more the Athenians had lost many men in the disaster of 454 in Egypt. Thus the supply of unmarried male citizens decreased and this decrease may explain the time when the law of 451/50 was passed.[8]

The law of 451/50 made the Athenian concept of citizenship somewhat untidy. A pleader in a lawsuit stated the obvious when he told his audience:

> Marriage consists in this, that one has children and one intro-duces the sons to one's fellow *phrateres* and to one's fellow demesmen but one gives the daughters as one's own in mar-riage to men.[9]

The citizenship of male descendants was displayed through their membership in a phratry and in a deme. Women were not members of those organizations (on the phratry see below). Their citizenship was latent; it consisted in the capacity to bear children who would be citizens. Athenian law on citizenship would have been tidier, had it provided that a son should have citizenship if his father was a citizen, whatever the status of the mother. One can recognize the untidy aspect of the law by calling to mind the questions put to a candidate for the archonship. If the status of his father as a citizen were doubted, he could produce witnesses to his father's enroll-ment in a phratry and in a deme. But if the status of his mother were doubted, he could reply by asserting the citizenship of her parents; that is, he could produce witnesses to the enrollment of his maternal grandfather in a phratry and a deme, but for his mater-nal grandmother he could only assert the citizenship of her parents. There was thus the possibility of an infinite regress.

Late in the fifth century the requirements of the law of 451/50 were relaxed. Probably that law was neither repealed nor suspend-ed, but demes sometimes accepted candidates even if only one of the parents was a citizen.[10] Doubtless the reason for failing to en-force the law of 451/50 was shortage of manpower as the Pelopon-nesian War proceeded. Two measures were passed in 403/2 and re-stored rigor. One, proposed by Nikomenes, said that a child born after 403/2 should not have citizenship unless both its parents were citizens, but no inquiry should be held towards enforcing this rule on children born before 403/2. The other, proposed by Aristophon, provided that the children of a male citizen and a female alien should be *nothoi*.[11]

Nothos has often been translated as "illegitimate"; the definition of this condition will be considered later in connection with marriage. Here note will be taken of the position of *nothoi* in relation to the law of inheritance. Athenian law recognized kinship (*anchisteia*) as far as first cousins and the children of first cousins. Relatives within this degree had right of inheritance and took part in the legal procedure consequent upon homicide.[12] A law current in the fourth century and cited in disputes about inheritance said that a *nothos* of either sex born after 403/2 was excluded from the *anchisteia*.[13] The references to 403/2 may suggest that the condition of *nothoi* was better before that year. But it may have been better only because the laws of inheritance, like the law of 451/50 on citizenship, were not being upheld.

Evidence of a sort on the condition of *nothoi* before 403/2 is provided by a scene in the *Birds* of Aristophanes, a play produced in 414. When Poseidon and Herakles visit the new city of the birds, Pisthetairos startles Herakles by telling him that he is *nothos*, since his mother was an alien (ll. 1650–52). This implies that the legislation of 451/50 did not merely deny citizenship to the children of mixed marriages but also declared them *nothoi*. Pisthetairos proceeds to quote two laws which disappoint Herakles of his prospect of inheritance (ll. 1660–66). The first law says that the *nothos* shall have no *anchisteia*, if there are "legitimate" (*gnēsioi*) children. The second says that if there are no legitimate children, the next of kin are to share the property. If these two laws, uttered in the comedy, are drawn from Athenian statutes, they appear to come from different periods. For the first, denying succession to the *nothos* if there are "legitimate" children, suggests that the *nothos* would have some prospect of succession where there were no "legitimate" children, but the second law denies the *nothos* that prospect.[14]

The following conclusions are to be drawn on the relation of *nothoi* to inheritance. Under the legislation of 403/2 the *nothos* had no capacity to inherit from his father. This exclusion was probably already provided in the legislation of 451/50. But the restriction of the fourth-century provision to children born after 403/2 and the two laws presented in a comic scene in the *Birds* suggest that *nothoi* may have had some capacity to inherit before the laws of 451/50 and 403/2 were passed. This suggestion is supported by two obscure pieces of evidence. One is the mention of *notheia* in the same scene of the *Birds*; the word is explained by Byzantine scholars as meaning a limited sum which a father could give or bequeath to his *nothoi*.[15] The other evidence is the references to a gymnasium frequented by *nothoi* at Kynosarges;[16] these seem to indicate that for a time there were *nothoi* of good social, though not necessarily legal, standing. In general in classical law, that is, in the provisions of 451/50 and 403/2, citizenship and *anchisteia* adhered closely together, but it is not unlikely that the condition of *nothoi* had once been rather better. That is, the condition of *nothoi* deteriorated somewhat, or to put the matter in its bearing on women, the rules concerning marriage became clearer and more strict.

The condition of marriages between citizens and aliens also deteriorated. The legislation of 451/50 and 403/2 merely imposed disabilities on the children of mixed marriages. The speech *Against Neaira*, delivered toward 340, quotes laws which added criminal penalties for the contracting parties.[17] The provisions may be paraphrased thus:

1. If a male alien lives in marriage with a female citizen, any Athenian may open suit against him. If he is convicted, he is to be sold into slavery, his property is to be confiscated and sold, and a third of the proceeds shall be assigned to the prosecutor.
2. The same provisions are to hold, if a female alien lives in marriage with a male citizen, and when the female alien is convicted, the male citizen is to be fined 1,000 drachmas.
3. If someone gives an alien woman in marriage to a male citizen as if she were a woman of his family, he is to suffer loss of civic rights,[18] his property is to be confiscated, and a third of it shall be assigned to the prosecutor. Any Athenian may open suit against him before the *thesmothetai*, as in the procedure against an alien who poses as a citizen.

It will be noted that under the first provision neither the female citizen who was married to a male alien nor her relative who had given her in marriage was penalized. No doubt it was presumed that the male alien had professed deceitfully to be a citizen and thus bore the whole blame for the anomaly of the mixed marriage.

By studying the fortunes of two people, Euktemon and Archippe, steps can be taken towards determining when the laws imposing these penalties were made. The affairs of Euktemon are known from the sixth speech of Isaios, which was delivered in 364 (6.14). Euktemon owned property in many parts of Attica, including a lodging house in the Peiraios and one in the Kerameikos. Among the slaves kept as prostitutes at the former lodging house was one called Alke. After a time Euktemon put her in charge of the lodging house in the Kerameikos and presumably manumitted her. She had two sons. Euktemon in old age grew tired of living with his wife and children in the family's residence. He took to visiting Alke at the house in the Kerameikos, sometimes he dined there, and at last he took up residence there. Alke told him, truthfully or otherwise, that he was the father of her elder son and persuaded him to present that son to a meeting of his phratry for admission. The proposal was opposed by Philoktemon, the eldest son of Euktemon and of his wife, the daughter of Meixiades. The members of the phratry voted against Euktemon's proposal. Thereupon Euktemon approached his friend Demokrates, who had a sister to give in marriage. They drew up a contract (engyēsis, see below) whereby Euktemon would marry the sister of Demokrates. In this way Euktemon threatened to produce children, genuine or supposed, with whom Philoktemon would have to share the inheritance. So through the mediation of relatives Philoktemon agreed to a compromise; he would withdraw his opposition to admitting Alke's son to the phratry, but that son should receive only one farm as his share of the inheritance. Thereupon Euktemon canceled his contract with Demokrates (6.18–24).

Philoktemon died in or about 376 (6.27). His dispute with his father took place some time earlier. The course of the dispute is known only from the account given by one party in a later lawsuit. The account may have been distorted. But at least it was plausible enough to be told in an Athenian court; that is, the maneuver attributed to Euktemon was possible. By intimidating the opposition Euktemon could get the son of Alke enrolled in his phratry, so that he would acquire citizenship and eventually own immovable property. By presenting the son of Alke as his own son Euktemon professed to live in marriage with Alke, a metic. His maneuver would have been hazardous if criminal penalties had already been available against a male citizen and a female alien for marital cohabitation. If such penalties had been available, Philoktemon would have been in a stronger position to resist his father.

The fortunes of Archippe have to do with the best-known bank in Athens of the fourth century. The bank was first owned, as far as is known, by two Athenians, Archestratos and Antisthenes. They acquired Pasion as a slave. As time passed, they manumitted him, entrusted management of the bank to him, and withdrew themselves from the bank. Pasion acquired Athenian citizenship and became owner of the bank. Before he acquired citizenship, he had married Archippe. She bore him two sons, Apollodoros and Pasikles. Pasion acquired Phormion as a slave, manumitted him later, and employed him as cashier in the bank. Pasion died in 370/69. Shortly before dying Pasion leased the bank to Phormion for eight years. When Pasion died, Apollodoros was already twenty-four years old, but Pasikles was a minor. The will of Pasion nominated Phormion and a certain Nikokles as guardians of Pasikles. It also assigned Archippe in marriage to Phormion with a dowry of three talents and 4,000 drachmas. The marriage followed about 368. Archippe bore Phormion two sons. In the course of 361/60 she died and Phormion received Athenian citizenship.[19]

Difficulty arises when one asks what the status of Archippe was during her successive marriages.[20] There is no evidence to show whether she was a citizen or an alien before her first marriage. Probably Pasion married her before he received citizenship, since their elder son, Apollodoros, was twenty-four years old in 370/69. It must be admitted that there is no clear indication of the date when Pasion acquired citizenship. A date before 386 has been proposed tentatively.[21] At least he had probably reached mature years before he received citizenship, since the grant of citizenship is likely to have been made as a reward for services to Athenians. Decrees granting citizenship often gave it to the honorand and his descendants. That evidently happened to Pasion, since his two sons acquired citizenship with him. A grant of this kind did not, as far as is known, mention the honorand's wife. There was no need to do so, since the citizenship of a woman consisted in the capacity to give birth to citizens; once a male honorand's children had received citizenship, the function of his wife's hypothetical citizenship had already been achieved. Yet if Archippe was indisputably an alien even after Pasion had received citizenship, their children might have suffered the disabilities imposed by the laws of 403/2. If on the other hand she was indisputably a citizen, whether since birth or in consequence of the grant of citizenship to Pasion, uncertainties might arise about her and her subsequent children after Phormion married her.

The only text alluding to Archippe's status suggests ambiguity. About 348 Apollodoros in the course of his quarrels with Phormion said that the latter had been at fault in taking Archippe under the alleged will of Pasion. Instead, Apollodoros asserted, Phormion ought to have claimed her "before the archon, if she was a citizen, or before the polemarch, if she was an alien."[22] Perhaps one may borrow a modern phrase and say that Archippe was a person of indeterminate nationality. Surely the law would be less able to tolerate such ambiguity after criminal penalties were introduced for mixed marriages.

A plausible occasion can be suggested for introducing the penalties and perhaps clarifying further the rules about marriage, citizenship, and inheritance. In 346/45 the list of citizens was revised. Within each deme the assembled demesmen voted on the claim of each putative member to membership. An adverse vote led to a hearing before a court.[23] The fact that the revision was held suggests that some people had exercised citizenship to which they were not entitled. One way in which this could come about is illustrated by the maneuver of Euktemon to get the son of Alke admitted to his phratry.

Women, Festivals, and Phratries

In the funeral speech Thucydides (2.38.1) made Perikles boast that the Athenians had instituted the greatest number of recreations from toil. Religious and civic observances provided festive occasions for women as well as for men. A chorus of women in the *Lysistrata* of Aristophanes told of festivals in which they professed to have participated in childhood and youth (ll. 641–47). Probably they spoke with comic exaggeration and each ritual act was performed by a few girls alone, who represented all those of their age.[24] At least the remarks of the chorus show that at the age of seven a girl could serve as *arrēphoros*, carrying symbols of Athena Polias in procession; at ten she could prepare dough for ritual cakes; later she could dress in saffron as a "bear" for Artemis Brauronia and carry in procession a sacred basket. There were festivals for women alone, notably the Thesmophoria. This festival was celebrated by the different demes. A litigant could boast that his mother had been chosen to preside at the Thesmophoria by the wives of the members of the deme, and on the occasion of that festival a wealthy man could be required to provide a feast for the wives of his fellow demesmen.[25]

Women, as noted previously, were not recorded as members of a deme; they took part in its festivals as wives of its members. Their relationship to the deme rested on a principle which is illustrated in a forensic speech delivered toward 360. In the previous generation Teisias had acquired a parcel of arable land on the slope of a hill. His neighbor was Kallippides, and their holdings were divided by a depression which provided a pathway down the slope. In stormy weather water flowed down the pathway. The water overflowed onto the land of Teisias and caused damage, so Teisias built a wall to keep the water out. In the next generation Kallikles, the son of Kallippides, sued the son of Teisias and complained that the wall had diverted water onto the land of Kallikles and caused damage. In the course of his defense the son of Teisias said that the actual loss incurred by Kallikles was small. To demonstrate this he cited a conversation between their mothers, and he remarked:

Before the other party engaged in malicious litigation, my
mother was on amicable terms with their mother. The women
used to visit one another, as was to be expected, because they
both lived in the countryside and were neighbors and because
our fathers were on amicable terms as long as they were alive.
(Dem. 55.23)[26]

In everyday life, as in the festivals of the deme, a married woman
derived her social relationships from her husband.

Besides being divided into demes since late in the sixth century,
male Athenians were grouped in older units of obscure origin, the
phratries (*phratria, phratriai*). Membership in these too was hereditary in the male line. A likely theory says that phratries arose in the
uncertain conditions of the Greek dark ages, when humble men
sought the protection of powerful families. A strong family or *genos*
collected a following by extending hereditary protection to humble
men in return for loyalty and services, and it honored them by calling them its *phrateres*, a designation in which the Indo-European
word for "brother" survived.[27] In the fourth century several phratries are known in each of which a named *genos* played a part.[28]

By the fourth century the phratries had long ceased to serve as
channels for any political power which the *genē* may once have
wielded, but they continued to flourish in social life. When a man
married, he offered a sacrifice, the *gamēlia*, and invited the members of his phratry to take part in it. On the tenth day after the birth
of a child the father offered a sacrifice, the *dekatē*, but this celebration was probably on a smaller scale; relatives and perhaps other
friends were invited, but there may have been no general invitation
to the members of the phratry. The *dekatē* was the occasion when
the father gave the child a name, and this was true both for male
and for female children. At two later times as the child grew up the
father offered sacrifices, the *meion* and the *koureion*, at the annual
festival of the Apatouria, which was celebrated by the different
phratries. These two sacrifices may have been offered only on behalf of male children. Perhaps the *meion* was offered while the
child was still an infant and the *koureion* when he approached
puberty.[29]

These rituals were to a large extent informal festivities and had little legal significance. More importance attaches to the occasion when the son was approaching manhood and his father introduced him to his phratry. Now the father swore to the child's parentage, there was opportunity for challenge and argument, and the members of the phratry voted on the question whether they were satisfied of the son's descent and should admit him to membership in the phratry. Practice among phratries varied. In at least one the formal introduction took place when the koureion was offered, and in at least one other the formal introduction took place a year after the koureion.[30] Phratries may have varied in their procedures for admitting new members. Claiming his inheritance, an adoptive son told how the deceased had introduced him and the members of the phratry had voted to add him to their written list; he commented: "Their rules have such a high degree of precision" (Isai. 7.16 fin.).[31] Presumably some phratries were not so careful.

The importance of admission to membership in the phratry is illustrated by the story of Boiotos. He was the eldest son of Mantias and was born about 382. Shortly after the boy was born Mantias divorced his wife, Plangon. She returned to the house of her brothers and took Boiotos with her. Boiotos was brought up in the house of his maternal uncles and as a boy he took part in a chorus of their phylē, Hippothontis, although Mantias belonged to the phylē Akamantis. Mantias married a second wife and she bore him a son, Mantitheos. When Boiotos came of age, he opened legal proceedings to compel Mantias to recognize him as his son. The dispute was submitted to arbitration. Mantias agreed in advance to accept the testimony of Plangon and he gave her a bribe of 3,000 drachmas to testify that Boiotos was not his son. Plangon accepted the present, and speaking on oath before the arbitrator, she said that Mantias was the father of Boiotos and of Pamphilos, a son whom she had borne later.

These events are known from the speeches delivered by Mantitheos in two later lawsuits against Boiotos.[32] Mantitheos adds that in consequence of the testimony of Plangon Mantias had Boiotos and Pamphilos enrolled in his phratry at the Apatouria. He continues by saying that Mantias died before these two sons were enrolled in his deme, but Boiotos went to the demesmen and had himself enrolled. There may have been some delay. If Boiotos was born about 382, he may have opened proceedings about 364 or soon after, but Mantias as general conducted an expedition to the coast of Macedon in 359 and must have died about 358. The impressive scene where Plangon testified before the arbitrator became notorious.[33] Since that occurrence was remembered, Boiotos doubtless had little difficulty in convincing the demesmen of his descent. Even so, the story as told by Mantitheos implies that admission to a phratry created a strong presumption of true descent and would carry weight with the demesmen when a candidate was presented for admission to a deme. Similarly other speeches delivered in disputes about inheritance cite both admission to the phratry and admission to the deme as proof of descent or adoption.[34]

It is therefore a matter of some importance to determine the relationship of women to the phratry. Three forensic speeches provide indications. The third speech of Isaios was delivered in a dispute for the estate of Pyrrhos. Phile claimed the estate on the grounds that she was the daughter of Pyrrhos; she was represented by her husband, Xenokles. The speaker of the extant speech opposed her claim. At 3.73–76 he argued that Pyrrhos would have introduced Phile to his phratry if he had acknowledged her as his legitimate daughter. The speaker produces witnesses to show that Pyrrhos did not offer the *gamēlia* to celebrate his union with Phile's mother and did not introduce Phile to his phratry. It is to be noted that the speaker does not mention any prospect of adding Phile's name to a list kept by the phratry. He speaks solely of "introducing (*eisagein*) her to the *phrateres*."

The other two speeches are the fifty-seventh of Demosthenes and the eighth of Isaios. The former was delivered in court by a man whose citizenship was challenged in his deme when the list of citizens was revised in 346/45. He set out to rebut in turn the allegations that his father was not a citizen (57.18–30) and that his mother was not a citizen (57.30–45). To prove his father's citizenship he called as witnesses his father's surviving relatives (57.20–22) and some members of his father's phratry, *genos*, and deme (57.23). To prove his mother's citizenship he called her surviving relatives as witnesses (57.37–39). He also called their fellow *phra-teres* and fellow demesmen as witnesses, but he called them to attest, not that the mother belonged to the phratry or the deme, but that her alleged relatives were indeed her relatives (57.40, 57.69). Again the speaker of the eighth speech of Isaios claimed the estate of Kiron on the grounds that his own mother was the daughter of Kiron. He mentioned phratries twice (8.18–19). He said that Kiron on marrying offered the *gamēlia* and invited the members of his phratry. He said that his own father introduced him to his phratry and swore to his descent and that the members of the phratry accepted this declaration without questioning it.

Neither of these two speeches says that the woman whose status was crucial to the dispute was recorded as a member of a phratry, although any such record would have assisted the case. Admittedly practice in different phratries may have varied. But it would be gratuitous to suppose that the cases for which speeches are extant were exceptional and that women were normally enrolled in phratries. The proper inference is that women were not so enrolled.[35] Again, in view of the phrase about "introducing" Phile to the phratry (Isaios 3.73–76) it may well be supposed that male Athenians sometimes took their daughters and their wives to festivals celebrated by their fellow *phrateres*, but that does not mean that women were presented for admission with sworn testimony or recorded in any list. There was not necessarily any need for exactitude in admitting people to festive celebrations. It will be remembered that Boiotos as a child took part in the chorus furnished by the *phylē* of his maternal uncles, not that of his father. Inclusion on a list with sworn testimony and a vote was another matter; it had a bearing on title to citizenship and to inheritance. The relation of women to phratries supports the hypothesis that a woman derived her social and legal relationships from her man, that is, from her father or brother before marriage and from her husband afterwards.

Marriage

An Athenian woman did not marry; she was given in marriage. A law is quoted by Pseudo-Demosthenes to show who has the right to give a woman in marriage:

> Whatever woman is pledged on just terms to be a wife by her father, or by her brother who has the same father, or by her paternal grandfather, the children born of her shall be legitimate (gnēsioi) children. (46.18)

The word used here for wife is not gynē, the customary word of classical prose, but the archaic damar. The language of law could be conservative. The verb translated as "pledge" is engyān. It and its noun engyēsis are crucial for understanding classical marriage. It might equally be translated "entrust."

Engyēsis was an oral contract, made between the man who gave the woman into marriage and the bridegroom. The form of words is known.[36] The man giving the woman said: "I pledge (such and such a woman) for the purpose of producing legitimate (gnēsioi) children." He uttered the verb engyō in the active. Uttering the same verb in the middle voice, the bridegroom replied: "I accept the pledge." The woman could be referred to in the passive participle. She was not a party to the contract but its passive object. The same verb was employed in the procedure for personal surety for repayment of a debt. The creditor "pledged" (active) the debtor (passive) to the person who offered himself as surety; the latter "accepted the pledge." The procedure of surety did not create a permanent relationship. It entrusted the debtor to a third person to ensure that the creditor could recover the loan. Marriage by engyēsis did not create a new community; it entrusted a woman to a man for the large but not unlimited purpose of bearing him heirs.[37]

The man who gave the woman in marriage had been her kyrios (guardian, master) up to that point. When marriage was concluded, the husband became her kyrios. Engyēsis did not complete the conclusion of marriage; it needed to be followed by ekdosis, the transfer of the woman to the bridegroom's dwelling. Engyēsis could be revoked, as is illustrated by the contract between Euktemon and

Demokrates. But *engyēsis* was more than a betrothal, since it was part of the procedure transferring *kyrieia* to the bridegroom.

The variable element in *engyēsis* was the dowry. In Athens dowry (*proix*) had a precise sense. It was a sum of money or valuables transferred from the woman's original family to the bridegroom for the woman's upkeep. If it was not a sum of money, it had to be assessed at a monetary value, so that the woman's original family could recover it if the marriage was dissolved.[38] When property other than money was given as dowry, that property was sometimes said to be given "in lieu of dowry."[39] The possibility of *engyēsis* without dowry is mentioned by a litigant hypothetically,[40] but no actual occurrence is known. Since the dowry was intended for the support of the woman, the husband had to refund it if the marriage was dissolved. If he did not refund it, the woman's relative(s) had an action against him and this action was called the *dikē sitou* or "action for grain."[41] While the marriage lasted, the husband had full authority to administer the dowry. If, however, he fell into debt, his creditors might seize his property, but an attempt could at least be made to prevent them from seizing his wife's dowry.[42] The dowry, administered by the husband, was distinct from the woman's paraphernalia, which were at her disposal. The stock phrase for her paraphernalia was "clothes and gold jewelry" (*himatia kai chrysia*), although their nature might vary.[43]

What happened to the dowry if the woman bore children and later died? An answer can be derived from the story of Archippe, which illustrates further features of dowry. As will be remembered, she was first married to Pasion and she bore him two sons, Apollodoros and Pasikles. When Pasion died in 370/69, Apollodoros was twenty-four years old and Pasikles was about ten years old.[44] In accordance with Pasion's will Phormion married Archippe about 368. As plaintiff in a trial held about twenty years later,[45] Apollodoros mentioned the dowry which Archippe brought to Phormion, and listed its components thus:

> a talent from Peparethos,
> a talent from here,
> a lodging house worth 100 minai,

female slaves,

the gold jewelry,

and the other things of hers. (Dem. 45.28)

Apollodoros stated monetary values for the first three items and these amounted to three talents and 4,000 drachmas. Since he did not state the value of the slaves, the jewelry or "the other things," it is likely that these were not part of the dowry but Archippe's paraphernalia. Later in the same speech (45.74) Apollodoros said that the dowry was five talents; he may have reached this tendentious figure by including an approximate estimate of the paraphernalia.

Archippe bore Phormion two sons.[46] Meanwhile Apollodoros and his wife had two daughters. Shortly before her death Archippe gave a present of 2,000 drachmas to these two girls, her granddaughters.[47] She died late in the winter of 361/60.[48] Thereupon Apollodoros opened proceedings against Phormion and demanded 3,000 drachmas, a small cloak, and a female slave. The case went to arbitration. Phormion complied with the recommendation of the arbitrators that he should hand over 3,000 drachmas to Apollodoros. Thus Apollodoros together with his daughters received 5,000 drachmas in all. The later speech which mentions this settlement says that Apollodoros received a quarter of the maternal property.[49] There were indeed four sons whom Archippe had borne, Apollodoros, Pasikles, and the two sons of Phormion. If the 5,000 drachmas which Apollodoros with his daughters received was a quarter of the whole, the total property to be divided at Archippe's death was three talents and 2,000 drachmas. This is close to the dowry of three talents and 4,000 drachmas which she had brought to Phormion. Evidently, if a woman died leaving sons, her dowry was to be distributed among them equally. One can only conjecture what would happen if she left daughters and sons; perhaps the sons divided the dowry equally but contributed to the eventual dowries of the daughters.

The behavior of Archippe is easy to understand. As she grew old, she preferred the children of her current marriage to those of her first marriage. Besides, Apollodoros had already shown his quarrelsome nature; after Phormion had married Archippe, Apollodoros had made the marriage grounds for opening an action against him, although nothing came of it.[50] When Archippe knew that she had not long to live, she tried to meet the eventual claim of her eldest son by giving his daughters a present of 2,000 drachmas. But her wishes were in vain. After her death Apollodoros had no difficulty in bringing about equal division of her dowry. The case illustrates the fact that a woman could not alienate the dowry.

A dispute in another family also bears on the question of distribution of the dowry after the woman's death. Mantias was survived by three sons, born of two wives. Since all three sons were recognized as his, they divided his property between them equally. But a dispute arose about the dowries of their mothers. Mantitheos, whose version alone has survived, said that his mother had brought a dowry of one talent, but that the dowry of one talent and 4,000 drachmas promised with Plangon had not been paid, since her family had fallen into debt. Pending litigation, the three men did not divide the dwelling house of Mantias but set it aside to meet these claims.[51] The outcome of the case is not known. At least it provides no objection to the view offered here.

The legal passivity of the woman in marriage is illustrated by the consequences of adultery. The Athenian concept of *moicheia* was more comprehensive than the modern word "adultery." *Moichos* was the word both for the seducer who took another man's wife by persuasion and for the rapist who took her by force.[52] The speaker of Lysias 1.32–33 argued that the adulterer who gained his aim by persuasion was more harmful than the one who employed force, since the former corrupted the woman's mind and alienated her affection from her husband. That was an advocate's argument and presumably he thought that it would carry weight with his audience, but it was not a statement of law. The law took no account of the woman's wish in relation to *moicheia*. It offered the aggrieved husband a remedy against the adulterer.[53] If he pursued the remedy successfully, he was required to divorce his wife under pain of loss of civic rights. The woman was then excluded from public temples; if she entered a public temple, she could be ill-treated in any manner short of infliction of death.[54] The exclusion from temples may reflect considerations of ritual purity. The woman taken in adultery was not treated as criminally guilty or legally liable; for she was not tried. She was a passive object in adultery, as in the conclusion of marriage.

The law imposed loss of civic rights (*atimia*) on the husband who failed to divorce his wife after winning his case against the adulterer. The penalty can be explained as an attempt to deter a man from prostituting a woman and blackmailing the customer by calling her his wife. There may have been an additional consideration. The dowry was intended for the upkeep of the woman and was therefore to be returned with her on divorce. No text says explicitly whether the dowry had to be refunded even if a man divorced his wife in consequence of adultery. The coherence of principles in the Athenian law of marriage suggests that it did have to be refunded in that event. So a penalty as severe as loss of civic rights might be needed if an aggrieved husband reasserted his honor by proceeding against the adulterer and was reluctant to part with a large dowry.

Marriage by *engyēsis* and *ekdosis* was not the only form of marital union recognized by the Athenians. If a man died intestate leaving a daughter but no sons, his nearest male relative succeeded to the estate and was required to take the daughter in marriage. If he refused her, the estate and the woman passed to the next among the relatives in a fixed order.[55] The heir could not take the estate if he refused to take the woman. If he was already married and wished to accept the estate with the woman, he had to divorce his wife.[56] The woman was said to be *epiklēros*, that is, "upon the estate." She was adjudicated to the relative by the archon and the act of adjudication was called *epidikasia*.[57] If more than one relative claimed the estate and the woman, the archon called a court into session to judge between them. If the deceased left more than one daughter, they were adjudicated to the relatives in a sufficient number. The word *epiklēros* has sometimes been translated "heiress." This rendering is acceptable, provided that one recognizes that the *epiklēros* had no power to dispose of the property but was transferred with it. "Female orphan" would be an equally defensible translation.

Epidikasia of an *epiklēros* created a union which had the same validity as marriage by *engyēsis*.[58] But the purpose was different. A man who took an *epiklēros* in marriage could not alienate the property which he acquired thus. It passed to the sons of himself and the *epiklēros*, when those sons were two years beyond puberty; the sons were then required to support their mother.[59] *Epidikasia* provided for the continuity of the line of the deceased by bringing in a man to manage the property and beget heirs to it. A law attributed to Solon required the husband of an *epiklēros* to engage in intercourse with her at least three times a month.[60] *Engyēsis* on the other hand enabled the bridegroom to beget heirs of his own. By the fourth century *epidikasia* of an *epiklēros* was becoming infrequent. Adoption and bequest[61] provided a more flexible way of solving the predicament of a man who had a daughter but no sons. The law only allowed such a father to give or bequeath his property if he gave his daughter in marriage to the chosen heir.[62]

By imposing this restriction the relatively flexible law of the classical period tried to achieve a purpose recognized by the more rigid institution of *epidikasia*. Indeed the Athenian law of inheritance as a whole is an impressively efficient system. But difficulty arose if a man died leaving a daughter but no sons and the daughter was still very young. An occurrence of this kind is illustrated by the third speech of Isaios, *On the Estate of Pyrrhos*. Pyrrhos had no sons. His sister had two sons, Endios and the speaker of the extant speech. Pyrrhos adopted Endios. When Pyrrhos died, Endios succeeded to the estate and held it for more than twenty years (3.1). Endios died a year before the extant speech was spoken (3.2). When Endios died, Phile claimed the estate and said that she was the daughter of Pyrrhos; she was represented by her husband, Xenokles (3.2). Her claim was opposed by the speaker's mother, and the speaker represented her (3.3). The speaker admitted that Endios had given Phile in marriage to Xenokles (3.45, 48–49, 51–52, 58). He said that Xenokles and Phile had been married more than eight years at the time of the speech (3.31). If she was given in marriage when she was about fourteen years old, as was usual in Athens, she can scarcely have been more than two years old when Pyrrhos died. So one can reconstruct the circumstances. When Pyrrhos looked ahead to his death, he did his best for his infant daughter; he adopted Endios and entrusted care of her to him. Endios could conceivably have remained celibate for a dozen years or more with a view to marrying

Phile, but he may have had good reasons for not doing so; an Athenian married a wife who could bear him sons while he was still in the prime of life and could bring them up to maturity. Endios in turn did his best for Phile; he brought her up and gave her in marriage to Xenokles. The outcome of the case is not known.

In addition to marriage by *engyēsis* and by *epidikasia* unions of a less solemn kind are attested. The key word is *pallakē*, "concubine." The speaker of Isaios 3.39 says:

> Those who give their womenfolk into concubinage exact stipulations beforehand about the things to be given to the concubines.

The remark implies that even in concubinage the woman was not a contracting party but was given by her relatives.[63] Demosthenes (23.53) cites a law that states the circumstances in which homicide is justified. They include killing the intruder whom one takes with one's wife or one's mother or one's sister or one's daughter or with the concubine whom one keeps for begetting free children. The provision was probably old, for it uses the older word, *damar*, for wife. The law offers the same protection to a man's union with the concubine whom he keeps for begetting free children as to his union with his wife. Possibly the term *pallakia* was vague and covered unions which varied in degree of permanence; the law only protected some of them.

Economic considerations may have determined whether a woman was given into engyetic marriage, as it may be called, or into concubinage. Athenian families gave large dowries with their daughters, but if the family was destitute, it could not give a dowry; instead it could give the woman into concubinage and try to gain stipulations for her support. Concubinage is not often mentioned in extant speeches and this relative silence is easy to explain. When a dispute about inheritance arose and turned on a question of paternity, the one party might try to show that the mother was given in marriage by *engyēsis*, but the other might insist that she was prostituted indiscriminately and so one could not identify the father of her child. So much is suggested by the speech *On the Estate of Pyrrhos*. Xenokles said that the mother of Phile was given in marriage to Pyrrhos by *engyēsis*. His adversary offered apparently powerful arguments to destroy the testimony to the alleged contract of *engyēsis* (3.18–26) and insisted that the mother of Phile had been prostituted indiscriminately (3.13–15). Possibly she could have been called the *pallakē* of Pyrrhos, since he acknowledged Phile as their daughter in entrusting care of her to Endios, but it was not in the interests of either party to the lawsuit to say that Phile's mother had been Pyrrhos' concubine.

Since there were unions less solemn than marriage by *engyēsis* or *epidikasia*, the question arises, what was the status of the son of such a union in the law of inheritance? Was he *gnēsios*, that is, entitled to inherit, or *nothos* and not so entitled? The story of Mantias may provide an answer to this question. As will be remembered, he married Plangon as his first wife and she bore him Boiotos, but he divorced her soon afterwards and married again. His second wife bore him Mantitheos. While his second wife was still alive, Mantias resumed associating with Plangon. After his second wife died, he continued the association, although he did not take Plangon into his house.[64] During this period of renewed association Plangon bore another son, Pamphilos. Later, when Boiotos opened proceedings against Mantias and the latter agreed to abide by the testimony of Plangon, she declared on oath that Mantias was the father of Boiotos and Pamphilos. In consequence Pamphilos was entitled to citizenship and a third of the inheritance of Mantias.[65] Pamphilos was conceived and born long after the marriage of his parents had been dissolved. Surely the conclusion cannot be escaped that the law of inheritance and citizenship inquired only into the identity of the actual parents and their status as citizens; the nature of the union between the parents, whether a marriage brought about by *engyēsis* or *epidikasia* or a less solemn association, was a matter of indifference to the law.

The same principle is illustrated by the statements made by the speaker of the third speech of Isaios. He insisted that the mother of Phile had not been contracted to Pyrrhos by *engyēsis* but had been prostituted, Pyrrhos being one of her customers. Yet he recognized that Endios had given Phile in marriage to Xenokles by *engyēsis*. That is, provided that the parents of Phile were known to have been citizens, she could be given in marriage to a citizen with the purpose of bearing him heirs who would inherit his estate and citizenship.

One must recognize an important difference between Athenian marriage and marriage in many modern systems of law. The latter accept a principle derived from Roman law of the *Digest*, that marriage is brought into being by the consent of a man and a woman to live together as husband and wife. This principle recognizes the personality of the woman; unlike in Athens, she is a party to the contract of marriage. The same principle creates a distinction between a valid marriage and an actual union which does not amount to a valid marriage; if the full consent of either party is lacking, the union is not a valid marriage, even though it may bear children. In Athens, on the other hand, the woman's consent was not required, since she was not a party to a contract but an object. She could be given in marriage by her *kyrios* through *engyēsis* or adjudicated in marriage by *epidikasia*. Moreover, these two procedures, *engyēsis* and *epidikasia*, differed from one another in content and purpose. There was no single element to make a union into a valid marriage. There was no definition of marriage to draw a precise line between it and less regular unions. Athenian practice was not unlike that of early Roman law, where a child came under the *potestas* of its father and hence had right of succession if and only if both parents had Roman citizenship.[66]

The account of Athenian marriage presented here has to face difficulties of two kinds. One arises from the oath sworn by a father on presenting his son to his phratry. The other springs from the wording of a sentence imposed in 411/10. Several forensic speeches mention the oath sworn by the father to his fellow *phrateres*. Some of these say that the father swore that the son was born to him by a woman who was a citizen (*astē*) and *engyētē*, that is, married to him under a contract of *engyēsis*.[67] This wording suggests that *engyēsis* alone brought about a valid marriage. But in other allusions to the oath the wording differs. Perhaps not much significance should be attached to the allegation that Kallias introduced his son to the Kerykes, his *genos*, and swore that this was his *gnēsios* son. The speaker, Andokides, was reporting a scandal about Kallias, he had no need to adhere precisely to the wording of the oath, and the force of *gnēsios* is not yet clear. More weight should be attached to the inscription stating the rules adopted by the phratry of the Dekeleieis early in the fourth century. This provided that when a father introduced his son to the phratry, his witnesses should swear that the son was *gnēsios* and born of a woman who was *gametē*.[68] Conceivably the combination of the words *gnēsios*, used of the son, and *gametē*, used of the woman, was equivalent to *engyētē* of the woman, but nothing compels this supposition and the variation in wording would need explanation.

Still more weight should be attached to the utterance of the adoptive son in the seventh speech of Isaios, *On the Estate of Apollodoros*. Defending his title to the inheritance, the speaker says that Apollodoros adopted him and presented him to his *genos* and phratry for admission. The speaker continues:

> They have the same law, whether one introduces one's born son or an adoptive son. With one's hand upon the sacrificial victims one must swear that the son whom one is introducing, whether one's son by birth or by adoption, is the child of a female citizen and has been rightly born (*gegonota orthōs*). (7.16)

It would not be defensible to suppose that "rightly born" was a circumlocution for "born to a woman united by *engyēsis* to the father." For an adoptive son had not been borne by a woman united through *engyēsis* to the man who adopted him and presented him to the phratry. An oath declaring that the mother was the engyetic wife of the father was inapplicable when the adoptive son was presented to the phratry for admission. It was equally inapplicable when the candidate presented had been borne by a woman who as *epiklēros* had been adjudicated to her husband by *epidikasia*.

The conclusion to be drawn about presentation of sons to the phratry is that the father swore to the purported circumstances of the child's origin, whatever they might be. If the father and mother had been married by *engyēsis* and *ekdosis*, the father said so in his oath. If the father had adopted the son, he swore an oath in vaguer terms which covered this circumstance. If the parents had been united by *epidikasia*, an appropriate form of words must have been available for the oath. One would like to know what Euktemon swore when he brought about the admission of Alke's son to his phratry (see above), but he may have perjured himself.

The other difficulty arises from the misfortunes of Archeptolemos and Antiphon. When the revolution of 411 was reversed, they were prosecuted and convicted for their share in it. The sentence included loss of civic rights (*atimia*) for their descendants, "both *nothoi* and *gnēsioi*."[69] *Atimia* was a penalty imposed only on citizens.[70] It would seem to follow, first, that *nothoi* descended from Archeptolemos and Antiphon would have been citizens but for the sentence and, second, that the Athenians drew a clear distinction between *nothoi* and *gnēsioi*. The second conclusion would imply in turn that the Athenians had a precise definition of marriage, to distinguish it from other unions, and therefore that they recognized a single element which defined a union as valid marriage. Yet these conclusions are incompatible with the succession of Pamphilos to a third of his father's estate, with the giving of Phile in marriage to a citizen, and with the absence of any element common to *engyēsis* and *epidikasia*.

A different approach must be adopted. Even in the absence of a defensible definition of marriage, that is, even though the Athenians did not recognize any one element as raising a union to the level of marriage, it was possible to distinguish between unions which were solemn and relatively lasting, on the one hand, and brief or casual unions on the other. The least disputable examples of the latter were adulterous unions where the woman was acknowledged to be the wife of another man. By *nothos* the Athenians may have meant the offspring of a brief or casual union, even though they did not say precisely what feature made a union lasting and solemn. In the absence of clear definition disputes could arise, as happened in the case of Phile and the estate of Pyrrhos. The sentence imposed on Archeptolemos and Antiphon deprived their descendants of civic rights, even if those descendants had been begotten in casual associations. The purpose of the provision of *atimia* in the sentence was to deprive the descendants of civic rights. By extending the disability to *nothoi* the sentence provided that persons suspected of descent from Archeptolemos and Antiphon should not enjoy the benefit of any doubt about their parentage.

The Kyrios and Property

It was easy to dissolve a marriage in Athens and no cause needed to be stated. A man could dissolve his marriage by sending the woman away from his house. He did not need to carry out any registration of the divorce, but he had to restore the dowry to the woman's original family and he could be sued if he failed to do so. A woman could dissolve her marriage by leaving her husband's house. She returned to her family of origin and came under the care and authority of her nearest male relative; he became her *kyrios* and her husband ceased to be her *kyrios*. Her divorce had to be recorded with the archon, and in this procedure of recording the woman was represented by her new (or renewed) *kyrios*. The clearest illustration of the practice is provided by the sister of Onetor. She was given in marriage to Aphobos, the guardian of Demosthenes, in Skirophorion (the twelfth month) of 367/66. The suit which Demosthenes brought against Aphobos was pending in 366/65 and 365/64 and came to trial in 364/63. In Posideion (the sixth month) of 364/63 the woman left Aphobos, she returned to Onetor, and Onetor registered the divorce with the archon.[71]

It has been suggested that the divorce initiated by a woman had to be recorded with the archon because it brought the husband's authority over her to an end and this fact needed to be made known publicly. In practice a woman could only carry out divorce with the collaboration of her nearest male relative. Consequently, if the husband began to waste or embezzle the dowry, the only remedy was divorce initiated perhaps in form by the woman but in fact by her nearest male relative. This predicament is illustrated by the story of the daughter of Smikrines in Menander's *Epitrepontes* (see chapter 1).

A woman had to have a *kyrios* at all times. Before marriage her *kyrios* was her nearest male relative, usually her father, or if he was dead or in foreign captivity or otherwise incapacitated, her brother, or her grandfather or her uncle if she had no brothers. In consequence of marriage her husband became her *kyrios*. But marriage did not extinguish the rights of her former *kyrios* over the woman and her dowry. It put those rights into abeyance, but they were revived if the marriage came to an end through death of the husband or dissolution.

The disabilities of women in relation to transactions in property are stated in the tenth speech of Isaios. The pleader argues that his adversary cannot maintain that a supposed act of adoption was carried out under any will of Demochares, for Demochares died before coming of age (10.4, 7), and he continues:

> It is impossible for a child to make a will. For the law explicitly forbids a child or a woman to contract for the disposal of anything of a value above one *medimnos* of barley. (10.10)

A woman could take part as buyer or seller in retail trade on a small scale at the market. But she could not engage in transactions beyond the value of one *medimnos* of barley, and so she could not engage in transactions in immovable property or make a will.

Some cults offered women opportunities of activity and self-expression, and in these they could dispose of movable property of relatively low value. An inscription of about 240 records honors accorded to a priestess of Athena Polias. It mentions a dedication which she had made and a sum of 100 drachmas which she had contributed to an ancestral sacrifice.[72] The dedications to Artemis Brauronia were made solely by women. They consisted of jewelry and fine clothing.[73] So they recall the phrase "clothes and gold jewelry," which were the expected items in a woman's paraphernalia, as distinct from dowry. Dedications were made to Asklepios both by men and by women. The objects dedicated were vessels of bronze and stone, sums of money (less than 100 drachmas), and reproductions of parts of the body.[74] The consent of the woman's *kyrios* is not recorded for any of these dedications to deities, but none of them was large in value and none involved a transfer of immovable property.

The restriction excluding Athenian women from major transactions in property has sometimes been taken to mean that with the consent of her *kyrios* a woman could carry out such transactions.

Against this view it has been objected rightly that there is a remarkable absence of evidence for Athenian women engaging in major property transactions even with the consent of the *kyrios*. Inscriptions of Hellenistic date from other Greek cities show women
disposing of land and large sums with the consent of their *kyrioi*,
but amid the many inscriptions found in Hellenistic Attica there
are none of this kind. The earliest Athenian inscription reporting
women as owners of land is of Hadrianic date.[75] Similarly, forensic
speeches, with one exception, fail to show Athenian women engaging in major property transactions with or without the consent of
their *kyrioi*.

The exception is the forty-first speech in the Demosthenic corpus, *Against Spoudias*, and it calls for note. Stylistic tests suggest
that it is a speech composed by Demosthenes at an early stage in
his activity, toward 360.[76] The speaker's name is not known and he
will here be called S. The circumstances leading to his disputes
with Spoudias were, according to S's account, as follows.

Polyeuktos of Thria had two daughters but no sons. He gave his
elder daughter in marriage to S and promised him a dowry of 4,000
drachmas, although he delivered only 3,000 drachmas. He adopted
Leokrates, the brother of his wife, as heir and gave him his younger
daughter in marriage. But Polyeuktos quarreled with Leokrates,
took the younger daughter from him, and gave her in marriage to
Spoudias. Spoudias also bought a slave from Polyeuktos; the agreed
price was 200 drachmas, but Spoudias did not pay it. Polyeuktos
during his final illness told a witness that Spoudias still owed him
200 drachmas for the slave. During the same illness S approached
Polyeuktos and raised the issue of the 1,000 drachmas still owed to
him as part of the dowry. The two men agreed that the dwelling
house of Polyeuktos was worth 1,000 drachmas, and the dying man
assigned it to S in his will.

The wife of Polyeuktos survived him. According to S, Spoudias
borrowed 1,800 drachmas from her. When she in turn was dying,
her brothers, who included Leokrates, came to her and questioned
her. In response to them she drew up a document recording the loan
of 1,800 drachmas and the sum of 200 drachmas owed by Spoudias
for the slave whom he had bought. After her death the relatives

gathered and her two daughters recognized her seals on the document. Spoudias and S each made a copy of the document and entrusted the original to a third person. In accordance with the will of Polyeuktos, S tried to collect the rents from the dwelling house, but Spoudias prevented him, and this was the occasion for the lawsuit.

In the speech S mentions further disputes, about a bowl and jewelry which had been pawned, about a bed-tester, and about a sum of 100 drachmas which his wife had contributed to the Nemeseia in honor of her deceased father. But these valuables were relatively small; they were no greater than the dedications of objects and money to Artemis Brauronia and to Asklepios, and so they do not bear on the question of the participation of women in major transactions.

Women play a part at three points in the story told by S.

1. Allegedly the widow of Polyeuktos lent 1,800 drachmas to Spoudias (41.8–9).

2. When the widow was dying, she wrote a document to record the debts of 200 drachmas and 1,800 drachmas as owed by Spoudias, and after her death her daughters recognized her seals to this document (41.9, 20–24).

3. At an earlier stage, when Polyeuktos wrote his will in his last illness, the wife of Spoudias was present. Spoudias was invited to attend but excused himself because of business and said that his wife would represent their interests sufficiently (41.17).

At the first of these points there appears to be a transaction by a woman involving a value far exceeding a *medimnos* of barley. Some have tried to escape the anomaly by saying that the transaction took place within the family and perhaps lacked legal significance.[77] But it had enough legal significance to figure as an item in a forensic dispute. A different explanation can be offered. S called the delivery of 1,800 drachmas to Spoudias by the widow of Polyeuktos a loan, but it may not have been a loan and Spoudias may not have asked the widow for it as a loan. Possibly Spoudias told the widow that he was the heir, as perhaps he was. That is, the delivery of the sum of money to Spoudias by the widow may not have been a transaction; the money had come into the hands of the widow because of her husband's death and Spoudias may have told her that it was rightfully his.

A comparable, though somewhat hypothetical occurrence, is mentioned in the speeches of Demosthenes against his former guardian, Aphobos. When Demosthenes opened proceedings, Aphobos told the arbitrator that the father of Demosthenes had buried four talents in the ground and entrusted knowledge and control of that money to his prospective widow.[78] The widow of Polyeuktos and perhaps the widow of the elder Demosthenes could have knowledge and hence actual control of sums of money, but that does not amount to lawful authority to dispose of money. If a confidence trickster persuades a minor heir to surrender valuables to him, the delivery is not a valid transaction, even though the thief may not be caught. The story told by S is surprising. Since Polyeuktos had two daughters but no sons, he ought to have adopted two heirs and given his daughters in marriage to them. Possibly he did, but S misrepresents as dowries and loan the shares which he and Spoudias received in the inheritance.

At the other two points where women play a part in the story told by S, their function is that of witnesses. The widow of Polyeuktos drew up a document to record debts, and her daughters recognized her seals. The wife of Spoudias attended the deathbed of Polyeuktos to represent her interests and those of her husband; that is, she could alert Spoudias if anything were done to harm those interests. These women did not carry out transactions, but they were not mere objects of transactions, as in the conclusion of marriage. They had at least the rudimentary personality required in order to testify. This conclusion will acquire importance when one asks why the law imposed disabilities on women.

Aristotle: Women as Perpetual Children

In the course of the first book of the *Politics* Aristotle studies the household as a stage in social organization more elementary than the city. He says that the household embodies three relationships of authority and the three kinds of authority differ. The rule of the master over the slave is despotic, that of the male over the female is civil, and that of the father over the child is royal (1.1259a37–1259b12). He adds the following statement in explanation:

> There is a difference of character between the rule of the free over the slave and that of the male over the female and that of the man over the child. In all of these the elements of the mind are present, but they are present in different ways. For the slave does not possess the faculty of deliberation at all. The female possesses it but in an indecisive form. The child possesses it but in an imperfect form. (1.1260a9–14)

Previously Aristotle has maintained that the natural slave is someone "who participates in reason sufficiently to perceive it but not to possess it" (1.1254b22–23). That is, the person whose natural endowment fits him to be a slave can understand a rational instruction but cannot propound one. This account of the natural slave explains what Aristotle means in saying that the slave does not possess the faculty of deliberation at all. His remark about the child is easy to understand; in his opinion the child's faculty of deliberation will become effective when the child grows up, but is merely latent as long as he is a child. His remark about the female is to be explained from the Greek belief that women, being less strong than men, are less able to restrain their impulses; in women the faculty of deliberation is indecisive in that it does not succeed in asserting itself over the desires.

In shorthand form, Aristotle's view was that women are children who never grow up. Those who find this view strange should find it even stranger that modern society has put an end to two of Aristotle's domestic relationships of authority, by abolishing slavery and by asserting the equality of the sexes, but preserves the third type of authority unimpaired. Strange or not, Aristotle's belief about the faculty of deliberation in women deserves some attention, since it may have been widely held among Greeks and so it may be the reason why Athenian law imposed disabilities on women.

Aristotle's view may have been plausible because there was customarily a marked difference in age between bride and bridegroom. The texts illustrating the ages are well known and require only brief notice. Suing his guardians, Demosthenes (27.4, 29.43) said that his sister was five years old when his father died, and so it could be expected that she would be given in marriage ten years later. Xenophon (*Oikonomikos* 7.5) gives an imaginary conversation between Sokrates and Ischomachos; the latter tells how he married a wife when she was not yet fifteen years old and at first she was sharply hostile to him, but when she grew less recalcitrant, he preached her a sermon, of which he was naively proud. Much earlier Solon (fr. 27, ll. 9–10 West) said that a man should marry between the ages of twenty-eight and thirty-five. Hesiod (*Works* 695–98) recommended that a man should marry when he was about thirty and take as wife a woman who was four years past the onset of puberty. Aristotle himself (*Politics* 7.1335a6–35) argued vigorously against early marriages. He concluded that a man should marry when he was about thirty-seven and a woman should be given in marriage when she was about eighteen. The tenor of his argument implies that women were often given in marriage at an earlier age. Evidently women were commonly given in marriage soon after puberty made marriage and childbearing possible. The age of men at marriage may have varied a great deal. At least a man was much older than his bride, except perhaps when a woman was given to a second husband, and so he could regard her as a child.

Objections to Aristotle

So far this chapter has been mainly concerned with deficiencies in the status of women. It has noted that in marriage and in adultery the law regarded them, not as parties to a transaction or a misdeed, but as passive objects. Although women could engage in retail trade on a small scale and could dispose of the trinkets which they brought as paraphernalia into marriage, they were excluded from major transactions in property. A woman had to have a *kyrios* at all times, and although her *kyrios* was expected to provide for her, she had no independent recourse against him if he did not attend to her interests. She could dissolve her marriage by leaving her husband, but she had to have a male relative willing to accept her, and his collaboration as *kyrios* was required to register the divorce. Women could be regarded as children incapable of growing up. If one thinks further on these lines, one may incline to say that in Athenian law women were not persons in the legal sense of beings who could sue and be sued.

Such an account would be mistaken. Several features of law and of language presuppose that women could form serious purposes, such as would have effect in legal dealings. In the speech *Against Spoudias* two sisters recognized their mother's seals on a document which their mother had drawn up when she was dying. In the document the mother recorded two debts allegedly owed by Spoudias. Some time previously one of the sisters had attended her father's deathbed in order to watch over her husband's interests. Again, when Mantias submitted his dispute with Boiotos to arbitration, he agreed to abide by the sworn testimony of Plangon on the question of who was the father of Boiotos. There can be no doubt of the capacity of Athenian women to testify.

Their relationship to property is more difficult to describe. Archippe in old age tried to distribute her dowry among her sons at her discretion. After her death Apollodoros overturned her dispositions and he achieved this without difficulty. Yet at least her attempt was not dismissed as absurd. Moreover, a feature of language concerning the final distribution of the dowry calls for note. Pleading in support of Phormion and addressing Apollodoros, Demosthenes says: "When you demanded proportionate distribution of the maternal property . . ." (36.32). That is, the dowry which accompanied the mother is spoken of as *ta mētrōia*, "the mother's property." This is the language of ownership.

In forensic speeches women are said to take action at law in order to assert rights to property. Thus in the dispute about the estate of Pyrrhos both Phile and the mother of the speaker of the extant speech claimed the inheritance. Each of these women was represented by her *kyrios*, but each of them was said to make the claim herself. In such a context the relation of the woman to her *kyrios* was the same as that of a modern litigant to his attorney. It would be mistaken to say that a litigant lacks personality because he has an attorney to represent him.

Women could inherit property from a man who died intestate. If he left no children, the order of succession was as follows.

1. The estate passed first to the deceased's brothers begotten by the same father and to the children of those brothers.
2. If there were no relatives of type 1, it passed to his sisters begotten by the same father and to their children.
3. If there were no relatives of types 1 or 2, it passed to the cousins of the deceased on his father's side and to the children of those cousins.
4. If there were no relatives of types 1, 2, or 3, it passed to the relatives of the deceased on his mother's side in the same order.[79]

It is to be noted that the estate could not merely be transmitted through women but could be inherited by women including sisters and female cousins, for the general term "cousins" includes both sexes. Doubtless the women were to be represented by their *kyrioi*, but the language of law spoke of the women themselves as becoming owners by inheritance.

Women could likewise inherit property under a will. The possibility is well illustrated by the fifth speech of Isaios, *On the Estate of Dikaiogenes*. Dikaiogenes II was killed in battle in 411. His will assigned a sixth of his property to each of his four sisters and a third to his cousin, Dikaiogenes III, whom he adopted (5.5–6). Twelve years later Dikaiogenes III contrived to acquire the whole inheritance. The speaker, himself the son of one of the women, says that by this maneuver Dikaiogenes III deprived the four sisters of their shares (5.7–9). The dispute continued with ramifications. Each of the four women had a husband to represent her. At the later stage, when the extant speech was delivered, the speaker pleaded as *kyrios* for his mother. But the women are spoken of as acquiring and therefore owning property by inheritance. Similarly in the Pseudo-Demosthenic speech *Against Makartatos* a woman is said to have claimed the estate of Hagnias as his next of kin and to have won her case in court (43.3–6).

Further speeches of Isaios tell of women inheriting property, sometimes after litigation. The seventh speech says that Apollodoros made a will, bequeathing his property to his uterine sister and providing for her marriage to a certain Lakratides (7.9). The litigant's adversary is identified as the wife of Pronapes (7.18; cf. 7.45). Again, the estate of an *epikleros* is said to be hers (10.14) and she is said to be *kyria* of it (10.23). The complicated story told in the eleventh speech of Isaios includes an occasion where a man adopted his niece as his heir in his will (11.8) and one where a woman sued a distant male relative for an inheritance and won (11.9). But particular interest attaches to the following passage in the same speech:

> It came about that Stratokles received a fortune of more than two and a half talents in addition to his original property. For at death Theophon, the brother of the wife of Stratokles, adopted one of his daughters and left her his property, comprising land at Eleusis worth two talents, 60 sheep, 100 goats, furniture, a fine horse which he rode as an officer of cavalry, and all his other goods. Stratokles became *kyrios* of this property for nine whole years. Then he left property worth five talents and 3,000 drachmas including his own patrimony but excluding the property which Theophon had given to his daughter. (11.41–42)

Here the daughter of Stratokles is said to have inherited property under the will of Theophon. Stratokles is said to have received the same property and become *kyrios* of it, but it is distinguished from his own property.

Whether Athenian women could own property, beyond trinkets and paraphernalia, depends on a question of definition, and it is an important question. The Greeks, it has been maintained, regarded ownership of property as essentially a right to use the property, and so the power to alienate, being the extreme kind of use, was the test of ownership.[80] If this test is applied, it follows that a woman did not own her dowry. When women are spoken of as having property, their *kyrioi* have full authority to administer it. Yet in such cases the *kyrios* is not said unconditionally to own the woman's property; notably in the case of the daughter of Stratokles, mentioned above, the property which the father left at death is distinguished from that of his daughter. Likewise, if a married man fell into debt, his creditors could seize his property but he could at least try to prevent them from seizing his wife's dowry.

A positive account of ownership, an account, that is, which defines ownership as authority to use and in particular to alienate property, has obvious attractions but leads to difficulties. In the first place the use which an owner can make of his property varies from one municipal system of law to another. In a modern city, for example, a man may own a house and a garden, but local ordinances will usually forbid him to keep pigs in his garden. It is not often true that one can do whatever one likes with one's own. The restrictions vary with the positive law of the community. Yet assertions of ownership—statements like "John Doe owns this garden," "This book belongs to Richard Roe," "That is my automobile"—are fully intelligible to a listener, even if he has not studied the laws of the locality.

Again, it may happen that an investor entrusts property, often in the form of money, to an entrepreneur. Then the entrepreneur has extensive authority to administer the property, but the investor may still be considered the owner. This condition is illustrated by Athenian speeches arising from loans made for maritime ventures. For example, the thirty-fifth speech in the Demosthenic corpus tells how the speaker and his partner, an alien from Karystos, lent 3,000 drachmas to Artemon and Apollodoros for a voyage to Pontos (35.7–8). Artemon and Apollodoros already had another 3,000 drachmas, and with the whole sum of one talent they were to buy 3,000 vessels of wine (35.18). The contract provided that they should take the wine to Pontos and sell it there; with the proceeds they should buy a new cargo; they should bring this to Athens and sell it there. Within twenty days of their return to Athens they should refund the loan, and until they did so, the speaker and his partner "should be owners of the cargo."[81] While the contract was in force, Artemon and Apollodoros had extensive authority to administer the property lent to them, but their creditors were still held to own that property.

In loans for maritime ventures the entrepreneur, who administered the property lent to him, could be said to be *kyrios* of that property, but expressions stating ownership, expressions of the type "our property" and "someone else's property" uniformly specify the investor (or creditor) as the owner.[82] In other enterprises too *kyrios* is used of the man to whom an owner entrusts property for commercial management. When Pasion put Phormion in charge of much of the business of the bank, he is said to have made him "*kyrios* of much property."[83]

A comparable distinction between the owner and the administrator of property has to be drawn where there is a minor heir. The minor is indubitably the owner of the property, but he has no power to use or alienate it. Instead it is administered for him by a guardian or trustee. In Athens the guardian of the minor could be called *kyrios* of the minor's property.[84] The administrator's authority to manage the property was limited. Judging from the speeches of Demosthenes against his guardians, some of the limitations could only be made effective after the minor came of age, but it is to be noted that at a much earlier stage Demochares, the brother-in-law of the widowed mother of Demosthenes, interceded successfully with Aphobos, the trustee, on behalf of the widow.[85]

Enough has been said to show that a positive account of ownership, an account starting from the owner's rights to use and alienate the property, is unsatisfactory. People other than the owner may have rights which bear on the property and limit the owner's rights. In particular, apart from the owner, there can be an administrator, whose authority over the property may be extensive or restricted, and in Athens such an administrator could be called *kyrios* of the property. A negative account of ownership is to be preferred. That is, a person is owner of property if all other persons in the world are denied access to that property. In other words, "This is my automobile" means "No one else can touch this automobile." This account has the merit of accommodating without difficulty restrictions on the owner's right to use his property; "This is my automobile" does not mean "I am licensed to drive this automobile." It should also be noted that a negative account treats ownership, not primarily as a relation between a person and a thing, but as a relation between persons, namely between one person, the owner, and all other persons.[86]

A negative account of ownership has to admit that sometimes persons other than the owner may have a right of access to the property. On the one hand the owner may create such rights by lending or leasing his property to a borrower or tenant. Since the relationship is contractual and arises with the owner's consent, it does not impair the proposed account of ownership. On the other hand that account is impaired somewhat if the law gives an administrator access to the property because the owner is incapacitated, for example, by being a minor or insane. But this modification to the negative account of ownership does not suffice to refute that account, since the administrator is a specific person and he has access to the property for the specific purpose of protecting the owner's interests.

On a negative view of ownership an Athenian woman was the owner of her dowry and indeed of any other property which she might acquire by inheritance. Other persons, for example, her husband's creditors, were not allowed access to her property, but her *kyrios*, a specific person, had authority to administer her property for the specific purpose of her upkeep and the protection of her interests.[87] This authority included representing her at law. Her relationship to her property and to her *kyrios* was the same as that of the minor heir. Thus in regard to property the condition of Athenian women conforms to Aristotle's view that women are children who never grow up. Even so it is to be noted that *epitropos*, the word for the guardian of a minor heir, is not used of the *kyrios* of a woman; presumably the two kinds of protective authority were distinguished.

Another obstacle to Aristotle's view arises from the law of homicide. A woman suspected of homicide was not assigned to her *kyrios* for domestic discipline but tried in a public court, just as a male suspect was tried, the difference being that the woman's defense was delivered by her *kyrios*. Texts illustrating this are few but adequate. Aristotle (*Magna Moralia* 1188b31–37) tells of a woman who gave a man a drug in the belief that it was a love philter, but it caused his death. She was tried before the Areopagos but acquitted because the killing was unintentional. The first speech of Antiphon was delivered by a man who was prosecuting his stepmother on a charge of poisoning his father fatally. Her own son defended her. He probably said that she had thought that the draught was a love philter and had intended to recover her husband's affections, which were becoming alienated. In the *Trachinians* of Sophokles Deianeira fears that Herakles, her husband, has become estranged from her. So she sends him a garment impregnated with the blood of the monster Nessos, in the belief that this will restore his affections. When she begins to suspect that her gift may do Herakles harm, she explains her fears to the chorus, and they comment:

> But when people have erred involuntarily, the resentment towards them is mild, and you should benefit from that mildness. (ll. 727–28)

Their allusion to the legal concept of involuntary homicide is unmistakable.

The three illustrations have much in common. It is perhaps to be inferred that Athenian men were preoccupied with the danger of being poisoned by jealous wives. Women could also be tried for other offenses. Neaira, the defendant in the case for which the fifty-ninth speech in the Demosthenic corpus was written, was accused on the grounds that, being an alien, she was living with a citizen as his wife. It is not known whether a child suspected of homicide was tried in court.[88] But since a woman could be prosecuted for crime, and since a woman could sue in court for an inheritance, it follows that the law recognized women as persons. That is, although they required representation at law, they could sue and be sued. Aristotle's theory of women as perpetual children explains their need for representation but does not do justice to their legal personality. An alternative hypothesis will be offered in chapter 7.

THREE

Women in the Laws of Gortyn

. . . .

Sind nun die Elemente nicht
aus dem Komplex zu trennen,
was ist denn an dem ganzen Wicht
original zu nennen?

(If, then, the elements cannot be separated out from the compound, what in the
whole bairn can be called original?)—Goethe, *Selbstbildnis*

Sources

The town of Gortyn stood in antiquity in the central part of south-
ern Crete, in a plain at an appreciable distance from the sea. Dis-
coveries made there between A.D. 1857 and 1884 recovered the
twelve columns of an inscription in a good state of preservation.
The text had been inscribed on an arc, some 30 feet in length, of a
circular wall; if the circle was completed, it had a diameter of
nearly 100 feet. The forms of the letters, compared to those on
coins, suggest that the inscription was cut in the fifth century B.C.
Later, perhaps in the first century B.C., the wall was dismantled and
erected anew at a different place to support a theater. At its original
location it had been part of a building, perhaps a court of law.

The inscription has come to be called "the law code of Gortyn."
It is indeed a series of laws. Most of them begin with a protasis in
the form "If anyone does such and such a thing," or "Whoever does
such and such a thing," and continue by saying in the apodosis
what consequence is to follow or what remedy is to be provided.
But although the authors of the text arranged the laws systemati-

cally, their work is not as comprehensive as the word "code" might lead one to suspect. The text includes, for example, provisions on some delicts but none on homicide. Again, there are elaborate rules saying how an heiress is to be given in marriage but none about giving any other woman in marriage. The people of Gortyn must have had laws, written or customary, on marriage and homicide. The inscribed text is itself complete, for it opens by invoking "Gods," and its last column ends in the nineteenth line, whereas the other columns run to 53, 54, 55, or 56 lines each. But presumably the inscription gives only a part of the body of law observed in Gortyn. The reason for inscribing these laws escapes conjecture.[1]

Apart from being perhaps the most handsome of the inscriptions recovered by exploration in Greek lands, the code promises to be a singularly valuable source of information about law and society. But to understand it one must study some crucial and recurrent terms. Occasionally these are defined in the text. Thus the "heiress" is defined at VIII 40–42:

> Let a woman be a *patrōiōkos*, if she has no father or brother begotten by the same father.

Again, the meaning of terms can sometimes be inferred from the provisions. This can be illustrated from monetary units. Payments to be made are stated sometimes in drachmas and sometimes in staters. One needs to ask, how many drachmas was the Cretan stater worth? An answer can be reached by combining two passages. First, the code opens with provisions against a claimant who seizes a man without first gaining the judgment of a court. The judge is to condemn the claimant to a fine and order him to release the captive within three days. The text continues:

> But if he does not release him, let him condemn him to pay a stater in the case of a free man but a drachma in the case of a slave for every day until he releases him. (I 7–11)

This rule implies that the stater and the drachma differed in value, that is, the stater was not worth one drachma. The second passage (II 2–10) states payments to be made for rape and the relevant parts can be summarized thus:

1. For rape of a free person by a free person the payment shall be 100 staters.
2. For rape of a free person by a slave the payment shall be twice as much.
3. For rape of a serf by a free person the payment shall be 5 drachmas.
4. For rape of a serf by a serf the payment shall be 5 staters.

Since serfs were a subdivision of slaves, as will be noted below, it follows from the combination of these four rules that the stater was worth two drachmas.

Yet several terms crucial for understanding the inscription cannot be explained from it alone. They concern the differences of legal status among the inhabitants, subdivisions of the citizens and classification of them by age. One can explain these terms by drawing on literary sources of later date, and these now deserve to be reviewed. There are four to be noted.

(1) Composing a universal history about the middle of the fourth century, Ephoros included an account of the Cretan constitution. It is known from a summary by Strabo the geographer (10.4.16–22, 480–84 = FGrHist 2A:70, F149). It is particularly useful in telling of *agelai* and *syssitia*, the units in which citizens were grouped for education, including military training, and common meals. It also has the following statements about marriage customs:

> All the men are compelled to marry at the same time among them when they graduate on the same occasion from the *agela* of the children. They do not take the girls whom they have married to their own dwellings at once but only when the brides are ready to manage the households. If a woman has brothers, her marriage portion is half of a brother's share. (20, 482 fin.)

That a sister's share in the parental inheritance was half of a brother's share is confirmed, with a restriction, in the code (IV 31–48). A provision of the code (II 20–23) about adultery with a free woman "in the house of her father or her brother or her husband" may be explained if after her marriage a woman remained for some time in her original dwelling. But the alleged rule requiring all men to marry on the same occasion, when they came out of the system of public education, has no bearing on anything in the code and no support in the other evidence. That does not necessarily mean that the rule rests on a misunderstanding by Ephoros or Strabo, but it should not be made a basis for further inference.

(2) Aristotle included a brief and critical account of Crete among the exemplary constitutions surveyed in the second book of the *Politics* (1271b20–1272b23). Possibly he drew on Ephoros.[2] He too tells of the common meals and he asserts that women participated; he says that there was common feeding for "women, children, and men" (1272a21, in that order). In accordance with the habit of Greek authors, he does not keep to technical terms. When he says that the soil is tilled for the Cretans by *perioikoi*, these are probably the *woikees* of the code.

(3) Dosiadas, who lived perhaps in the third century B.C., wrote a work on Crete and a passage from its fourth book is quoted verbatim by Athenaios (4.143a–d = *FGrHist* 3B:458, F2). The passage deals only with the town of Lyttos and gives details on the common meals. Each dining hall accommodated the citizens of one *hetaireia*. Each citizen contributed a tenth of his crop, but at the meal each adult received an equal amount of food, though the younger men got smaller portions. A woman presided at the meal and assigned the best portions to men distinguished for valor or wisdom. It will be noted that the remarks of Aristotle and Dosiadas diverge on female participation in the common meals. Practice may have varied from town to town or from period to period. At least women were not wholly excluded.

(4) Finally, something can be learned from Byzantine scholars. Hesychios, who probably compiled his dictionary in the fifth century A.D., explains the word *apagelos*. The works of Eustathios, who lived in the twelfth century, include a *Commentary on the Odyssey* with a note on *apodromos*.[3]

On the basis of the code and these literary sources the next section will describe the social institutions of Gortyn. Attention will then be given in successive sections to the main parts of the code concerning women: to the provisions about the heiress, to those about sexual offenses, and to the property rights of different members of the family. A concluding section will draw a comparison with Athens.

Social Institutions

The primary distinction among the inhabitants of Gortyn was between the free (*eleutheroi*) and the slaves (*dōloi*) (I 1). The latter were further divided into serfs (*woikees*) and domestic slaves (or "slaves within," *endothidioi dōloi*), as appears, for example, in the provisions on sexual offenses (II 2–45). The serf could occupy a house and possess farm animals with some security; he could own enough money to pay fines; he could take a wife and there were rules governing distribution of property, if a serf's marriage was brought to an end through separation. The domestic slave had far less protection, as will become clear when the rules on sexual offenses are considered, and he can surely be equated with "the slave bought from the marketplace" (VII 10–11).

Among the free there were likewise two subdivisions. The word *eleutheros* without specification meant a free person of full rights. Free persons of lower status were called *apetairoi*. The payment for committing rape on a fully free person was 100 staters, but the payment for committing rape on a person belonging to the household of an *apetairos* was 10 staters (II 2–5). Dosiadas explains that citizens were grouped in *hetaireiai*, and for celebrating the common meals each *hetaireia* had its own dining hall. In Greek cities membership in subdivisions of the body of citizens was usually hereditary. The Cretan *hetaireiai* may have resembled the phratries attested in Athens and elsewhere, although to say that is to explain the unknown by the little known. Possibly the *hetaireiai* had previously served for military and other purposes but survived into the time of Dosiadas for common meals only. An *apetairos* was evidently a free man who did not belong to any *hetaireia*. How the *apetairoi* arose can only be conjectured,[4] but the question is not of concern here.

Free persons of full rights belonged to units called *pylai*. When allowance is made for differences of dialect and orthography, the *pyla* is equivalent to the *phylē* attested in Athens and elsewhere. So it may be reproduced in translation by *phylē* or by the latinization "tribe." Presumably *phylai* were few in number and hereditary in membership.

Citizens, that is to say, free persons of full rights, were divided on the basis of age, and classification by age is important in the laws concerning marriage and inheritance. For females the significant age was twelve years. The code (XII 17–19) says that a *patrōiōkos* is to be given in marriage when she is twelve years old or older. Before the age of twelve a woman was *anōros* or *anēbos*; once she had reached that age she was *ēbionsa*, a term for which *ōrima* occurs as an alternative once in the code (VIII 39). Modern expressions such as "being a minor" and "having come of age" will serve as renderings.

For male citizens there were distinctions of age. They are mentioned in the following provisions about the marriage of an heiress:

> If the heir who is entitled to marry the *patrōiōkos* is *anōros* or if the *patrōiōkos* is *anōros*, let the *patrōiōkos* have the house, if there is one, but let the heir entitled to marry her receive half of the revenue from everything. But if the heir who is entitled to marry the *patrōiōkos* is *ēbion* and *apodromos* and the *patrōiōkos* is *ēbionsa* but the heir does not wish to marry her, let the *patrōiōkos* have all the property and the proceeds until he marries her. But if the heir is *dromeus* and the *patrōiōkos* is *ēbionsa* and willing to be married but the heir does not wish to marry her, let the relatives of the *patrōiōkos* bring the case to court and let the judge adjudicate that he shall marry her within two months. (VII 29–47)

Here the words *anōros* and *ēbion* are mutually exclusive and easy to understand. A man is *anōros* if he is too young to marry, but he is *ēbion* if he is old enough to marry. The two adjectives have this same implication for males as for females, although it cannot be taken for granted that the same age of twelve conferred capacity for marriage on the man as on the woman. Again, the word *dromeus* occurs elsewhere in the code and specifies a man who is not merely *ēbion* but has reached the age for exercising the plenitude of rights.

Some transactions, including a gift made by a husband to his wife and the division of an inheritance among heirs, require the presence of three witnesses who must be free and *dromees* (III 21–22, V 53–54); a man cannot alienate the property of his deceased wife unless the children consent and are *dromees* (VI 31–36). The code provides (XI 50–55) that some suits against a woman after divorce can only be initiated in the presence of a witness who has been *dromeus* for fifteen years or more. In view of its patent derivation from *dromos* ("racecourse"), the word *dromeus* may refer to participation in gymnastic and military exercises.

The sentence in the middle of the passage quoted above speaks of an heir who is *ēbiōn* but *apodromos*. This is the only occurrence of the word *apodromos* in the code. Byzantine erudition makes interpretation possible. Eustathios explains the word *apodromos* thus:

Others use the word *apodromos* in other ways. They say that in Kyrene they call the *ephēboi* "triakapoi" and in Crete they call them "apodromoi" because they do not yet take part in the common races.

Eustathios equates the Cretan *apodromoi* with the *ephēboi* attested best at Athens; *ephēboi* were young men undergoing military training in their eighteenth to twentieth years.[5] Hesychios attributes the word *apagelos* to the Cretans and explains it as "the child not yet taking part in the *agelai*, the child up to the age of seventeen years." It will be noted that in the words *apodromos* and *apagelos* the prefix *ap-* has the force of saying that someone is "not yet" admitted to something, whereas in *apetairos* it indicates permanent exclusion.

It should accordingly be supposed that the male child was *anōros* for the duration of his first seventeen years. But after he had completed that time he became *ēbiōn* and was admitted to an *agela* for two years of military training. When those two years were completed, he became *dromeus*. The word *ēbiontes* did not mean the class of men aged between seventeen and twenty years; it meant all who had attained maturity at the end of their first seventeen years of life, and so it included old men. Similarly the word *apodromoi* did not mean the class of men aged between seventeen and twenty years; it meant all who had not yet become *dromees* on completing their training in an *agela*. There was no single word for young men in their eighteenth and nineteenth years;[6] to specify them one had to employ both words, *ēbiōn* and *apodromos*, as the code does in the sentence under consideration.

The code employs two words for relatives, *epiballontes* and *kadestai*. *Epiballontes* is used frequently for relatives when they are presented as heirs. The verb of which *epiballontes* is the participle has still wider usage in the code. If a dispute arises about property alleged to belong to a mother or a wife, the parties are to plead their case "where it belongs (*epiballēi*), before the judge as is prescribed for each action" (VI 25–31), that is, in the appropriate court. Again, if someone ransoms a fellow citizen out of foreign captivity, the former captive on return "shall be in the power of the man who ransomed him until he repays *to epiballon* (the sum due, VI 46–51). The related noun *epabola* occurs in the sense of "due share"; in some circumstances the relatives of a deceased person are to sell the inheritance by auction and then "let each receive his *epabola*" (V 50–51). *Epiballontes* can usually be translated as "heirs." It is not known how far the Cretans traced kinship in recognizing the right of heirs to inherit. Athenian law recognized kinship as far as first cousins and the children of first cousins. Probably Gortynian law too set a limit to recognized kinship (this is suggested by rule 6, below).

The other word, *kadestai*, is more troublesome. In Attic and other dialects, as far as is known, this word means relatives by marriage. A *kados* or *kēdos* was a tie of personal loyalty, such as could be brought into being by a marriage alliance. But several passages in the code indicate that in its usage *kadestai* was not restricted to relatives by marriage but included all relatives. For example, if a woman after divorce gives birth to a child, it is to be brought to the house of her former husband in the presence of three witnesses. If the husband does not accept the child, the mother is free to rear or expose it. "On the question whether the child was brought to the husband's house, the oath of the *kadestai* and the witnesses is to prevail" (III 44–52). Surely *kadestai* here does not mean persons to whom the woman was formerly related by the marriage recently dissolved. The same conclusion can be drawn from some of the provisions about giving a *patrōiōkos* in marriage. If the heir, being *dromeus*, does not wish to marry the *patrōiōkos*, "the *kadestai* of the *patrōiōkos*" can get a court order requiring the heir to marry her within two months (VII 40–47). If on the other hand there are no heirs, "the *kadestai* of the *patrōiōkos*" are to make a proclamation in the *phylē*, inviting anyone to marry her (VIII 13–17). Obviously the *kadestai* of the *patrōiōkos* are not persons related to her by marriage, since she has still to be given in marriage. Again, if a free man is taken in adultery, the aggrieved husband is to make an announcement in the presence of three witnesses to the *kadestai* of the captive, requiring them to ransom him within five days (II 28–31). The *kadestai* to whom this announcement was to be made can scarcely have been restricted to persons related to the captive by marriage, although these may have been included. Indeed in this passage, as in the rule about the woman who bears a child after divorce, it should be presumed that the *kadestai* of the principal person included his or her father.

The best solution to the question of the Gortynian meaning of *kadestai* consists in saying, not that *epiballontes* and *kadestai* are different sets of relatives, but that they are relatives regarded from different aspects. Relatives are called *epiballontes* when they are entitled to an advantage in consequence of their relationship to the subject. Relatives are called *kadestai* when, in consequence of the relationship, they are required to take care of the subject or perform an act for his benefit.[7]

Finally, before approaching the substantive provisions of the code, something needs to be said about the officers administering justice in Cretan cities. The explanation amounts to a digression, justified because some of the officers are mentioned in provisions about women and the family. Moreover, procedure before the various officers is both similar to that in Athens and different from it, and the comparison may have a bearing on conclusions to be drawn at the end of this chapter and in chapter 7.

In classical Athens nearly all lawsuits proceeded in two stages. At the first stage the parties appeared before a magistrate, who was often one of the nine archons, and he conducted a preliminary inquiry (*anakrisis*). This inquiry did not produce anything in the nature of a verdict or recommendation but merely served to clarify the issue. At the second stage the parties pleaded in turn before a body of *dikastai* or judges. These usually numbered 201, 401, or 501, according to the importance of the dispute. They heard the pleadings of the two parties and decided the issue by vote. In Rome a somewhat similar division of the action into two stages characterized the formulary procedure, which flourished from the second century B.C. into the Principate. At the first stage, the proceeding *in iure*, the parties appeared before the praetor. They outlined their grievances, counter-grievances, and defenses. In the light of these the praetor drew up a formula, which was an instruction to a judge; it defined the issue which the judge was to determine. The praetor also appointed a single judge or *iudex*. At the second stage, the proceeding *apud iudicem*, the parties presented their evidence and arguments to the judge and he decided the issue stated in the formula.

The way the procedure by two stages worked is best attested in Rome, and its value needs to be clarified. When a dispute begins, the parties often argue at cross-purposes. That is, when the plaintiff has stated his grievance, the defendant in reply may or may not deny the facts alleged by the plaintiff, but he may assert some further consideration. If, for example, the plaintiff says that the defendant has seized property belonging to the plaintiff, the defendant may admit or deny seizing the property but he may say also or instead that for some further reason the plaintiff is not the rightful owner. There are then two sets of allegations as to fact, those made by the plaintiff and those made by the defendant; each set of allegations may be true or false. The dispute cannot yet be presented to a court for final judgment, since even if the court discovers the truth about one set of allegations, that may not suffice to determine the respective rights of the two parties to the thing in dispute. Before the case can go to court, the issue must be joined; that is, the issue must be stated in a way which encompasses the allegations of the two parties and makes clear their bearing on the right to own the thing in dispute.

At Rome the proceeding *in iure* was the occasion for joinder of the issue. The formula issued in consequence by the praetor could be complex. In addition to the allegation made by the plaintiff, it could mention both an *exceptio*, a further consideration alleged by the defendant, and a *replicatio*, the plaintiff's answer to that consideration. The *iudex* then had to inquire into the truth of every set of allegations. The formula told him how to bring his findings of fact to bear on the dispute, so that he could issue a judgment. Furthermore the praetor, an annual officer, issued at the beginning of his tenure of office an edict; in it he stated the types of case in which he would "grant a trial" (*iudicium dare*), that is, issue a formula and appoint a judge. Each successive praetor tended to repeat the edict of his predecessor, sometimes adding new clauses. Moreover, provincial governors often modeled their edicts on that of the urban praetor. In this way the praetor's edict became a fruitful source of law both at Rome and in the provinces.

In Athens the eventual development was different, although it may have begun from a similar starting point. Little is known about the *anakrisis* of the magistrate. Presumably it was at first the occasion for joinder of the issue. But in the fourth century a modification was made. Laws were passed defining a number of grounds on which the defendant could deny the admissibility of the plaintiff's plea, without admitting or denying the plaintiff's allegation. For example, the defendant might object that the plaintiff's claim had already been judged in a previous trial or had been arbitrated and both parties had agreed to the arbitrator's recommendation. This objection was not unlikely to be made if a dispute of a previous generation was renewed in the next generation, as there were no official records of trials or of arbitrators' awards and one had to produce witnesses to show that a trial or arbitration had taken place. Again, the defendant might object to the plaintiff's plea by saying that there was no magistrate authorized by law to bring a plea of that kind into court; the modern equivalent consists in saying that the law does not provide a remedy. A defendant's objection to the admissibility of the plaintiff's plea was called a *paragraphē*. Its effect was that the magistrate called the court of numerous *dikastai* into a prior session to determine the factual truth of the defendant's objection (for example, "Has this dispute indeed been judged in an earlier trial?"). At this prior session the roles of plaintiff and defendant were reversed, with the original defendant speaking first. If the court found that the original plaintiff's plea was admissible, there was a further session to determine the truth on that issue. If the defendant had recourse to *paragraphē*, the magistrate's *anakrisis* was reduced to a formal occurrence, called *proanakrisis*.[8]

Compared to Roman proceedings *in iure*, Athenian *paragraphē* was rigid. If the defendant wished to challenge the admissibility of the plaintiff's plea, he had to allege a ground recognized by the positive law. The formulary procedure was more flexible because the Roman praetor exercised greater authority than the Athenian archon; in devising new formulas the praetor was limited only by his own imagination and good sense. But features of similarity between Athenian and Roman procedure are easy to recognize. In the cities of Crete little is known about procedure, but two agents engaged in the administration of justice are to be distinguished. They are the *kosmos* and the *dikastas*. Aristotle (*Politics* 2.1272a7) says that there were ten *kosmoi* in each Cretan city. An early inscription from Dreros suggests that the share of each *kosmos* in the administration of justice was the most serious part of his functions.[9] Many passages of the code entrust duties and authority to the *dikastas*. He is always spoken of in the singular; presumably he acted alone, like the Roman *iudex*.

The Gortynian *dikastas* performed functions of two kinds, which are distinguished thus in the code:

> On matters which the written laws say that the judge shall judge according to the testimony of witnesses or according to an oath of denial, he shall judge in accordance with the written laws, but on other matters he shall make a determination on oath in the light of the pleadings. (XI 26–31)

That is, on some matters the laws provided that the oath of a specified person was decisive. An illustration is provided by the rule, noted above, about a woman who bore a child after divorce (III 44–52). If her relatives and their witnesses testified that they brought the child to the house of her former husband, their sworn testimony was to prevail; that is, their testimony was recognized by the law as outweighing any denial which the former husband might make, and so there could be no further argument and there was no discretionary choice for a judge to make. Again, on some matters the code provided that a person who was sued could clear himself of liability by taking an oath of denial. For example, the laws say what property a woman was to take as hers if she left her husband in consequence of dissolution of the marriage (II 45–III 12). If she took property beyond her share, she was to pay five staters and restore the thing taken. The law continues:

> But if she denies the allegation, let the *dikastas* order her to take an oath of denial by Artemis before the statue of Artemis the Archeress in the Amyklaian temple. If anyone takes anything from her after she has sworn the oath of denial, let him pay 5 staters and restore the thing. (III 5–12).

Here the woman's oath of denial was to be accepted as final proof. In short, in some cases the law provided that the sworn testimony of witnesses or sometimes of a party could not be rebutted, and in these cases the *dikastas* had the merely declaratory function of giving judgment in accordance with the sworn statement. But on other matters the judge had authority to make a discretionary decision; before doing so he had to take an oath and listen to the arguments on both sides. The distinction between the two functions of the judge resembles the distinction recognized in the opening clause of the oath sworn by Athenian *dikastai*:

> I will vote in accordance with the laws and the decrees of the people of Athens and of the Council of Five Hundred, and on matters where there are no laws I will vote in accordance with the most just opinion.

In Gortyn, as in Athens, it was assumed that the positive law had provided in advance for some occurrences and told the judge what to do about them, but on other matters he was authorized to make a discretionary decision in the light of the pleadings of the parties.[10]

It is likely that the task of the *kosmos* in administering justice resembled the *anakrisis* of the Athenian magistrate and Roman proceedings *in iure*. It was the occasion for joinder of the issue, before the case was sent to a *dikastas* for judgment.[11] It is also likely that procedure in two stages, attested in Athens and Rome and discernible in some other Greek communities, had a common origin in all places. There is much to be said for the theory that the state first began to restrict self-help when a putative culprit, fleeing from an aggrieved person, sought the protection of a public officer. The officer extended temporary protection to the putative culprit (the defendant, *ho pheugōn*, "the one who flees") until the issue could be judged, and called a court, whether of one or of many judges, into session to judge the issue. If the court found for the plaintiff (*ho diōkōn*, "the one who pursues"), the temporary protection came to an end and the plaintiff could continue his interrupted act of self-help. If the court found for the defendant, the state did what it could to protect him further.[12] One may wonder whether the similarities of procedure between Rome, Athens, and other Greek cities were due to mutual influence, and something may be said about that in chapter 7. At the end of the present chapter the question will be recognized, how to account for similarities between Athens and Gortyn in substantive law concerning women.

The Heiress

A long section of the code (VII 15–IX 17) consists of rules concerning the *patrōiōkos*. This section opens with provisions saying to whom the *patrōiōkos* is to be given in marriage (VII 15–VIII 40). Next the *patrōiōkos* is defined (VIII 40–42): a woman is *patrōiōkos* if neither her father nor any brother begotten by the same father is alive. Rules follow finally about administration and alienation of the property of the *patrōiōkos* (VIII 42–IX 17). This arrangement of the provisions suggests that in making rules about the *patrōiōkos* the legislator thought that the most important task was to give her in marriage.

The rules for giving a *patrōiōkos* in marriage may be numbered and paraphrased as follows.

Rule 1. The *patrōiōkos* is to be given in marriage to the eldest brother of her father. If there are more than one *patrōiōkoi* and more than one brothers of the father, order of age is to be observed. If the brothers of the father are dead but sons of those brothers survive, the *patrōiōkos* is to be given in marriage to the son of the eldest brother. If there are more than one *patrōiōkoi* and more than one sons of the deceased brothers, the order of age to be observed is that of the deceased brothers. Each heir (*epiballōn*) is to marry only one *patrōiōkos*.

Rule 2. If the heir or the *patrōiōkos* is a minor (*anōros*), the *patrōiōkos* is to have the house, if there is one, but the heir is to receive half of the revenue from everything.

Rule 3. If the heir is of age (*ēbiōn*) but *apodromos*, and the *patrōiōkos* is of age, but the heir does not wish to marry her, she is to have all the property and the proceeds until he marries her.

Rule 4. If the heir is *dromeus*, and the *patrōiōkos* is of age and wishes to be given in marriage, but the heir does not wish to marry her, the relatives (*kadestai*) are to initiate legal proceedings and the judge is to order the heir to marry her within two months. If he does not comply, the *patrōiōkos* is to keep all the property and be given in marriage to the next heir, if there is one. But if there is no heir, she is to be given in marriage to the suitor of her choice from her *phylē*.

Rule 5. If the *patrōiōkos* is of age but does not wish to marry the heir, or if the heir is a minor and the *patrōiōkos* is not willing to wait, she is to have the house, if there is one in the city, and its contents, and she is to receive half of the other property, and she is to be given in marriage to the suitor of her choice from her *phylē*. The other share of the property is to be assigned to the heir.

Rule 6. If there are no heirs as recognized in the written laws, the *patrōiōkos* is to have all the property and be given in marriage to the suitor of her choice from her *phylē*. But if no member of her *phylē* is willing to marry her, her relatives are to make a proclamation in the *phylē*, asking: "Is no one willing to marry her?" If no member of the *phylē* marries her within thirty days of the proclamation, she is to be given in marriage to anyone else to whom she can be given.

Rule 7. This rule provides for the woman who has been given in marriage by her father or her brother but later becomes a *patrōiōkos* in consequence of their deaths. It assumes that her husband is willing to preserve the marriage; otherwise the provisions on divorce, given elsewhere in the code (II 45–IV 17) would doubtless apply. If the woman does not wish to remain married to her husband, the rule envisages two possibilities:

a. If the woman has borne children, she is to receive a share of the property "in accordance with the written laws" (that is, presumably rule 5 above) and she is to be given in marriage to another man of her *phylē*.

b. If there are no children, the woman is to have all the property and be given in marriage to the heir, if there is one, but if there is none, she is to be given in marriage "in accordance with the written laws" (that is, rule 6 above).

Rule 8. This rule provides for the *patrōiōkos* who has been given in marriage but whose husband later dies. Again, two possibilities are envisaged:

a. If the man dies leaving children, then if she wishes, the woman is to be given in marriage to any man of her *phylē* to whom she can be given, but she is under no obligation to accept a new marriage.

b. If the deceased leaves no children, the *patrōiōkos* is to be given in marriage "in accordance with the written laws" (that is, rules 1–6 above).

Rule 9. If the heir is not in this country and the *patrōiōkos* is of age (*ōrima*), she is to be given in marriage to the next heir "in accordance with the written laws" (that is, rules 1–6 above).

The rules about administering and alienating the property of a *patrōiōkos* deserve also to be numbered and paraphrased:

Rule 10. The paternal relatives are to administer the property, but the *patrōiōkos* is to receive half of the revenue, as long as she is a minor.

Rule 11. If the *patrōiōkos* is a minor and there is no heir, she is to have authority over the property and the proceeds, and as long as she is a minor, she is to be raised with her mother; but if there is no mother, she is to be raised with her mother's relatives.

Rule 12. If anyone marries a *patrōiōkos* in a manner contravening the written laws, the heirs are to lay information before a *kosmos*.

Rule 13. If a man owing money as a debt dies and leaves a *patrōiōkos*, she may mortgage or sell property to the extent of the debt by her own action or through the agency of her paternal or maternal relatives; such purchase and such mortgage shall be valid. If anyone acquires property by purchase or mortgage from a *patrōiōkos* in any other circumstances, the property shall belong to the *patrōiōkos*, and the person who sold or mortgaged it, if convicted, shall owe a payment in twice the value to the person who acquired the property by purchase or mortgage, and he shall make good any further loss in simple restitution. This rule shall be valid from the time when it was written, but there shall be no liability for earlier transactions.

It is noteworthy that rules 4, 5, 6, and 7 allow the *patrōiōkos* some freedom to choose among suitors. Indeed female choice might be extended far under rule 4, if an adult heir was willing to refuse the *patrōiōkos* collusively. On the other hand the legislator has brought in female choice through the back door, so to speak. His primary aim has been to specify the man who has the right and duty to marry her. One would like to know whether a woman who was not a *patrōiōkos* had any freedom to choose among suitors. Rule 7 may suggest that she did not have any such freedom. For under that rule a woman already given in marriage by her father or brother acquired a limited freedom of choice, if she later became *patrōiōkos*. But more will be said on this question when sexual offenses are discussed.

The primary aim of the rules is not merely to assign the *patrōiōkos* to a husband but also to ensure that she bears children. For under rule 8 the *patrōiōkos* whose husband dies may remain unmarried only if she has already borne children. In seeking a husband for the *patrōiōkos* the legislator has been guided by the rules on inheritance of property. These rules provide that the estate of a deceased man or woman is to pass to heirs in the following order (V 9–28):

1. The estate shall pass to the children, grandchildren, and great-grandchildren of the deceased.
2. If there are no heirs of class 1, it shall pass to the brothers of the deceased or the children of those brothers or the children of those children.
3. If there are no heirs of classes 1 or 2, it shall pass to the sisters of the deceased or to the children of those sisters or to the children of those children.
4. If there are no heirs of classes 1, 2, or 3, it shall pass to "those to whom it belongs (*epiballēi*) as source of the property" (the meaning is obscure).
5. Finally, "if there are no *epiballontes*," a provision of uncertain meaning follows.[13]

Evidently heirs of the first four classes were called *epiballontes*, the same word as is used for the heir who is to take the *patrōiōkos* in marriage.

In Athens likewise the order of succession to an *epiklēros* was the same as the order of intestate succession to property. But in comparison with the Athenian rules about the *epiklēros* the salient feature of the Gortynian rules about the *patrōiōkos* is their far greater elaboration. It is to be presumed that these rules, including those on administering the property of the *patrōiōkos* and including the sanctions in rules 12 and 13, were devised not in any spirit of utopian speculation but to meet actual predicaments. Why, then, did the people of Gortyn draw up more extensive provisions about the heiress than the Athenians?

The answer is to be found in the different degrees to which testamentary bequest was developed in the two communities. The Gortynian code provides (X 33–XI 23) for adoption of sons, a procedure scarcely distinguishable from testament.[14] Adoption was to be carried out at a meeting of the citizens in the place of assembly.[15] If there were no born children, the adoptive son inherited all the property and obligations of the adopter. But if there were born children, the adoptive son was to have a daughter's share, that is to say, half of a son's share (IV 39–43), in the inheritance. The adopter could revoke the adoption, but then he had to pay 10 staters to the man whom he thus renounced. A woman or a minor could not adopt a child, just as in Athens a woman or a child could not make a will.[16] The Gortynian rules say precisely what share the adoptive son was to have in the inheritance. The Athenian will in the fourth century was a more flexible instrument, although the stages by which it had developed are not known. Apart from specifying a main heir, the testator could leave legacies. When the elder Demosthenes died, he left a widow, a son aged seven, and a daughter aged five. His will entrusted these dependents to three guardians, who were also to administer the property until the son came of age. One of the guardians was told to marry the widow and another to marry the daughter when she should be old enough. Legacies were provided for the three guardians to induce them to carry out their trust conscientiously.[17]

In Athenian courts the rules about the *epiklēros* were cited in the fourth century but occasions for applying them were growing less frequent. A man who found that he was likely to leave a daughter but no sons could provide for her better by making a will; in it he adopted a son, who was required to marry the daughter. It appears that the Athenians and the Gortynians both recognized the same problem, of providing for the solitary daughter, but they reached different solutions. The Gortynians instituted an elaborate set of rules to meet every eventuality. The Athenians, on the other hand, allowed more testamentary authority to the father, since he was the person most likely to take thought for the welfare of his daughter. The contrast is between public regulation and private enterprise.

Yet although the two systems developed to different results, their starting point was the same. Both the Gortynians and the Athenians recognized the same problem, that of the solitary daughter; that is, both communities recognized the solitary daughter as a problem requiring thought for its solution. The first step taken by both systems towards a solution was the same. The female orphan was to be given in marriage to a man who would administer the property that went with her and beget heirs. To this rudimentary but important extent both systems sprang from the same assumptions about the place of women in society. Both systems considered the solitary woman an anomaly and tried to provide her with a husband and eventually with children.

Sexual Offenses

A continuous section of the code (II 2–45) deals with sexual offenses. It opens with the phrase "If anyone copulates by force with a free person, male or female . . . ." Thus Gortynian law agreed with modern thought in recognizing sexual offenses as a single category, and in this it differed from Athenian law. Athenian laws were classified according to the officer authorized to uphold them. There were (at least) two procedures to deal with the adulterer. In one of them the aggrieved husband, having recourse to *apagōgē*, brought the offender to the Eleven. The other procedure was the *graphē adikōs heirchthēnai hōs moichon* (the suit alleging that someone had been unjustly seized as an adulterer), and this fell within the province of the *thesmothetai*. The law of homicide, upheld by the king-archon, had an exception granting impunity in some circumstances for killing the lover taken with one's wife or some other female members of one's household. The male citizen who prostituted himself suffered diminution of civic rights, and if he contravened the restriction on his rights, he could probably be brought before the Eleven by *apagōgē*.[18]

The Gortynian code distinguishes sexual delicts of four kinds (II 2–28). The word "by force" (*kartei*) is employed in defining the first two. They may be numbered, paraphrased, and in part translated, as follows.

Delict 1. "If anyone copulates by force with a free person, male or female, he is to pay 100 staters." If the victim is a member of the household of an *apetairos*, the payment is to be 10 staters. If the aggressor is a slave and the victim is a free person, the payment is to be twice as large. If a free person copulates by force with a male or female serf, he is to pay 5 drachmas. If a serf copulates by force with a male or female serf, he is to pay 5 staters.

Delict 2. "If anyone deflowers by force a domestic female slave, he is to pay 2 staters. But if she has already been deflowered, for an offense committed by day he is to pay 1 obol and for an offense committed by night he is to pay 2 obols. The oath of the female slave is to prevail."

Delict 3. "If anyone tries to copulate with a female free person who is under the care of a relative (*kadestas*), he is to pay 10 staters, provided that a witness testifies."

Delict 4. "If anyone is taken in adultery with a free woman in the house of her father or her brother or her husband, he is to pay 100 staters; but if an another's house, he is to pay 50 staters." If the woman is the wife of an *apetairos*, he is to pay 10 staters. If a slave is taken in adultery with a free woman, the payment is to be twice as large. If a slave is taken in adultery with the wife of a slave, he is to pay 5 staters.[19]

The first two delicts may be called "rape," and the third may be called "attempted seduction." The rules listed above are followed in the code by provisions about the procedure to be followed when a man is taken in adultery (II 28–45). These also deserve to be paraphrased.

1. If the man taken in adultery is free, the captor is to make an announcement in the presence of three witnesses to the relatives of the captive, and the announcement shall require them to ransom him within five days. If the man taken in adultery is a slave,

the captor is to make the announcement in the presence of two witnesses to the master of the slave. If the captive is not ransomed, the captors may do with him whatever they wish.

2. If the captive says that he was taken by trickery, the captor is to swear that he took him in adultery and not by trickery. If the payment at issue is 50 staters or more, the captor is to swear as one of five men who swear the same oath. If the woman is the wife of an *apetairos*, the captor is to swear as one of three men who swear the same oath. If the woman is the wife of a serf, his master and one other are to swear the oath.

The procedural rules, especially the first, indicate that the provisions about adultery have come into being because the state has imposed restrictions on self-help. The aggrieved husband who captures an adulterer has him at his mercy, but the law intervenes to facilitate ransom and specify the rate of ransom. It should not necessarily be assumed that the statutory rates were always observed with precision. In any actual case bargaining is likely to have taken place; the statutory rates provided a starting point or a guide for negotiation. In the light of the procedural rules, it is clear that the payments for adultery (delict 4) were not fines paid to the state but amounts paid to the aggrieved person. The same is doubtless true of the payments for other sexual offenses and other transgressions recognized at Gortyn. The code includes a law of delict, not a law of crime.[20]

Of the four delicts the second, rape of a domestic female slave, requires only brief attention. Probably the payment was to be made, not to the slave, but to her master. For if, like the slave bought from the marketplace (VII 10–11), she was property of her master, she was to be protected against intruders but not against her owner.[21] The payments for rape of a domestic female slave are lower than those for other sexual offenses; that is, she was thought to deserve less protection. It is by contrast remarkable that her oath was to prevail if dispute arose on the question whether rape had taken place; her sworn testimony could not be rebutted. Thus although the domestic female slave had lower status than anyone else, she had the rudimentary personality required to testify. It may be noted that the code has no rule about homosexual rape of a domestic male slave; presumably that could be committed with impunity.

The third delict has been discussed well by others, and for the most part their findings need merely be noted.[22] The woman under the care of a *kadestas* is probably the *patrōiōkos*, the woman whose father and brothers have died, so that she is under the care of an uncle or more distant relative. Admittedly it was argued above that in some passages of the code *kadestai* include even the closest relatives, but "a woman under the care of a *kadestas*" seems a strange way to refer to a woman who had a father or brother alive to give her in marriage (cf. rule 7 above). At least the expression "under the care of a *kadestas*" must include the *patrōiōkos*, even if it is not restricted to her. In some circumstances a *patrōiōkos* could choose among her suitors. So she might entertain suitors. A suitor for a wealthy *patrōiōkos* might engage in attempted seduction, as distinct from forcible rape, in the hope of thus bringing about marriage. The rule about the delict says that the suitor is to make a payment of 10 staters if a witness testifies to the offense. In effect the rule might encourage the woman's relatives to supply a chaperone when she entertained suitors.

If this interpretation is right, the question arises, why does the law say what to do about attempted seduction but not add a further remedy if the attempt succeeded? Conjecturally one may reply that success in the attempt at seduction was tantamount to marriage, and the code had rules about the marriage of a *patrōiōkos*, including a procedure to be followed if she were married in a manner contravening the rules (rule 12 above).

The first and fourth delicts need to be compared with one another. The laws provide a scale of payments for rape and for adultery. The amount varies with the status of the offender and of the woman. Similarity in the scales for the two offenses will become evident if the amounts and their applicability are tabulated.

1. If the offender is free and the woman is a free person of full rights, the payment is 100 staters
   a. for rape, and
   b. for adultery committed in the house of the woman's father

or brother or husband (but for adultery committed elsewhere the payment is reduced to 50 staters).

2. If the offender is free and the woman is a member of the household of an *apetairos*, the payment is 10 staters
   a. for rape, and
   b. for adultery.

3. If the offender is a slave and the woman is free, the payment is doubled
   a. for rape, and
   b. for adultery.

4. If the offender is free and the woman is a serf, the payment is 5 drachmas
   a. for rape (but the laws have no provision for adultery in these circumstances).

5. If the offender is a serf and the woman is a serf, the payment is 5 staters
   a. for rape, and
   b. for adultery.

In the different circumstances determined by status the payments for the two offenses, rape and adultery, are the same, with two exceptions. Neither exception is important. First, if adultery was committed elsewhere than in the house of the woman's father or brother or husband, the payment was reduced. For if a married woman strayed away from a place of safety to a place where a stranger could take her, the offender might plead this as a mitigating circumstance, to borrow a modern term; he had not defied the householder's authority blatantly. Second, the laws do not say what was to be done if a free man committed adultery with a female serf. The likely explanation is that sexual intercourse between a free man and a female serf was treated as rape. For the difference in status made the woman unable to resist the man's advances.

In the main, then, the payments for adultery are the same as those for rape. The exercise of force by the offender was essential to the concept of rape (*kartei oipēn*). From the agreement between the scales of payment it follows that, once a woman had been given in marriage, intercourse with her by a man other than her husband was penalized just as if it were carried out by force. That is, once a woman had been given in marriage, her consent or her refusal of consent to intercourse with a stranger no longer had any legal effect. But before the woman was given in marriage the situation was different. Except for the special case of the third delict (attempted seduction of a woman under the care of a relative), the laws have no provision about a man who copulates with an unmarried woman without exercising force, that is, if she consents to the union. The explanation that springs to mind is that a union to which the unmarried woman consented constituted marriage.

This conclusion does not mean that the people of Gortyn had reached the view, expressed in the *Digest*, that marriage is brought about wholly and solely by the consent of the man and of the woman.[23] The provisions about the *patrōiōkos* (rule 7 above) recognize the woman who has been given in marriage by her father or brother and later becomes *patrōiōkos* through their deaths. Since a father or a brother could be said to give a woman in marriage, it is not likely that his role in the transaction was legally negligible. But the conclusion drawn here implies that the woman's consent played some part, recognized by law, in bringing about her marriage, even if she was not a *patrōiōkos*. If that is true, it will explain why the rules about the *patrōiōkos* restrict the rights of the *epiballontes* and allow her some degree of choice among suitors.

Property within the Family

Four passages of the code deal with the proprietary rights of husband, wife, and children. The passages concern:

1. Disposal of property when a marriage ends through divorce or death (II 45–III 44).
2. Division of parental property among children (IV 23–V 9).
3. Division of an inheritance among heirs (V 28–54).
4. Protection of property of a member of the family against encroachment by other members of the family (VI 2–46; cf. XI 31–45).

The second of these passages may be considered first, since it reveals ideas which are basic to the code but strange to the modern mind. This part of the code (IV 23–V 9) authorizes the father to divide his property among his children but says that he is under no obligation to divide it as long as he lives. The mother is given the same authority over her property. One exception is made to the parent's lifelong possession of the property. If someone is ordered by a court to make a payment, his share of the property of his parents is to be handed over to him without delay. When a man dies, his sons are to have his house(s) in town and their contents; his other property, except for rustic dwellings and farm animals in the possession of serfs, is to be divided among his children so that each daughter receives half as much as each son. When a woman dies, her property is to be distributed in the same way. If there is a house but no other property, the same proportion is to be observed (presumably the house is to be sold). If the father wishes to make a gift to his daughter at her marriage, he is to respect the same proportion; that is, he can give her half the eventual share of a son.

Elsewhere gifts within the family are mentioned. A father may make a gift to his daughter, but it is restricted, evidently to her eventual share of the inheritance (VI 1–2). A man may make a gift to his wife, but it is restricted "according to the written provisions" and there must be three witnesses who are free and *dromees* (III 20–22). The later part of the code (from XI 24 onwards) is inscribed in a different hand and may consist of supplements. It includes a statement that there are to be no actions in court over gifts made by son to mother or by husband to wife before these laws were passed and in accordance with the provisions previously in force, but for the future such gifts are to be restricted by the current provisions (XII 1–5). Although these rules allow some freedom of gift within the family, they are designed in the main to restrict that freedom. Gifts outside the family are not envisaged at all, and although adoption could have the effect of bequest or gift, the share of the adoptive son in an inheritance was limited. The underlying assumption is that although the father and the mother can administer their property, the children are entitled to their shares. Other passages too in the code will accord with the notion that the parents are regarded more as temporary administrators and trustees of a lasting fund than as absolute owners. Probably commerce was less highly developed in Crete than in Athens, and so there was less occasion for allowing the owner to alienate property and engage in speculation.

The rules about dividing parental property among children are followed by those stating the order of succession (V 9–28). These have already been noted. They are followed in turn by rules governing division of an inheritance among heirs (V 28–54). These are straightforward. If some of the heirs wish to hold the property in common but others wish to divide it, the *dikastas* shall entrust it to the latter until division takes place. If the heirs cannot agree on dividing up the assets, these are to be sold by auction so that each heir can receive his share of the proceeds. The division must be carried out in the presence of at least three witnesses who are free and *dromees*. The preference of the law for dividing the property over holding it in common is easy to explain. If some of the heirs wished to divide the property, it would not be feasible to compel them to hold it in common with the others.

The rules governing disposal of a woman's property when her marriage ends (II 45–III 44) are more elaborate than those which can be discovered in Athens. If a marriage is dissolved, the woman is to have "her own property, which she had when she came to the man, and half of the proceeds if these are from her own property, and half of what she has woven inside (her husband's house), and 5 staters if the man is the cause of the divorce" (II 46–54). Rules are laid down for resolving disputes which may arise if a man denies that he is the cause of the divorce, if the woman takes additional property from him, and if a third person helps her to do so. If a marriage is brought to an end through the death of the husband, there are two possibilities. First, if children survive, the widow, if she wishes, may be given in marriage again, keeping her own property and anything which her husband has given her "according to the written provisions" in the presence of three witnesses. But if the woman takes property of the children, the law provides an action for recovering it. Second, if there are no children, the woman is to have her own property and half of what she has woven inside her late husband's house; she is to receive her share of the proceeds from within the house along with the heirs and whatever her husband gave her "in the manner that is written" (III 29–30). If she takes anything else, the law provides an action for recovering it. If, further, a marriage comes to an end because the woman dies and she is childless, her heirs (*epiballontes*) are to receive her property and a half of what she has woven in her husband's house and a half of the proceeds from her property.[24] Finally, if the marriage of a serf is terminated through separation, the woman is to keep her own property; if she takes anything else, the law provides an action for recovering it.

This section of the code, dealing with disposal of property when a marriage is terminated by dissolution or death, says nothing about the case where the mother dies leaving children. For that case was covered by the rules enabling children, grandchildren, and great-grandchildren to inherit. Among the provisions concerning widows it is to be noted that a widow who already has children may be given in marriage again, "if she wishes." It is implied that she may remain single, if she wishes. There was a similar provision about the widowed *patrōiōkos* (rule 8 above). Thus the law assumes that a woman has some obligation to bear children. Only after she has borne children who survive does she acquire freedom to remain single if her husband dies.

The student of Athenian law is likely to be impressed by the emphasis placed on the woman's rights to property if the marriage is terminated. In Athens the dowry was intended for the woman's support. If the marriage was dissolved, the dowry returned with the woman to her original family; if on the other hand the woman bore sons and died later, the sons inherited the dowry. One could even speak of the dowry as belonging to the woman; for as will be remembered, after Archippe had died and her dowry had been distributed equally among her four sons, Demosthenes (36.32) called it "the mother's property." But the Athenian dowry only belonged to the bride in the minimal sense that others were not supposed to encroach on it. It was managed for the woman by her husband, and the only safeguard against mismanagement was the possibility of divorce, but for that the woman needed the collaboration of her original family. In Gortyn, on the other hand, the laws specify more fully what belongs to the woman. In addition to the property which she brought into the marriage (equivalent to the Athenian dowry), the woman may own, depending on the circumstances, a share in the proceeds of that property and in things which she has produced during the marriage. The laws even provide judicial procedures to resolve disputes about the extent of the woman's property.

This part of the code does not say who is to administer the woman's property while her marriage continues. Some light is thrown on this question by the further section which protects the property of each member of the family against encroachment by other members (VI 2–46). The section begins with rules to be observed while the parties are alive (VI 2–31). No one is to acquire the property of a father from his son by purchase or mortgage, although one may acquire from the son property which the son himself has acquired or inherited. Similarly a father is not to alienate property of his children which they themselves have acquired. Furthermore no one is to acquire by purchase or mortgage or pledge[25] the property of a wife from her husband or that of a mother from her son. If a woman's property is alienated in contravention of this rule, the property is to revert to the woman, and the man who alienated it is to pay twice its value to the person who acquired it; he is also to make good any further loss. "But transactions carried out in the past are not to be actionable." Thus the code states a sanction and a prohibition against retroactive enforcement for the rules against alienating a woman's property but not for those against alienating that of a father or of his children. Presumably the protection of a woman's property was an innovation and needed an explicit sanction for enforcement.

The same section of the code proceeds to rules about administering a mother's property if she dies leaving children (VI 31–46). The father "is to have control" (karteron ēmēn) of her property, but he is not to alienate it by sale or mortgage, unless the children consent and are dromees. If he alienates it in contravention of this prohibition, the property is to revert to the children, and the man who alienated it is to pay twice its value to the man who acquired it; he is also to make good any further loss. If the father marries another woman, the children "are to have control" (*karterons ēmēn*) of their mother's property.

Again, comparison with Athenian law is instructive. The Athenian wife or mother was under the *kyrieia* of her husband or of her adult sons after his death. It has been maintained that the section of the Gortynian code which protects the property of the wife or mother "is a law abolishing the economic power of the *kyrios*."[26] That judgment may be excessive. Admittedly the word *kyrios* does not occur in the code. But the phrase "to have control," noted in the previous paragraph, is suggestive. After the mother has died, the father is "to have control" of her property, unless he marries again, and if so, the children are "to have control" of their mother's property. The father's "control" does not authorize him to alienate the property. Surely "control" means routine administration of the property. If so, it is possible that while a married woman was alive, her husband or, after his death, her son had "control" of her property, that is, he conducted the routine administration. That this was indeed so is suggested by the fact that the rule forbidding husband or son to alienate the property of wife or mother was an innovation accompanied by an explicit sanction.

One more passage in the code mentions separate property of husband and wife. It occurs among the laws which are probably supplements. It reads:

> If someone dies owing a debt or after losing a lawsuit, the heirs to the estate may have the property, provided that they are willing to pay the sum determined in the lawsuit and pay the debt. But if they are not willing to do so, the property is to belong to those who won the lawsuit or to the creditors, and the heirs are not to incur any further liability. The father's property is to be liable for the father's debts, and the mother's property is to be liable for the mother's debts. (XI 31–45)

In short, a Gortynian woman could be sued in court and could lose her case. This indeed follows from her capacity to own property. An Athenian woman too could sue and be sued. An Athenian woman was represented in court by her *kyrios*. That may have been true of the Gortynian woman also. In the role of women in litigation there may have been little material difference between Athens and Gortyn. But the difference in spirit between Athenian speeches and the language of the code of Gortyn in relation to women is palpable.

Gortyn and Athens

Earlier in this chapter a comparison was drawn between procedural law in Athens and in Gortyn. In their developed form the two systems had an important difference. Each case was judged by a single judge in Gortyn but by a board of numerous judges in Athens. But the two systems also had a feature of similarity. In each the definitive trial of a case was preceded by a preliminary hearing before a magistrate. This preliminary hearing was probably the occasion for joinder of the issue, although in Athens in the fourth century its significance was diminished through the growing popularity of *paragraphē*.

Likewise in substantive law concerning women comparison between Gortyn and Athens reveals features of difference and similarity. When a husband was to be chosen for a woman, the Athenians did not allow any legal effect to her own wishes, although kind fathers may have consulted the preferences of their daughters.[27] In Gortyn the woman's choice, though subject to limits, played a part, certainly if she was a *patrōiōkos* and probably even if she was not. In Athens the dowry, though intended for the woman's support, was administered by the husband and his discretionary power was large; the woman was said to bring her dowry "into his *oikos*."[28] In Gortyn, on the other hand, the law recognized the woman's property as fully hers and safeguarded it against embezzlement, although the sanction was an innovation made when the code was drawn up.

Yet at a deeper level there are similarities. At Gortyn, as at Athens, a woman was given in marriage by her father or brother (VIII 20–21; cf. rule 7 above). If she had no father or brother, the law stated rules for giving her in marriage. That is, both the Gortynians and the Athenians recognized the heiress or female orphan as an anomaly; the single woman had to be assigned to a man, and both systems started by assigning her with the property to the heir, although Gortynian law added further refinements. In Athens a woman's citizenship was latent and consisted in capacity to give birth to citizens. In Gortyn a woman had some obligation to bear children; only the widow who had already borne children was free to remain single. In both systems adultery was an offense committed by an intruder against the husband; the character of the deed was not affected by the presence or absence of the woman's consent. Although in their treatment of women the two systems developed to significantly different results, they started out from the same assumptions and goals.

FOUR

Women in Sparta and in Hellenistic Cities

. . . .

Eine Frau spricht so, die weiss, was es wert ist,
einen Mann im Hause zu haben.

(So speaks a woman who knows what it is worth to have a man in the
house.)—G. Gaiser, *Eine Stimme hebt an* (1950)

Dearth of material compels this chapter to be short. Inscriptions of Hellenistic date tell of women in several cities but reveal little about the way private institutions worked. Sparta, the subject of the first section, is known from literary sources, but because of the provenance of these Sparta is seen through Athenian or atticizing eyes. The Athenians found it funny or shocking that Spartan women engaged in gymnastic exercises. In the *Lysistrata* of Aristophanes a Spartan woman comes to join the Athenian women who have conspired to end the Peloponnesian War. The Athenians admire her physical condition, and she explains: "I do physical jerks and jump striking my heels against my rump" (l. 82). Xenophon and Aristotle stand out among authors who provide information on Sparta. The former's treatise *The Constitution of the Lakedaimonians* is devoted largely to praise of military practices but includes statements about marriage customs. Aristotle, though not an Athenian, can scarcely be distinguished in culture from the Athenians, among whom he spent much of his life. He gave a short account of the Spartan constitution, including the condition of Spartan women, in the course of the second book of the *Politics* (1269a29–1271b19). He was much concerned to say what was wrong with the Spartan constitution. If Aristotle had written an account of the constitution of paradise, he would have said what was wrong with it. Plutarch's *Life of Lykourgos*, composed in the first century A.D. or early in the second, has relatively full information of varying value on Spartan institutions but adds little on women to the earlier sources.

Inquiry into Spartan institutions is restricted by sources far inferior to those for the law of Athens and for that of Gortyn. For the latter two cities the material, in spite of defects, is relatively informative, and so one can hope both to recognize rules and to penetrate to the concepts and aims which gave rise to them. The information on Sparta, on the other hand, is provided by foreigners, who were on the watch for curiosities. Part of the information may be no better than travelers' tales, but it is difficult to say what part.[1]

Sparta

Aristotle (*Politics* 2.1269b19–23) says that the Spartan legislator provided discipline for the men, to train them in endurance, but neglected the women; the latter, he continues, "live licentiously in every form of license and luxuriously." For boys there was public education, beginning at the age of seven years and concluding with two years of military training when the young man was eighteen to twenty years old.[2] Xenophon says that in Sparta girls engage in physical training as much as boys do; he mentions competitions in running and strength. Plutarch likewise attests competitions in running, wrestling, and throwing the discus and the javelin for Spartan girls.[3] Evidently discipline was imposed on Spartan girls, and any license they enjoyed was only attained after they grew up.

Aristotle has more precise things to say about the property of Spartan women. He writes:

> Nearly two-fifths of the whole territory is owned by women, since there are many heiresses and Spartans give large dowries. (*Pol.* 2.1270a23–25)

His statement about two-fifths of the territory has often been accepted, but it can only have been an approximation, since he is not likely to have had an up-to-date survey of Spartan landholdings to draw on. That he was talking in casual terms is suggested by his remark about heiresses. For a woman only became an heiress when the hazards of mortality deprived her of her father and brothers, and such accidents are not likely to have continued with uniformity long enough to contribute to any concentration of property in the hands of women. The Spartan heiress will require attention shortly. Meanwhile it should be noted that Aristotle's word for "dowry" is the Athenian word, *proix*. If the Spartan dowry was legally similar to the Athenian dowry, it was only owned by the woman in the negative sense defended in chapter 2. Perhaps, on the other hand, in Sparta as in Gortyn the dowry was the woman's property, protected effectively by law against mismanagement or embezzlement by the husband. But if so, it is not unlikely that in Dorian Sparta, as in Dorian Crete, a daughter's property, which she took with her on marrying, was limited to her statutory share in the parental estate.

In short, Aristotle's statement is difficult to interpret and defend. But it must be admitted that in the fourth and third centuries Spartan wealth came to be concentrated in a few families. Aristotle may be right in suggesting that women had something to do with this. The explanation should perhaps be sought in the tendency of rich people to marry rich people.[4] That is, wealthy bachelors chose the daughters of wealthy families as brides, and wealthy parents of daughters sought out wealthy men as sons-in-law. This factor could contribute to the concentration of wealth among a few families, provided that the incidence of early mortality was severe enough to counteract the effects of dividing parental inheritances among children. Decline of the Spartan population is notorious.

There remains good evidence for saying that some Spartan women had effective control of plentiful wealth. It concerns Kyniska, the daughter of King Archidamos II (469?–428/26) and sister of King Agesilaos (399–360). In the second century A.D. Pausanias the traveler reported that Kyniska was the first woman to breed horses and win a victory at Olympia; later, he added, other women, especially Spartan women, won Olympic victories. He told of a statue of her, set up at Olympia, and he said that the base bore representations of a horse-drawn chariot and a charioteer. A fragment of the base has indeed been found at Olympia. It bears a dedication in verse by Kyniska for winning the chariot race; she adds that she was the first woman to win the prize.[5] The winner of a chariot race was the owner of the horses, not the charioteer. To compete was a mark of wealth, since horses require a great deal of grass and grazing land is not plentiful in Greece, although Lakonia and Messenia have fertile plains. To compete in a chariot race was also a mark of ostentation. The victory of Kyniska shows that she differed from Athenian women, not only in controlling wealth, but also by putting her wealth on display.

The question of the status of the heiress in Sparta can lead to further conclusions. Aristotle calls her by the Athenian word, *epikleros*. But Herodotos (6.57.4) uses the word *patrouchos* for the Spartan heiress. It is not unlikely that Aristotle has chosen the Athenian word for the sake of his public and Herodotos has preserved the Spartan word. *Patrouchos*, appearing in Gortyn as *patrōiōkos*, says that the woman "has her father's property"; *epikleros* says that she is "upon the estate." But not much should be made of the difference in etymology, since "having" can be ambiguous.

It is more to the point that Herodotos mentions the heiress in summarizing the prerogatives of Spartan kings; he says that the king judges who has the right to marry a *patrouchos* "if her father has not pledged her in marriage." It would be fruitless to ask whether the king judged disputed cases on his own authority or, like an Athenian archon, called a court into session to adjudicate. It is to be noted that Herodotos, writing about a century before Aristotle, mentions this function of the king but Aristotle does not. Indeed the latter says:

> As it is, one may give the heiress to the bridegroom of one's choice, and if one dies intestate, whoever one leaves as heir may give her to the bridegroom of his choice. (*Pol.* 2.1270a26–29)

The first of these provisions is indicated by Herodotos (6.57.4) and is similar to Athenian practice; an Athenian who had a daughter but no sons could adopt an heir and give him the daughter in marriage. The second provision goes somewhat beyond Athenian practice. If an Athenian died leaving a female orphan with little or no property, the next of kin had the choice between marrying her and providing a dowry in order to give her in marriage.[6] Aristotle in telling of the Spartan custom does not have in mind impoverished heiresses, for he has offered frequency of heiresses as a reason why much land was controlled by women.

Some readers, noting the provisions which Aristotle states about Spartan heiresses, have supposed that the king's power to adjudicate them had been abolished since the time of Herodotos.[7] The inference is neither necessary nor likely. Whenever a transaction takes place, disputes can arise from it. If there is no court to judge a dispute, an aggrieved party may have recourse to self-help. But if in the time of Herodotos the king served as judge in disputes over heiresses, it is not likely that those disputes had reverted to the sphere of self-help by the time of Aristotle. If, for example, under the second of the provisions mentioned by Aristotle two men each asserted that an heiress had been given to him by her father's heir, it is likely that there was a judge to settle the dispute and in view of the statement of Herodotos it is likely that the judge was the king. The silence of Aristotle is no argument against royal jurisdiction over heiresses in his time, and the silence of Herodotos is no argument against the existence in his time of the freedom attested by Aristotle for giving heiresses in marriage.

Accordingly the implications of Herodotos' statement need to be recognized. The heiress was assigned, in case of dispute, by the king. The inheritance went with the heiress. It follows that any control which she had over the property was limited. Moreover, the existence of a customary or statutory law empowering the king to adjudicate the heiress has an implication for the marriage of other women. The law only inserted a public officer to assign the heiress because she had no father or brother to give her in marriage. That is, Spartan law on marriage began at least from a condition in which the father or brother chose a husband for the woman.

A similar conclusion is to be drawn from the oddities which travelers noticed in Spartan marriage customs. Xenophon tells of two practices which he found distinctive. First, an elderly man with a young wife could bring in a young man to beget children. Second, a man who desired children but not marriage could beget children by a married woman after persuading her husband to allow this. Xenophon adds two explanations: the women were pleased to hold two households together, and the husbands were pleased at gaining for their sons brothers who strengthened the family without acquiring a claim on its property.[8] The explanations may be Xenophon's own, but they imply that the inheritances were not pooled when a woman bore children to two men; each group of sons inherited only the property of their own father.

Consequently the first of the two practices mentioned by Xenophon is scarcely distinguishable from the rules observed in Athens. An Athenian husband could part with his wife and arrange for her to be given in marriage to another man. A good illustration is provided by the story of Menekles. His first wife bore him no children and died. Afterwards he approached a family which consisted of two brothers and two sisters. He had been a friend of their late father, and now the two brothers gave him their younger sister in marriage. The brothers went into military service under Iphikrates in Thrace. They saved some of the wealth which they acquired. On returning to Athens they found that their elder sister had borne her husband two children, but Menekles was still childless.

> A month or two later Menekles approached us. He expressed high praise for our sister, but he said that he was perturbed because he was growing old and was childless. He thought that our sister ought to get a better reward for her merits than to share a childless old age with him. It sufficed that he himself should suffer the misfortune. He asked us to do him the favor of giving her in marriage to another man with his own concurrence. We urged him to seek our sister's consent to the proposal; we said that we would do whatever she could be induced to agree to. At first she would not listen to his suggestion, but after some time had passed she gave her reluctant consent. So we gave her in marriage to Eleios of Sphettos. (Isai. 2.7–9)

From the context of the forensic speech it is evident that the sentiments reported were conventional.[9] The Athenian occurrence conforms to the first of the two practices attributed by Xenophon to the Spartans: an elderly man gave his young wife to a young man, so that she could bear children, and the children whom she bore to the young man would inherit only the property of their own father. It should be observed that in both cities the husband disposed of his wife, even though Menekles was kind enough to persuade her.

A later stage of development in the practices noted by Xenophon may perhaps be discerned in a statement of Polybios (12.6b.8). He reports two customs of the Spartans. First, a woman could be the wife of three men, or of four, or even of more if they were brothers. Second, a man who had begotten enough children could give his wife in marriage to a friend. The second of these customs is the same as the first of the practices noted by Xenophon and agrees with Athenian practice. But the first of the customs reported by Polybios is polyandry in a fully developed form. Perhaps one may conjecture that the other practice noted by Xenophon—whereby a man who desired children but not marriage could beget children by a married woman with her husband's consent—was incipient polyandry, or polyandry not fully understood by Xenophon. Polyandry can be readily explained as a consequence of poverty. Possibly one dare call to mind a remark of Plutarch (*Lykourgos* 16.1), that in Sparta a child was examined at birth by "the oldest among its fellow tribesmen," and these decided whether to rear or expose it. In most Greek cities that decision was taken by the father. Public officials, anxious to rear prospective soldiers and unmoved by paternal sentiment, may have exposed too many female infants.

Such conjectures may not be fruitful. From the remarks of Xenophon and Polybios on marriage customs, as from the statement of Herodotos about the *patrouchos*, it appears that the Spartan woman was given in marriage by a man; in law at least she had little or no voice in the selection of her husband.[10] But marriage affects property, both immediately in the dowry or marriage settlement and subsequently through the creation of heirs. It follows that the rights of women over property were limited, even though a few Spartan women, such as Kyniska, had de facto control over wealth.

Hellenistic Cities

Women appear in a goodly number of inscriptions found in cities scattered widely in the Greek area. The inscriptions often tell of transactions in property. They have been studied extensively.[11] So the present section can be brief and restricted to an illustrative sample. It will be argued that the inscriptions indicate only in the vaguest outlines the nature and extent of female authority over property.

One may start with two inscriptions, which can be compared. One of them (*IG* VII, 3172) was found at Orchomenos in Boiotia; it was set up in the later part of the third century. It tells of Nikareta, the daughter of Theon, of Thespiai. She had made a series of loans to the city of Orchomenos. The people of Orchomenos fell into arrears with repayments. Finally a settlement was negotiated and by this Nikareta was to receive no less than 18,833 drachmas in satisfaction of her claims. The inscribed text recording the settlement opens by saying that it was made by Nikareta "in the presence of her *kyrios*, her husband Dexippos, the son of Eunomides," and with other men present.

In drawing on an inscription as evidence the historian must ask, who had the text inscribed and for what purpose? Even though a certain answer to these questions may not always be possible, they will at least protect him from the unconscious assumption that the inscription was made to provide him with information and by a disinterested party. It is a reasonable guess that the text found at Orchomenos was inscribed on the orders of the people of Orchomenos to obviate further disputes with Nikareta. The people of Orchomenos had an interest in recording the presence of Nikareta's husband as her *kyrios*. This is obviously true, if his consent was necessary to the validity of the settlement. But even if his consent was not necessary, the people of Orchomenos still had an interest in recording his presence to avoid future arguments. That is, even if Nikareta could have made the settlement on her own, it might conceivably have been argued afterwards, for example by her heirs, that the settlement was not her considered decision but had been brought about by deceit or other improper pressure. The recorded presence of her *kyrios* provided some guarantee against such embarrassments. Thus the presence of the *kyrios* does not show whether his consent was necessary to the validity of the settlement or of the transactions which led up to it. Even if his consent was necessary, there is no way of telling whether Dexippos exercised an effective restraint on the business dealings of Nikareta. It is even possible that the initiative in all the transactions came from Dexippos but he preferred to conduct them in his wife's name. The inscription noted the presence of other men at the settlement. Presumably they could be called as witnesses if it were challenged. Their presence does not tell the historian whether witnesses were necessary to the validity of the settlement or indeed whether witnesses had to be male.

The other inscription (*IG* VII, 43), also of the third century, is from Megara and tells about Arete, daughter of Aristandros, of that city, and about the village of Aigosthena, which was on the coast in the northwestern part of the Megarid. Arete had bought a garden from the people of Aigosthena for 1,000 drachmas. She dedicated half of it to "Poseidonios" and the community of Aigosthena.[12] Revenues from the land were to be added to the funds for the sacrifice and competition which the people of Aigosthena had voted to celebrate in honor of Poseidonios. The inscription records the dedication. The transaction, taking the form of purchase and dedication by Arete, amounted to an act of charity which she performed for the people of Aigosthena; she bought and gave the land where the festival was to be celebrated, and she endowed a fund for the expenses.

The text does not say that any *kyrios* took part in Arete's transaction. Rather than drawing an inference from this omission, one must again ask, who had the document inscribed? Possibly, in accordance with Greek habit, Arete had it inscribed to display her munificence. If so, the failure to mention a *kyrios* does not necessarily mean that no *kyrios* took part. Yet if the consent of a *kyrios* was required, the failure to mention him may suggest that his consent was easily given. Clearly there is room for more than one conjecture. The possibility will be entertained later that the consent of a *kyrios* to a woman's deeds degenerated into a mere formality of ratification.

These two inscriptions and many others of the Hellenistic period present women as financial benefactors of cities and other communities. Note should be taken of an explanation which has been suggested.[13] Greeks of the archaic and classical periods developed a distinction between public and private spheres of activity. The public sphere embraced the affairs of the city, industry and trade, and was proper to men. The private sphere was the household and was proper to women. But in the Hellenistic and Roman periods many cities became dependent, because of debt or for other reasons, on benefactions made by wealthy families, including families outside the city. In consequence the private sphere expanded. The distinct sphere of the city grew smaller and less distinct. Cities rewarded their benefactors, male and female, with honors and with election to magistracies. But it is to be observed that, although in this manner women received honorific titles and civic offices, they did not exercise political power.[14]

An inscription from Thera (*IG* XII, 3:330) tells a far more interesting tale than those considered hitherto. It is the will of Epikteta, inscribed on four tablets of marble which were part of a base supporting four statues. Epikteta was the wife of Phoinix. They had two sons, Kratesilochos and Andragoras, and a daughter, Epiteleia. The daughter was given in marriage to Hypereides, the son of Thrasyleon, and she bore a son, Andragoras II. The story told in the will runs as follows.

Kratesilochos died. So his father, Phoinix, began building a temple of the Muses in honor of Kratesilochos and of himself. Phoinix died before the work was completed, but Epikteta continued it. Andragoras died two years later. But on instructions which Andragoras had given her Epikteta completed the work, added a statue of Andragoras, and assigned a revenue of 3,000 drachmas to the association which was to conduct the cult. In her will Epikteta entrusted the temple to the care of Epiteleia. She forbade alienation of the temple. The priesthood was to be held by Andragoras II and afterwards by the eldest among the descendants of Epiteleia. Epikteta bequeathed the revenue of her other property to Epiteleia but provided that she should pay 210 drachmas to the cultic association each year in the month of Eleusinios. The will also provided that the relatives and other members of the association should gather each year in the month of Delphinios and offer sacrifices on three days: to the Muses on the nineteenth, to Phoinix and Epikteta on the twentieth, and to Kratesilochos and Andragoras on the twenty-first.

The will is followed by an inscribed list of people who are to be members of the association. The list begins with twenty-five masculine names, accompanied by patronymics, and the first of these is Hypereides, the son of Thrasyleon. Next the list provides that membership shall extend to the wives of these twenty-five men, to their daughters as long as these are under the authority of the fathers, and to their sons permanently together with their wives and descendants in the same way. The list proceeds to ensure membership to heiresses (*epiklaroi*) together with their husbands and children. It concludes with seven named women together with the husbands and daughters of some of them.

The treatment of daughters in this list reflects ideas familiar from classical Athens. A daughter who is not an heiress belongs at first to her father's family; so she is subject to his authority and she is a member of the hereditary association for the cult of Phoinix and the others. On marriage she ceases to be a member of her original family and of that association and she becomes a member of her husband's family. But if a woman becomes an *epiklaros* (the dialectal form of *epiklēros*) because her father dies and leaves no sons, she remains a member of her father's family for life. Her husband becomes a member of her father's family and begets heirs to it. Presumably Epiteleia became an *epiklaros* when Phoinix and his two sons died.

Again, Epikteta resembles the women of classical Athens in that she has a *kyrios*. The opening lines of the will say that it was made by Epikteta "with her *kyrios*, Hypereides, the son of Thrasyleon, and with the consent of her daughter, Epiteleia, the daughter of Phoinix." In Athens too a man might become *kyrios* of his mother-in-law if her husband and sons died. But Epikteta differs from

Athenian women in that she made a will. It is impossible to tell whether more weight should be attributed to the similarity or to the difference. For the record of the participation of Hypereides in the will does not show whether he exercised effective authority over Epikteta's transactions or merely carried out a formality of ratification. One cannot tell what would have happened if Epikteta and Hypereides had disagreed on the terms to be included in the will. Neither the testator nor the person who had the will inscribed had any desire to report any preceding differences of opinion within the family. When a historian tries to reconstruct the way the law worked, he may draw on sources of different kinds, if available; records of quarrels, such as Athenian forensic speeches, can be singularly revealing.

The most remarkable passage in the will concerns the revenue of 3,000 drachmas which Epikteta assigned to the association. This revenue is said to be derived from "parcels of land which she herself had acquired" (*autoktēta chōria*, l. 32). Another inscription from Thera (*IG* XII, 3:327) gives a letter from Ptolemy III Euergetes (246–221) ordering distribution of some named estates; one of them is specified as "what Timakrita had." In classical Athens a woman could be said to have property. Such expressions occur in forensic speeches, which tell of property inherited by women. But Athenian women do not appear in inscribed records of ownership of land before the time of Hadrian. Moreover, when Epikteta is said to have acquired land herself, the phrase suggests that she had acquired it not by inheritance but by her own efforts. Perhaps she had bought the parcels of land; perhaps, like Nikareta of Thespiai, she had lent money but had foreclosed on real security.

The will of Epikteta can easily be taken to represent an intermediate stage. Possibly in the classical period the restrictions on women in relation to property had been as narrow in Thera as in Athens; by the third century old customs were breaking down, women were exercising extensive authority over property, but mere relics of earlier rules survived in the institutions of the *kyrios* and of the *epiklēros*. But an alternative hypothesis is equally tenable. It may be that restrictions of the Athenian type had never obtained in Thera or in many other Greek cities; in many cities women may always have exercised large authority over property. On this view it becomes more difficult to explain the function of the *epiklēros* and of the *kyrios*, but not impossible. Hellenistic inscriptions from many parts of the old Greek area—that is, of the lands inhabited by Greeks even before the conquests of Alexander—show women making loans and benefactions, disposing of movable property, manumitting slaves, and even owning land. Often the consent of a *kyrios* is attested,[15] but by no means always. The possibility that the requirement of the consent of a *kyrios* began as an effective restriction and degenerated to a mere formality is suggested by the development at Rome, to be studied in chapter 5.

Alexander and his successors of the first generation founded settlements, as cities and military colonies, in much of the Near East. They brought in settlers from Macedon and Greece. Private law in the new settlements persisted in a relatively, though not wholly, uniform condition until the second century A.D., after which it yielded place increasingly to Roman institutions. Most of the evidence comes from Egypt, some from Palestine, and some from Dura-Europos on the middle Euphrates.[16] The settlers came to their new homes as individual and fully independent persons, no longer bound by ties of real or fictitious kinship as in the cities of old Greece. Women were in principle fully capable of owning property and disposing of it. In the earliest Egyptian documents concerning the property of Hellenistic women no *kyrios* is mentioned. Later he appears, but his task was merely to ratify the woman's acts and this task appears to have been treated lightly. Possibly Ptolemaic legislation had introduced the requirement of a *kyrios* on the Athenian model; it was not rooted in the fabric of society. People of both sexes had full capacity for adoption and bequest; that is, they could adopt and bequeath, and they could be adopted and inherit by will. The presence of born children did not restrict a parent's freedom of bequest. A widow had fully independent control over her minor children; she could commit her child into a course of training or contract it into employment or into marriage. The Athenians had put increasingly severe limitations on intermarriage between citizens and aliens, but there were no restrictions in Hellenistic Egypt. Marriage arose from actual cohabitation. The old institution of *engyēsis* disappeared,[17] as did the rules enabling relatives to claim an heiress. Marriage had minimal effects and could be terminated at will without formality. Neither adultery nor concubinage is attested in Greek papyri from Hellenistic Egypt; for it was easy to discard an old partner or acquire a new one.

Ptolemy III had dealings with Thera to the extent of ordering distribution of some estates there. Did the individualistic customs of Egypt and the other Hellenistic kingdoms influence the cities of old Greece? Was the authority which Epikteta of Thera and other women in the Greek homeland exercised over property, modeled on the independence which Greek and Macedonian women enjoyed in the new settlements in the Near East? More than one answer is possible. The function of this chapter has been to maintain that in studying the legal condition of Greek women outside Athens and Gortyn there is far more room for questions than for answers.

FIVE

Women in the Roman Republic

. . . .

Hinter jedem Ding oder Geschöpf, wenn es einem anderen ganz nah kommen
möchte, ist ein Gummiband, das sich spannt. Sonst könnten ja am Ende die
Dinge durch einander hindurch gehen.

(Behind every thing or creature there is a rubber band, which stretches, when it
would like to come very close to another. Otherwise things could in the end go
right through one another.)—R. Musil, *Der Mann ohne Eigenschaften* (1930)

For the sake of comparison with Greek cities this chapter will consider the legal condition of women in the Roman Republic. The
comparison promises to be instructive for two reasons. One is that
the Romans were highly articulate about their laws. They thought
and wrote about law; indeed they first developed law into a science.
Admittedly comparison of Greek conditions with the less literate
societies favored by anthropologists can be fruitful, and there is
no ground to belittle such work. But the Romans thought enough
about law and enough of their thought has been preserved to make
it possible to discern principles, aims, and concepts. The second
reason is that the Romans, at least in the early stages of their development, lived in economic conditions not unlike those of the
Greeks. The climate, the methods of agriculture, and the extent of
commerce were somewhat similar. If, to anticipate, Roman law in
relation to women proves to be markedly different from Greek law,
an economic explanation will not suffice.

The private law of the Roman Republic originated from a statutory code, the Twelve Tables. Tradition said, credibly enough, that
these had been issued in the middle part of the fifth century.

Schoolboys continued to study them in the time of Cicero. In the period of the Republic private law was elaborated for the most part not by statute but from two other sources. One of these was the edict issued by the urban praetor when he took office. In it he stated the rules which he would uphold, and he included specifications of the grievances for which he would grant a trial, as noted in chapter 3.[1]

The other source of law was the *responsa prudentium*, or answers given by respected jurists (*iuris consulti* or *iuris prudentes*) to questions of law put to them. Such questions might be put to them by praetors, by judges (*iudices*), or by private persons when these engaged in legal acts or litigation. The jurists taught law and wrote treatises on law. They developed the law by interpretation; that is, from acknowledged and often written rules they elicited principles to apply to cases not foreseen in those rules. The jurists are to be distinguished from men hired by litigants to plead cases (*advocati* or *causidici*). The latter were valued, not for any knowledge of the law which they might acquire, but for their skill in persuading their listeners. They were less esteemed than the jurists. It is difficult to specify the degree of authority which opinions delivered by jurists exercised. The emperors later gave select jurists "the right of answering with the weight of the emperor" (*ius respondendi ex auctoritate principis*), and the matter was finally settled in A.D. 426 by the so-called Law of Citations; in this the reigning emperors laid down somewhat mechanical rules to guide judges in choosing among the opinions of named jurists of the previous centuries.[2]

A grasp of the Roman concept of the family is fundamental to understanding the legal condition of women. So this chapter will deal first with the authority of the father and with acquisition of property. It will then proceed to marriage, its forms and consequences. The next topic to consider will be inheritance and the related matter of guardianship over minors and over women. Finally attention will be given to the bearing of the Roman comparison on Greek cities.

The Family and Acquisition

The clue to understanding the Roman family is to be found in the large authority exercised by the father over his children (*patria potestas*). Gaius the jurist, who wrote an introductory handbook of law in the second century A.D., remarked that the degree of authority exercised by the father was peculiar to Rome; he added that he recognized that the Galatians thought that they had something similar.[3] That is the language of a man who had taken care to verify his information. Evidently Gaius or his predecessors had studied the customs of other communities and found nothing like the authority of the Roman father. Doubtless the other communities studied included the Greek cities. It is a fair inference that no Greek city allowed the father such extensive authority over his children as he exercised in Rome.

Patria potestas was extensive in more than one way. The Twelve Tables (IV 2a) recognized the authority of the father to put his son to death. In duration the paternal authority continued until the father died (unless the father emancipated his son in a manner to be noticed shortly). On reaching manhood the son could exercise public rights and duties, including military service, voting, and eligibility for office, but he remained subject to the authority of his father. Consequently, as long as the grandfather was alive, he exercised authority over his sons and grandsons, and as long as the great-grandfather was alive, he exercised authority over his sons, grandsons, and great-grandsons. *Patria potestas* was also extensive in relation to property. Only the father could own property; that is, anything acquired by the child was owned by the father.[4] In Athens a law attributed to Solon provided that an elderly father could not claim support from his son unless he had taught the son a trade.[5] There was no need for any such provision in Rome.

The authority of the Roman father reflects a highly patriarchal concept of the family, in which the furthest living male ancestor in the male line, the *pater familias*, is alone fully recognized as a person at law. It points to an earlier condition, in which property belonged to the family as an immortal corporation and the current patriarch was merely the transitory representative of the corporation.[6] But there is no evidence that that earlier condition ever existed. Property was owned by individual persons as early as the time of the Twelve Tables, for these recognize the power of the owner to alienate property by bequest (V 3). Collective ownership by the family can easily be reconstructed from the *patria potestas*, but it may have existed, not as historical reality, but only as a phantom in the minds of those who developed Roman institutions.

The forms recognized by Roman law were few and simple and they could be employed for many purposes. One of them, *mancipatio per aes et libram*, or *mancipatio* for short, calls for note here. It was a conveyance whereby ownership of a thing could be transferred from one person to another. It required the presence of the person parting with the thing, the person acquiring it, a *libripens* or man holding bronze scales, and five witnesses. The person acquiring the thing held it (for example, a slave) with one hand; he held a piece of uncoined bronze in his other hand and said: "I declare that this slave is mine by the law of the Quirites, and be he purchased to me with this piece of bronze and these bronze scales." He touched the scales with the piece of bronze and gave the bronze to the person who was parting with the thing.[7] All the eight participants in *mancipatio* had to be Roman citizens.

This form was not a sale but a conveyance modeled on sale. It transferred a right, often a right of ownership. It was the required mode of conveyance for things known as *res mancipi*. These were slaves, certain beasts of draft and burden (namely oxen, horses, asses, and mules), land and buildings in Italy, and rustic praedial servitudes, that is to say, rights of way and rights of access to water. It is not clear why these, and only these things, were *res mancipi*. A suggested explanation is that these were the things which one required if one lived by farming in Italy.[8]

Mancipatio per aes et libram could be applied to purposes beyond the conveyance consequent upon sale and purchase. With modification it was adapted to provide a form of bequest. The testator bequeathed his property, his authority over his descendants, and his obligations, in short all his rights and duties. By the time of Gaius the testator first wrote his will on tablets of wax, naming his heir and stating full instructions. Then he carried out *mancipatio* of his estate to a person called the *familiae emptor*, but the latter had no function. The testator continued to have his estate until he died, and then the heir named in the will succeeded to it.[9] Again, *mancipatio* was adapted for the purpose of emancipating a son, that is, freeing him of the *patria potestas* of his father. With characteristic terseness the Twelve Tables say: "If a father sells his son three times, the son shall be free of the father."[10] This meant that the procedure for emancipating a son was triple *mancipatio* followed by manumission. The process of Roman thought is not difficult to discern behind the practice. If a father sells his son into slavery, he does not retain authority over the son. But in accordance with a principle familiar in children's games everywhere, an act carried out only once may have been performed in error, and even if it is repeated once, it may still be impugned, but when it has been done three times, there is no room for doubt. In consequence of emancipation a son passed out of the authority of his father and became a fully independent person (*sui iuris*). Therefore he lost his right to inherit from his father.

A further application of *mancipatio* and a provision about doing a deed three times will receive attention in connection with marriage. For the present it is to be observed that as a conveyance for property *mancipatio* was often inconvenient or impracticable. For example, as Rome dealt increasingly with other Italian communities, there were occasions for buying and selling things which were *res mancipi*, but all the parties to *mancipatio* had to be Roman citizens. The Romans surmounted the difficulties by recognizing prescription (*usus*) as a way of acquiring property. The periods required for acquiring prescriptive title were two years for immovable and one year for movable property, and these periods were already stated in the Twelve Tables (VI 3). That is, subject to important conditions, such as acquisition in good faith, uninterrupted possession for the prescribed periods ripened into ownership.[11] But since prescription could be invoked for acquiring property, surely it could also serve to bring about marriage.

Marriage

In consequence of birth the daughter of a Roman citizen, like the son, was subject to the father's authority. She could be given in marriage in any of several ways. One of these, *confarreatio*, was a religious ceremony in which the parties mixed flour together. It was required if the children of the marriage were to be eligible for some priesthoods, but it is of no interest here, since it was not legally fruitful. Another method was *coemptio*. This was an application of *mancipatio* to transfer authority over the woman from her *pater familias* to the husband. The authority which the husband acquired over the woman in consequence of *coemptio* or of *confarreatio* was called *manus* ("hand"). It was very similar to *patria potestas*. The wife was recognized as equivalent to a daughter, and she had a daughter's right of succession to her husband's property. Her husband, or rather his *pater familias*, became owner of her property.[12]

Ownership of property could be acquired by *mancipatio*. Ownership of property could also be acquired by *usus* (prescription). Authority (*manus*) over a woman could be acquired by *coemptio*, which was an application of *mancipatio*. It followed that authority over a woman could be acquired by *usus*; that is, if a man and a woman lived together, the woman became subject to the man's extensive authority. Since the woman was not immovable, the period of prescription which gave the man authority over her was a year. But a difficulty arose because cohabitation might be intermittent. The Roman solution drew on the assumption that doing a deed three times is decisive. If marriage came about by *usus* but the woman stayed away from her husband's house for three nights each year, she did not become subject to his authority. This rule was stated in the Twelve Tables (VI 5). A woman not subject to her husband's authority remained under the *patria potestas* of her *pater familias* and consequently had right of succession to paternal property.

Thus marriage came about in each of three ways (*confarreatio, coemptio, usus*) and it brought about unions of two kinds, which can be called "marriage with *manus*" and "marriage without *ma-*

nus." The latter could only come about through *usus* and only if the woman stayed away from her husband's house for at least three nights every year. The provisions for transferring authority over a woman from her *pater familias* to her husband may suggest that at the earliest time every married woman in Rome was subject to the *manus* of her husband. But marriage without *manus* is attested in the earliest documentary evidence that survives, for the Twelve Tables stated the rule about three nights.

These differences in marriage had no effect on the status of the children. Provided that the father and the mother were both Roman citizens,[13] the union was *iustae nuptiae* (lawful marriage), and the children came under the *patria potestas* of the father and had right of succession to his property. These consequences followed, even if the union were of short duration, divorce being easy.[14]

It is not unlikely that in early Rome marriage was preceded by a betrothal. In this the bridegroom and the man giving the woman in marriage exchanged promises (*sponsalia*) and these promises were actionable. But allusions in the comedies of Plautus show that by about 200 the betrothal had degenerated into a unilateral declaration of intent by the man who would give the woman in marriage. His utterance was no longer actionable but was merely a social convention.[15] There is a marked contrast with Athenian *engyēsis*, which was the most important step taken in bringing marriage about.

Something can be said about the relative frequency of marriage with *manus* and marriage without *manus* in the late Republic. In a forensic speech delivered in 59 Cicero speaks of marriage with *manus* in a way which implies that it was relatively uncommon, though by no means unknown. About half a century earlier Q. Mucius Scaevola delivered an opinion about the status of a woman whose marriage by *usus* begins on the first day of the year and she stays in her husband's dwelling until only three nights of the year are left, but she goes elsewhere for those three nights. His opinion was that the woman comes under the *manus* of her husband, for within a year of the marriage she only absented herself from his dwelling for two and one-half nights, since the new day and therefore the new year begin at midnight.[16] The question may have been hypothetical, but the fact that Q. Mucius Scaevola gave thought to it suggests that marriage with *manus* was still common.

Inheritance and Guardianship

The contrast between the Roman and the Athenian concepts of the family appears with clarity in the rules on intestate succession. If a man died without making a will and without leaving descendants, the Twelve Tables provided that his nearest agnate relative should succeed to his property. A man's agnate relatives are the people related to him by descent through male ancestors. His agnate relatives include his brother if begotten by the same father, his sister if begotten by the same father, his father's brother and sister if begotten by the same grandfather, and so on. Agnate relatives include women but they exclude persons related to the primary person through women. So they exclude the descendants of sisters and aunts. Agnate relatives are people who have been subject to the *patria potestas* of the same male ancestor, or who could have been subject to it if that ancestor had lived longer.[17] The insistence on succession by agnates, to the exclusion of other relatives, reflects a highly patriarchal concept of the family.

If a man died leaving a minor child of either sex, a guardian (*tutor*) was needed. If the child was a boy, guardianship (*tutela*) ceased when he reached puberty. But the Twelve Tables provided that a girl remained under guardianship all her life. Gaius found this difficult to explain and toyed with the possibility that the ancients had attributed frivolity to women.[18] The true explanation becomes apparent if one considers the different kinds of *tutor*.

A *tutor* could be appointed in more than one way. Sometimes the deceased father had designated a *tutor* in his will; he was then the *tutor testamentarius*. But if the deceased father had not done so, *tutela* passed to the agnate relatives in order of proximity. Such a *tutor* was called the *tutor legitimus*, since he was specified by the law embodied in the Twelve Tables (V 6). The *tutor legitimus* was doubtless the oldest form of the institution of *tutela*. Thus, in the absence of a will, the order of succession to guardianship of the deceased's children was the same as the order of succession to his

property. The guardian's authority over his ward, unlike *patria potestas*, was modest and sprang from the guardian's interest in the
ward's property; the guardian was the ward's eventual heir.[19] That
explains why guardianship over a male ward ceased when the boy
reached puberty; he could now beget heirs, who would displace the
agnate ascendants and collaterals from succession to his property.
The same principle explains why a female ward remained under
guardianship all her life. Her eventual children were not related
through a male ancestor to her deceased father, from whom she
inherited property, and so they could not displace her agnatic relatives from succession to her property.

The question then arises, how did marriage affect the status of a
female ward? The Twelve Tables said that if a woman was in the
tutela of her agnate relatives, one could not acquire *res mancipi*
from her by prescription (*usus*) unless the *tutor* consented.[20] This
restriction protects the interest of the agnates in the woman's property. For a man to acquire *manus* over a woman was similar to
acquiring property; the similarity becomes evident when it is recognized that what was acquired was neither a person nor a thing
but a right, in the one case a right of authority over a woman and in
the other a right of ownership over a thing. From the restriction in
the Twelve Tables it would seem to follow that a husband cannot
acquire *manus* over a woman without the consent of her agnatic
tutor. Indeed Cicero in the speech of 59 remarks that marriage
with *manus* requires the consent of all the *tutores*. From this evidence it has been suggested that, between the time of Q. Mucius
Scaevola and Cicero, jurists developed the doctrine that a wife did
not come under the *manus* of her husband unless consent was
given by her *tutor* of whatever kind or by her *pater familias*.[21]
Hence marriage could be without *manus* even if the woman was
not put to the trouble of staying away from her husband's dwelling
for three nights every year. This theory would explain how marriage
without *manus* had become common by the time of Cicero.

Two further developments in guardianship over women call for
note, since they increased female liberty. First, a husband who had
his wife in *manus* could grant her in his will the right to choose her
own *tutor*. This possibility is first attested in an occurrence of the

year 186. Hispala Fecenia had given information leading to the discovery of the Bacchanalian conspiracy. The rewards voted to her by the senate and ratified by the assembly included the right to choose a *tutor* "as if a husband had given her this right in his will."[22] It is implied that this right had been granted in wills before; one cannot tell how much older the practice was. Gaius (1.150–53) adds the important point that, once a woman had received the right to choose a *tutor*, she could dismiss the one she had chosen and choose another as often as she wished, unless the will prohibited this explicitly.

Second, at the woman's request, a praetor and a majority of the tribunes of the *plebs* could appoint a *tutor* to ratify her acts. This possibility is first attested at a somewhat earlier stage in the fortunes of Hispala Fecenia. She was a freedwoman and therefore a Roman citizen, for in Rome, unlike Greek cities, manumission conferred citizenship. When her *patronus*, her former master, died, she was no longer subject to anyone but fully independent (*sui iuris*). She had a lover and she wished to make a will, in which she would bequeath her property to him. But as a woman she could not perform any valid transaction without the collaboration of a *tutor*. So she approached a praetor and the tribunes and asked them to give her a *tutor* who would ratify the proposed will. They complied.[23]

One cannot tell how much older this practice was, nor can one discern stages of development in this or in the practice of granting a woman choice of *tutor*. In the time of Cicero the consent of a *tutor* was required probably for all transactions carried out in property by a woman; the requirement is attested, for example, if the woman wished to manumit a slave or make a binding stipulation.[24] But the *tutor* could no longer impede the woman's acts; he merely ratified them. One cannot but admire the ingenuity of Roman jurists. *Tutela* over women had begun as a restriction on their capacity to dispose of property, and that appears to have been its function in the Twelve Tables, if one may judge from the parts of them preserved. But by interpretation the jurists transformed *tutela* into a powerful engine for female liberty.[25] The modern mind often assumes that the proper way to reform private law is statutory legislation, a procedure which, though sometimes cumbersome, has the merit of allowing a hearing to many interests. But interpretation as a means of reform has at least one merit over statute. Statutes are precarious. If a reform is introduced by statute, it can be repealed by a further statute made by the same legislative authority, or it may sometimes be challenged as conflicting with rules of higher authority such as the provisions of a fundamental law or constitution. Reform by interpretation was free from this weakness, since interpretation preserved in form the restrictions which it circumvented in fact. In the time of Cicero a Roman woman might manumit a slave with the concurrence of a *tutor* who was a man of straw, but one could not challenge the former slave's freedom by saying that no *tutor* had consented to the manumission.

One may note finally the persons whose consent was required for marriage.[26] Originally a woman was given in marriage by her *pater familias*; her consent was not required, but the consent and indeed initiative of her *pater familias* were required both for marriage with *manus* and for marriage without *manus*. If she had no *pater familias*—if, that is, she was *sui iuris*—the consent of her *tutor* was required for a marriage with *manus* but not for a marriage without *manus*. It is not clear whether the woman's own consent, even if she were subject to a *pater familias*, had come to be required by the end of the Republic. On the man's side his own consent was required and that sufficed if he was *sui iuris*. If he was subject to a *pater familias*, the latter's consent to the marriage was required in the Republic and still in the early Empire. The trend of development fostered by the jurists was toward increasing individual freedom. Hence classical Roman law attained the doctrine, which is preserved in the *Digest*, that marriage springs wholly from the consent of the man and of the woman.[27]

Comparisons

It was seen above that the transactions of a Roman woman in property continued to be ratified by a *tutor*, even though his function degenerated from an effective restriction to a mere formality. This fact has a bearing on some of the Hellenistic inscriptions considered in chapter 4. These recorded transactions carried out by Greek women in the presence of their *kyrioi*. But from the mere reference to the *kyrios* in an inscribed record one cannot tell whether his participation was an effective restriction on the woman's freedom or a mere formality, as it became in Rome. Further comparisons between the types of authority exercised over Greek and over Roman women may be instructive.

A Roman woman could be subject to authority of different kinds. As a daughter she was subject to the *patria potestas* of her father or his *pater familias*. In consequence of marriage she could be subject to the *manus* of her husband. *Patria potestas* and *manus* were both severe; indeed they were very much alike, although the difference in name may conceal some difference in fact. After the death of her direct male ancestors in the male line, a woman, unless married with *manus*, became independent (*sui iuris*). She was still restricted by *tutela*, but this kind of authority was mild, springing as it did from the interest of her agnatic heirs in her property. In a Greek city, on the other hand, a woman was subject to authority of a uniform kind, *kyrieia*. It might be exercised, according to the circumstances, by her father, her brother, her uncle, her husband, her adult son or her son-in-law, or another male relative, but the degree of authority was the same, whoever exercised it. The nature of *kyrieia* may have varied from period to period and from city to city, as comparison between the rules current in Gortyn and in Athens suggests. But in any one city at one time *kyrieia* was uniform. The differentiated types of authority exercised over women in Rome arose from a highly patriarchal concept of the family. This concept gave the furthest male ancestor in the male line full control over his descendants and their property as long as he lived. The uniform authority exercised over women in Greek cities sprang from an assumption about the incapacity of women to carry out major transactions, an assumption which will be clarified in chapter 7.

Roman private law in relation to women underwent development in the direction of liberalization. This becomes evident when one studies the history of the *tutela* exercised over women. In general the law of the Republic underwent a comprehensive development from rigidity of rules and forms toward flexibility. That development is illustrated by the introduction of prescription as a mode of acquisition to escape the inconveniences of *mancipatio per aes et libram*.[28] There was likewise development toward flexibility in procedural law to meet more types of case, as the formulary procedure grew through the inclusion of more formulas in the praetor's edict. One may then suggest that Roman jurists were prompted to develop the law toward flexibility because of the rigidity which it exhibited in its pristine condition. In particular the enormous extent of *patria potestas* and *manus* gave the jurists occasion to devise ways of according freedom to women.[29]

A last observation needs to be made on comparing Roman law of the family with other systems. Long ago, in a work which has become a classic of legal thought (*Ancient Law*, first published in 1861), H. S. Maine discerned similarity between the family as recognized in Roman law and in Hindu law. He supposed that the same condition had once obtained in every society, including early Greece. Although many of his ideas continue to be fruitful, some inferences drawn hastily to Greek conditions have not been beneficial. Following Maine, many historians tried to elucidate Greek institutions from the pattern known somewhat better in Rome. Notably the *genos* attested fitfully in Athens and some other Greek cities was equated with the Roman *gens*. Happily these assumptions have lately been challenged; it is coming to be recognized that little is known about the *genos* and that that little allows many hypotheses.[30] The remark of Gaius about the unique extent of paternal authority in Rome should serve as a warning against any attempt to explain the Greek law of the family from Roman concepts and rules. The warning is reinforced by the contrast in the rules about intestate succession. In Athenian law the estate of a man who died intestate and left no descendants passed to relatives in four successive categories, and these were called *anchisteis*. In Athens, as in Gortyn, males and persons related to the deceased through males took precedence over females and persons related to the deceased through females. But persons related to the deceased through females were not excluded, as they were in Rome. The restriction of intestate succession to agnate relatives, together with provision for succession by ascendants, reflects a concept of kinship which is peculiar to Rome. That concept springs from a highly patriarchal notion of the family, a notion rooted in Roman *patria potestas*. The familial institutions of the Athenians, or indeed of the Gortynians, cannot be explained as due to a weakening of the more authoritarian rules preserved in Rome. No line of development leads from an agnatic rule of succession to the indiscriminate admission of cognates to the inheritance.

The Women of Homer

. . . .

Oh! let us never, never doubt
What nobody is sure about!
—Hilaire Belloc, "The Microbe," *More Beasts for Worse Children*

Much is said in the *Iliad* and more in the *Odyssey* about women, about how they behave, and about how they ought to behave. Although the poems do not belong to classical literature in the narrow sense, they were read and respected widely in the classical period; so it is to be expected that they influenced classical attitudes. One might, then, hope to reconstruct the legal condition of women portrayed in the poems and attribute it to an ascertainable time at which the poems were supposedly composed. In fact no such simple procedure is possible. On the one hand the condition of women in the poems proves on scrutiny to be elusive. On the other, questions of the date of composition and of the historicity of the society portrayed do not admit any clear answers, although modern research has discovered limits within which answers can be sought.

The first four sections of this chapter will draw information from the texts and the remaining two will inquire into the nature of the poems. The poems presuppose a recognized distinction between marriage and concubinage, and inquiry into this distinction will serve as a starting point. The section following that will consider the Homeric ways of bringing about marriage, especially the presentation of valuables (*hedna*) by the bridegroom to the bride's parents. It will next be necessary to look further into the special case of Penelope, special because to give a widow of mature years was not the same as giving a young girl in marriage. A pause will then be made to draw tentative conclusions, since the customs discovered in the preceding sections are different from those of the Athenians. The penultimate section will consider the transmission and origins of the poems; its aim will not be to propound a hypothesis but to recognize areas of uncertainty. The last section will return to the texts and reveal the degree of imagination with which the poets presented female figures, mortal and divine.

Marriage and Concubinage

When Odysseus had parted company with Kalypso and sailed away from her island, his raft was destroyed by Poseidon, but after two days and nights in the waves he was cast ashore on the island of Phaiakia. This island has an important position in poetic geography. Until he reached it, Odysseus wandered in a wonderland of monsters, witches, and other supernatural beings. Phaiakia, on the other hand, belonged to the real world, but situated as it was on the border of fairyland, it was free from the imperfections of the everyday world. Its king lived in a palace which was exempt from miracles, but unlike everyday palaces this one had walls of bronze, doors of gold, watchdogs of gold and silver, and other furnishings of exceptional quality (*Od.* 7.86–94). In the orchard attached to the palace the fruit trees bore fruit all the year round (7.114–21). So one might expect the king's daughter, who rescued Odysseus, to hold exemplary opinions about marriage. Nausikaa lives up to this expectation.

After she has supplied the shipwrecked fugitive with food and clothing, she gives him instructions (6.255–315). She will lead him through the fields, but when they approach the city, he is to wait near a grove of Athena. Nausikaa and her servants will continue their journey separately. Later Odysseus is to make his way alone to the palace. Nausikaa explains that the citizens would criticize her if they saw her bring a strange man into the city, since her deed would dishonor her native suitors. She adds:

Indeed I disapprove of any other woman who does such things,
any woman who against the will of her dear father and mother
mixes with men before public marriage takes place. (6.286–88)

Nausikaa here states two conditions which must be fulfilled if the
union of a woman with a man is to be approved. The consent of the
woman's parents is required, and the union must be public.

Nausikaa distinguished between approved unions and other
unions. The distinction is reflected in the language of the *Iliad* and
the *Odyssey*, for the poets call some children *nothoi* as opposed to
gnēsioi. At *Iliad* 11.101–4 Agamemnon advances on two sons of
Priam, who are in one chariot. The one, Isos, is *nothos* and is the
driver of the chariot; the other, Antiphos, is *gnēsios* and is the rider.
Similarly at *Iliad* 16.737–39 Kebriones, a *nothos* son of Priam, is
charioteer to Hektor. Among the Trojans Pedaios was a son of Antenor and was *nothos*, but Theano, the wife of Antenor, brought
him up in the same way as her own children to please her husband
(*Il.* 5.69–71). Likewise on the other side Telamon brought up his son
Teukros in his house, although Teukros was *nothos* (*Il.* 8.281–84).

References to concubines present a similar picture. Amyntor, the
father of Phoinix, kept a concubine (*pallakis*). So his wife, the
mother of Phoinix, was jealous and incited her son to seduce the
woman (*Il.* 9.448–53). Odysseus in disguise tells Eumaios a false
but plausible story of his origin. His father, Kastor, had many sons
who were *gnēsioi* and were borne by his wife (*alochos*). But the
speaker was borne by a female slave whom Kastor kept as his concubine (*pallakis*). Kastor himself honored the speaker equally with
his "straight-born" (*ithageneis*) sons. But when Kastor died, the
other sons divided the inheritance between themselves, leaving little for the speaker (*Od.* 14.199–213). When Eurykleia was young,
she was bought as a slave by Laertes, but he did not engage in
intercourse with her, since he feared the anger of his wife (*Od.*
1.430–33).

The passages reviewed so far show that apart from his wife a man
might take a concubine, most probably from among his female
slaves, but the children of the concubine were *nothoi* and had little
or no right of succession. There was, then, a concept of marriage

distinct from concubinage. This inference is confirmed by the behavior of the adjective *kouridios*. It is used of a wife, of a husband, and less often of things belonging to the married couple.[1] But the disabilities of a *nothos* could be surmounted. As noted above, Pedaios and Teukros were brought up on an equality with their legitimate half-brothers. Moreover, since Helen had no child after Hermione and Menelaos desired a male heir, he took a female slave as his partner and she bore him a son, Megapenthes. When Megapenthes was old enough, Menelaos found him a bride and gave a marriage feast. Evidently Menelaos intended Megapenthes to be his heir.[2] The case of Megapenthes and the treatment of Pedaios by Theano suggest that the inferiority of a *nothos* could be disregarded if the lawful wife of his father consented.

It is more difficult to discover what the essential element was in marriage to distinguish it from concubinage. What condition did a union have to fulfill, if in the opinion of the poets it was to be lawful marriage? Nausikaa implied that the union must be public and that the bride's parents must consent. Publicity was ensured in the marriage feast, a ceremony mentioned occasionally in the poems.[3] When Telemachos reached Lakedaimon, Menelaos was giving a marriage feast for both his children. His son, Megapenthes, was taking a local woman as wife. His daughter, Hermione, was to be sent as wife to the son of Achilles (*Od.* 4.1–19). Apparently a marriage feast could be held in the absence of the bridegroom. But the requirement of publicity says little about the nature of marriage, for one has still to ask, what fact about the union was made public? Possibly, in view of the other condition implied by Nausikaa, the fact to be publicized was the consent of the bride's parents. Indeed one may propound the hypothesis that the element essential to lawful marriage was their consent. A union with a servile or dependent concubine would not be marriage, since she had no parents available to give their consent. One may test this hypothesis by pursuing two lines of inquiry. One of them arises from the valuables conveyed from one party to another when marriage was contracted.[4] The other has to do with the prospects for Penelope in the absence of her husband.

Ways of Contracting Marriage

In many, though not all, Homeric marriages valuables called *hedna* (or *eedna*) are given by the bridegroom to the parents of the bride. The word occurs in some repeated phrases. A successful suitor is described as "having provided limitless *hedna*" (*Il.* 16.178; *Od.* 19.529). A man is said to have taken a wife "when he had provided countless *hedna*" (*Il.* 17.190, 22.472; *Od.* 11.282). The suitors for Penelope are spoken of as "offering *hedna*" (*Od.* 11.117, 13.378). Twice the suggestion is made that the suitors should each woo Penelope with *hedna*, and she should accept the one who provides most (*Od.* 16.391–92, 21.161–62). Eurymachos, one of the suitors, is said to "increase *hedna*" (*Od.* 15.18); the meaning is that he makes a very large offer. On first addressing Nausikaa, Odysseus says that the man will be most happy who takes her to his home "after prevailing with *hedna*" (*Od.* 6.159). In a repeated couplet advice is given to Telemachos: Penelope should go back to her father's house, and her parents "will arrange a marriage and fit together very numerous *hedna*, such as should properly follow on account of their dear daughter" (*Od.* 1.277–78 = 2.196–97). Here some readers have understood the word as meaning "dowry," that is, valuables conveyed by the bride's parents to the bridegroom or to the bride and bridegroom jointly. Against this interpretation it has been argued that the poet means that Penelope's parents "will contrive many fine gifts," "that is, attract rich *hedna*."[5] Certainly the force of "to fit together" is not clear and so the passage cannot be invoked as decisive evidence for a meaning of "dowry" in *hedna*.

The adjective *anaednos* is applied to a woman who is given in marriage without conveyance of *hedna*.[6] The verb *eednomai* is used in the middle voice of the father who gives his daughter in marriage (*Od.* 2.53); he receives *hedna*. The noun *eednotai* is used of the woman's kinsmen who are linked to the husband in consequence of marriage (*Il.* 13.382). The story of Ares and Aphrodite mentions *hedna* in an informative sentence. After Hephaistos has captured the lovers in his bed, he says:

Soon you two will not wish to continue sleeping. But my device and my chain will hold you, until the father repays to me in full the *hedna* which I handed him for his bitch-faced girl, since his daughter has beauty but no self-control. (*Od.* 8.316–20)

Thus *hedna* are valuables transferred by the bridegroom to the bride's kinsmen when marriage is contracted. They can be recovered if the woman proves unfaithful. This does not mean that marriage was a sale of the bride by her kinsmen to the bridegroom. Against such a view it has been observed that in the Homeric poems sale is rudimentary. It does not take place between people of the same community but only with foreigners or persons of unknown nationality, and the range of goods which change hands is limited; the goods are usually slaves, occasionally wine from Lemnos or Phoenician jewelry. It is not likely that a well-established custom of marriage would be modeled on a merely embryonic practice of sale.[7] A feature in the condition of Penelope when Odysseus is away confirms the conclusion that marriage was not regarded as a sale. It is suggested repeatedly that Penelope should go or be sent back to the house of her parents so that they can give her in marriage to a new husband.[8] This suggestion implies that the marriage of Penelope to Odysseus did not extinguish finally the legal relation of her parents to her; their rights in relation to their daughter may be in abeyance, as long as the marriage lasts, but will revive if the marriage comes to an end through the (presumed) death of the husband. In sale the vendor alienates wholly his right to the thing sold in consideration of the price which he accepts.

Provided that it is recognized that marriage had nothing to do with sale, the old-fashioned translation of *hedna* as "bride-price" is acceptable. Some have lately preferred "bride-wealth," but the term is clumsy and not clear. *Hedna* should be distinguished from the gifts (*dōra*) which might precede or accompany marriage as an embellishment. The father of the bride may give *dōra* with his daughter to the bridegroom.[9] Telemachos can undertake to give gifts to the suitor whom Penelope chooses as her husband (*Od.* 20.342). Suitors might give gifts to the people (*philoi*) of the woman whom they wooed; Penelope reminded her suitors of this custom (*Od.* 18.275–80) and thereby elicited gifts from them. Again, the father of a bride might give his daughter gifts when she set off for the house of the bridegroom, and these gifts could include slaves.[10] Gifts of this last kind are the bride's paraphernalia, known in classical Athens and other places. There is no trace in the Homeric poems of dowry in the strict Athenian sense of an amount of valuables assessed and entrusted to the bridegroom by the bride's family for her maintenance. Gifts in Homeric marriage are a ready way of establishing friendly relations or improving them. They are never integral to the conclusion of marriage, whereas *hedna* sometimes were.

Yet the poems tell of some marriages where there were no *hedna*. In studying these one may start from "marriage by prowess," as it may be called. A clear pattern can be recognized when a stranger does a man a great service and the beneficiary gives his daughter and other rewards to the stranger. Othryoneus came to fight in defense of Troy. He asked that Kassandra, the most beautiful of the daughters of Priam, be given to him without payment of *hedna*, and he undertook to drive the Achaians from Troy. Priam agreed to the proposal. But Othryoneus was killed in battle. On killing him Idomeneus boasted that the besieging force would have brought the most beautiful of the daughters of Agamemnon and given her in marriage to Othryoneus, had he fought for them (*Il.* 13.363–82). A bargain of a similar kind will come about if the father of a woman offers her in marriage to a man to induce him to desist from inflicting an injury on the father. Agamemnon offered Achilles his choice among Agamemnon's three daughters, also a gift of seven towns, provided that Achilles would desist from his anger and return to war (*Il.* 9.144–57, 286–99). In this offer, as in the story of Othryoneus, it is assumed that a daughter is a valuable asset to her family of origin and so she may be given as a reward to a man who has done that family a service.

The pattern is similar if the father gives his daughter to a man who has performed deeds of prowess, even though these deeds do not bring immediate benefit to the woman's family. The king of Lykia set Bellerophon a series of heroic tasks. When Bellerophon had performed them, the king gave him his daughter and half of the kingdom (*Il.* 6.191–93). A man who had slain the Chimaira,

defeated the Solymoi, and overcome the Amazons was a good ally
to have in case of future emergencies. The same principle of honor-
ing outstanding achievement with the gift of a bride is illustrated
by the stylized story of the woman who was to be given in marriage to the man who could string a composite bow and shoot an
arrow through the heads of twelve axes. Another illustration should
probably be found in the marriage of Tydeus, mentioned briefly by
his son Diomedes (*Il.* 14.119–25). Tydeus left Pleuron, where he
had been born, and settled in Argos after wandering. He married a
daughter of Adrastos and became owner of a rich house and extensive land. Diomedes does not specify any deed performed by Tydeus
but adds: "He excelled all the Achaians with the spear." In the
same way Alkinoos, the paramount king of the Phaiakians, conceived admiration for Odysseus, who had come to him in disguise.
He expressed the wish that Odysseus would accept his daughter in
marriage and settle to dwell in the kingdom; Alkinoos would give
him a house and possessions (*Od.* 7.311–15).

One may accordingly distinguish between "marriage with *hedna*" and "marriage by prowess." In the latter a successful suitor
takes up residence in the house or kingdom of his father-in-law. But
the two kinds of marriage do not coincide in any simple way with a
distinction between virilocal and uxorilocal residence. If Othryoneus had survived and driven the Achaians away, it is not clear that
he would have resided in Troy afterwards. If Achilles had accepted
Agamemnon's offer in *Iliad* 9, it is not clear that he would have
taken up residence in the Peloponnese instead of returning to the
kingdom of Peleus. The place of residence is indifferent to the Homeric concept of marriage. Moreover, the two ways of bringing
about marriage, by prowess and by *hedna*, both spring from the
same principles. The fundamental assumption is that each member
of a family is of value to that family. Therefore, if a suitor is to take
a woman as wife from the family, he must give the family benefits
or at least provide a reliable prospect of future benefits. He may win
his bride by driving away the enemies who attack her father's kingdom, or by overcoming Amazons or Solymoi he may show that her
family can count on him for beneficial deeds in future. If he has no
opportunity to perform deeds of prowess, he can win the esteem of

his bride's family, which is usually represented by her father, by giving large *hedna*.

Since the two ways of bringing about marriage, distinguished here as "marriage with *hedna*" and "marriage by prowess," sprang from the same principles, they could be combined. At two passages in the poems there are suggestions, though only suggestions, that they were combined. The passages concern Iphidamas and Penelope. Iphidamas was brought up in Thrace by his maternal grandfather, Kisses. When the boy grew to manhood, Kisses would not let him leave. Instead Kisses gave his daughter to Iphidamas in marriage (*Il.* 11.225–26). The reader may well classify this union as "marriage by prowess"; one presumes that Iphidamas had shown outstanding promise, although the poet has not said so. When the Achaians went to war, Iphidamas came to the defense of Troy. He was killed in battle by Agamemnon. The poet comments that he had no joy of his wife, although he had given much for her; he had given a hundred oxen and promised a thousand smaller animals, goats and sheep together (*Il.* 11.243–45). The gifts are not here called *hedna*. The case is not clear, but there is no objection to supposing that Iphidamas both showed promise of prowess and gave *hedna*.

When Penelope set her suitors the contest with the bow, prowess was envisaged as the mode for bringing about marriage. Yet several passages in the *Odyssey* suggest that she will be given in marriage with *hedna* in the absence of Odysseus.[11] One might infer that the two modes of contracting marriage were compatible. But the inference can be escaped if one supposes that the poets have moved from one mode to the other because of the demands of the story. Yet a remark made during the contest with the bow may provide a further indication that the poets considered the modes compatible. The first of the suitors to make the attempt is Leodes. When he finds that he cannot string the bow, he says that his fellows are to try but many will be humiliated by failure. He continues:

Now someone hopes in his heart and schemes to marry Penelope, the wife of Odysseus. But when he has made his attempt on the bow and discovered the truth, let him seek out some other of the well-robed Achaian women and woo her with *hedna*. But she would then marry the man who provides most and comes as is destined. (*Od.* 21.157–62)

Does "she" in the last sentence mean Penelope, or the eventual bride of a man who fails in the contest? The same couplet in which this sentence occurs has been uttered two days previously by Antinoos, when he proposed a plan to the other suitors, and by "she" Antinoos certainly meant Penelope (*Od.* 16.391–92). The identical wording of the two remarks may suggest that Leodes, like Antinoos, means Penelope when he says that "she" would marry the man who provides most. On the other hand, in the preceding phrase Antinoos refers to Penelope when he says, "Let him seek her and woo her with *hedna*," but Leodes, uttering the same words, refers to another woman, the eventual bride of a man who had failed in the contest with the bow. Possibly the poets have repeated the couplet incongruously.

No secure conclusion can be drawn from the passages concerning Iphidamas and Penelope. In composing these passages the poets may or may not have recognized that they were combining distinguishable modes of bringing about marriage. The question is not of great moment, for as expounded above, the two modes rest on common principles. The basic requirement towards bringing about marriage was that the prospective son-in-law should win the esteem of the woman's father. He might do so by performing deeds of beneficial prowess, by demonstrating his capacity to perform such deeds, or by giving *hedna*. The importance of mutual esteem is revealed by Alkinoos, when he notices that Odysseus weeps on hearing the song of Demodokos. He asks whether a son-in-law or a father-in-law of the stranger perished at Troy, "for those are the people most dear after one's own blood relations."[12]

Before leaving Homeric modes of bringing about marriage it must be admitted that another way of explaining *hedna* might be attempted. This alternative explanation starts from the principle that each member of a family has a value to that family. If a stranger kills or kidnaps a member of the family, the family can demand compensation in valuables and back up the demand with a threat of retaliation. The compensatory payment is called *poinē*.[13] Then surely, if a stranger takes a female member of the family by force to be his consort, the family can retaliate or accept compensation in valuables. According to this way of thinking Homeric marriage would arise from marriage by capture. *Hedna* would be an anticipatory payment of compensation; the suitor pays in advance instead of confronting the family with an accomplished fact and bargaining with them under threat of retaliation.

Against this explanation it should be urged that there are very few indications of marriage by capture in the poems. When Briseis laments the death of Patroklos, she says that he comforted her after Achilles had killed her husband and sacked her city, and that he undertook to make her the lawful (*kouridiē*) wife of Achilles (*Il.* 19.295–98). In the *Thebais* Oineus received Periboia as his share of the spoils when the war against Olenos was completed, and he made her his wife.[14] But the treatment of prisoners of war is arbitrary. It does not offer insight into regular customs, since one party is overwhelmingly more powerful than the other.

There remains a possible illustration of marriage by capture where the parties are of equal power. That is the taking of Helen by Alexander. While she is in Troy, she is presented as the wife of Alexander, not as a mere concubine. In the scene of the watching from the walls, when the poet first presents her to the audience, Priam addresses her as "dear child" (*Il.* 3.162, 192) and she calls him "dear father-in-law" (172). Later, in speaking to Hektor, she regards herself as the wife of Alexander and even wishes that she had been the wife of a better man (*Il.* 6.350). In the course of the fighting suggestions are made occasionally that the Trojans might bring the dispute to an end by paying compensation. In response to a proposal of Antenor for restoring Helen, Alexander insists that he will keep her but expresses himself willing to restore the possessions which he took with her and to give additional valuables. The Achaians refuse this offer (*Il.* 7.362–64, 385–93, 399–404). Later, when Hektor awaits the charge of Achilles, he considers whether he might offer to restore Helen and the possessions taken with her and to make additional payments, but he recognizes that Achilles would not accept the offer (*Il.* 22.111–25). But these passages say nothing about established custom; they mention possible compensation in the course of ephemeral suggestions for negotiation.

There is a more promising approach to settling the dispute over Helen when a truce is made, so that Menelaos and Alexander can fight a duel, and there is a hint of a compensatory payment, but it is made in a significant context. Agamemnon speaks of three possible outcomes for the duel (*Il.* 3.281–91). If Alexander kills Menelaos in the duel, he is to keep Helen and the possessions, and the Greeks will sail away. Second, if Menelaos kills Alexander, the Trojans are to restore Helen and the possessions, and they are to pay an appropriate sum to the Greeks. But third, if the Trojans refuse to honor their obligations after Menelaos has killed Alexander, Agamemnon will stay and fight the war to an end. In this speech Agamemnon mentions an eventual payment to be made by the Trojans, but it is not the type of payment which a hypothesis of marriage by capture and compensatory payment requires. The payment is only to be made if the Trojans have to restore Helen. No compensatory payment is to be made if the outcome of the duel allows Alexander to keep her.

In short, the occurrences in the poems which might be explained as marriage by capture are better understood as plunder in warfare. They do not suffice to show that the poets recognized a regularized notion of marriage by capture, and therefore no such notion can serve to explain marriage with *hedna*. One may also dismiss as unimportant the few occasions in the *Odyssey* where a master gives his servant a female consort. Sometime before setting off for Troy Odysseus gave Eumaios a house, a plot of land, and a wife (14.64). Again, when Odysseus prepares to attack the suitors and reveals his identity to the swineherd and the cowherd, he promises them that in the event of victory he will give them wives, possessions, and houses near his own (21.214–15). Because of the overwhelming disparity of power between master and servant no inference can be drawn about law or custom in these cases. The gift of a wife to the servant, like the other gifts, springs wholly from the master's will and any consequent issues, such as succession of eventual children to property, will depend on his discretion.

The Prospects for Penelope

Because of the words uttered by Nausikaa to Odysseus the hypothesis was propounded that in Homeric thought the consent of the bride's parents was the element essential to marriage and distinguished it from concubinage. Study of the ways of bringing marriage about has confirmed and enlarged this hypothesis. The bride's parents do not merely consent to the marriage. Her father gives her in marriage. He gives her to a man who has won his esteem by prowess or by promise of prowess or by giving *hedna*. So far nothing has been found to suggest that the consent of the bride herself was required. The hypothesis has still to be tested by scrutiny of the condition of Penelope.

Before Odysseus left for Troy, he advised Penelope to wait until Telemachos reached manhood and then to marry a new husband of her own choice (18.266–70). His utterance was advice, not an exercise of authority. It implies that Penelope would become free to marry and that she would be free to choose her husband. Many remarks in the *Odyssey* recognize her freedom of choice. Athena in disguise gives advice to Telemachos in the first book; if Penelope's desire is to be married, he should send her to her father's house so that her parents may give her in marriage (1.275–78). On the next day Antinoos says to Telemachos (2.113–14): "Send your mother away and tell her to accept in marriage the man whom her father recommends and whom she herself approves." His words are peremptory but even he recognizes that Penelope has some freedom of choice. Later Telemachos explains to Eumaios that his mother is in two minds, whether to stay with him and take care of the house or to follow the one among the suitors who is best and makes the largest offer (16.73–77).

In setting the contest with the bow (21.68–79) Penelope says that she will follow the winner; by thus exercising choice she implies that she has the right to choose. The same right is implied by statements of Athena (13.379–81) and of Telemachos (16.126–27) to the effect that Penelope does not send the suitors away but postpones the decision. It is also implied by the trick which Penelope played on the suitors when she bade them wait until she had finished weaving a shroud for Laertes (2.89–109, 19.138–56). If she had to abandon the trick when it was discovered, this does not imply that the suitors had authority to make her marry but only that they were importunate. Again, when Athena went to Lakedaimon and urged Telemachos to return home, she told him that Penelope's father and brothers were advising her to accept Eurymachos in marriage, and she implied that Penelope was likely to follow this advice (15.16–26; cf. 19.157–61). But Athena spoke of advice, not of an exercise of authority. Some passages envisage that Penelope will eventually be given in marriage by Telemachos (1.292, 2.223) or by her parents (2.50–54, 195–97) and do not mention explicitly her choice, but they do not exclude that right.

As noted, Odysseus had advised Penelope to stay in his house until Telemachos reached manhood. Her condition changes in the course of the poem, because in a series of steps the adulthood of Telemachos is made manifest. The poet allows the listener first knowledge of this development when Penelope bids Phemios desist from singing of the return of the Achaians; Telemachos corrects her and tells her to go back to her quarters, to attend to her own tasks, and to supervise the maidservants; he concludes that the story to be sung by the bard "is of concern to all the men and most of all to me; for I have authority in the house" (1.346–59). It had not always been so. As Eurykleia explains to Odysseus later, while Telemachos was a growing child, Penelope did not let him give orders to the maidservants (22.426–27). His approach to manhood is made publicly manifest when through heralds he summons the assembly of the Ithakesians and announces his intention of equipping a ship and sailing in search of news of his father. When he carries out this undertaking, it is beyond dispute that he has come of age.

The response of the suitors is a plot to kill Telemachos in ambush on his return (4.625–73). Their prospects have changed now that Telemachos is no longer a child. Previously the hand of Penelope was not all that they sought in wooing her. The extent of their ambitions, though rarely mentioned, is revealed by a remark which Eurymachos makes after the fight in the hall has begun and Odysseus has killed Antinoos. He says that Antinoos was to blame for the evil deeds and that he brought them about not so much because he desired marriage with Penelope as because he wished to be king of Ithaka (22.50–53). A few days earlier Telemachos told Theoklymenos that Eurymachos was the best man in Ithaka and most likely to marry Penelope and take the prize (geras) of Odysseus (15.521–22). These passages show that the kingdom was to pass with the hand of the queen to the successful suitor. That, at least, was the condition until Telemachos showed that he was mature and able to defend the prerogatives which he inherited from his father. Once that had happened, the suitors could only gain the kingdom if Telemachos was removed. Since they planned the killing of Telemachos as a joint enterprise, they spoke of dividing the kingdom among themselves thereafter and assigning the palace to Penelope and the one who would marry her.[15]

Once Telemachos has proved his manhood, he is master of the estate of Odysseus. Consequently Penelope finds that she need no longer stay in the house of Odysseus in order to preserve the inheritance for her son. Instead people whom she respects, notably her parents, urge her to marry, and as she recognizes, it would now be to the advantage of Telemachos for her to marry; the suitors would then depart and cease to be a burden on the estate (19.157–61, 524–34). Yet she is reluctant to go.

The passages reviewed in this section show uniformly that Penelope is entitled to choose a suitor and even to refuse them all and to stay with Telemachos in his paternal house. Her will is recognized as decisive. In this her condition differs from the many cases reviewed in the previous section; for in each of those cases a woman was given in marriage by her father, and although it was not denied explicitly that a father might take his daughter's preference into account, the woman's own will was not considered important enough for the poets to mention her consent.

The difference may, however, arise, not from any divergence in the customs regulating marriage, but from Penelope's factual condition as a woman of mature years and experience. To find out whether this is so, one may ask, what is the sanction which deters Telemachos from giving Penelope in marriage, once he has become master of the estate and could free it of the burden of the suitors by sending her away? Telemachos answers this question. When the

assembly has gathered in Ithaka, Antinoos tells him to send his
mother away and bid her accept the suitor whom her father recommends and she prefers. Telemachos replies:

> Antinoos, it is not feasible for me to send away from the house
> against her will the woman who bore me and reared me. My
> father is elsewhere in the world, whether he is alive or dead. It
> would be an evil thing for me to make a large repayment to
> Ikarios, if voluntarily on my own initiative I send my mother
> away. Then I shall suffer evils at the hands of her father, and a
> god will inflict others on me, since on departure from the
> house my mother will call down hateful furies with her curse.
> Besides there will be the resentment of public opinion towards
> me. So I will never utter the word of dismissal. (2.130–37)

In this utterance the opening reference to the woman who bore and
reared Telemachos may allude to his filial sentiment. He proceeds
to state three deterrents, which are not sentimental but material.
They arise from the predictable response of Penelope's father, her
own curse and the spirits to execute it, and public opinion. The
remark about Penelope's father should not be understood as an allusion to repayment of a dowry. Rather, Telemachos would antagonize
Ikarios by sending his daughter away and would have to buy back
his goodwill with large gifts. It is clear that in this speech as a
whole Telemachos does not specify any rule of customary law to
prevent him from sending Penelope away. So much is evident from
the multiplicity of the deterrents. Telemachos could send Penelope
away, but the factual balance of forces in the human and divine
spheres would inflict on him consequences more severe than he is
willing to accept. Telemachos speaks in the manner of a good law-
yer, who is not content to tell the client what he is entitled to do
but warns him of the probable consequences of the proposed deed.
Penelope's right to choose among the suitors and even to reject
them all springs from her individual condition. She is a woman of
mature years who has brought up a son. (It should perhaps be called
to mind that at Gortyn the widowed *patrōiōkos* was free to remain
single, provided that she had already borne children: see rule 8 in
chapter 3). Moreover, she has a father to protect her, she can call up

spirits of vengeance by her curse, and she has the approval of public opinion.

Provisional Conclusions: Homeric and Athenian Customs

A member of a family is at once an asset and a burden to his relatives. He is a burden because he has to be fed, clothed, lodged, and protected. He is an asset because he can do his relatives services, by tilling the soil, by protecting them against attack, or in other ways. If the member of the family is female, her capacity to give birth to children may be a direct or an indirect asset.

Customs of marriage, which transfer women out of the family, may take account of either aspect or both; they may recognize the woman as asset and/or as burden. In the principles governing Athenian marriage by *engyēsis* the aspect of burden was recognized. A father tried to find a good husband for his daughter and supplied a dowry for her maintenance because her upkeep was an acknowledged burden. A father who had a daughter but no sons could adopt a male heir, provided that he gave his daughter in marriage to the adoptive son; the upkeep of the woman was an encumbrance on the estate. Athenian recognition of the aspect of burden does not mean that the aspect of asset was disregarded. On the contrary marriage created a tie between father-in-law and son-in-law, because a woman's father showed esteem for a man in selecting him as bridegroom; to give one's daughter (or sister or other female relative) was to confer a valuable asset.

Homeric marriage recognizes only the aspect of asset. A father gives his daughter to a man who has done the family a great service, or whose talents promise a good ally, or who gives generous *hedna*. Even though the case of Penelope is unusual in that as a mature woman she has a voice, probably a decisive voice, in choosing a husband, the aspect of asset is evident here too. Penelope is so valuable an asset that many suitors come and compete for her.

The Athenian and Homeric concepts of marriage are so markedly different that one cannot have developed from the other. If, for example, it is supposed that the classical Athenian custom arose among people who had previously practiced the Homeric custom, a disturbing factor must have intervened and changed the direction of development decisively. The Athenian custom cannot be explained from features inherent in the Homeric custom. These considerations lead to the question of the historicity of Homeric society. Were Homeric practices, including in particular marriage practices, observed at some time and place, and if so, at what time and what place, or were they fictitious? The next two sections will try to answer that question.

Transmission of the Poems

A work of fiction can be of value to the social historian if it portrays conditions obtaining at the time when it was composed. For example, Hans Fallada's *Kleiner Mann—was nun!* was published in 1932 and describes the conditions of its time. When Fallada wrote it, he could not know that in 1933 political changes would put an end to the unemployment and misery which he described. The same author's *Der Alpdruck* was published in 1947 and describes the conditions following straight after the German surrender, when everyone who had access to drugs took them. Fallada, who died in February 1947, could not foresee the economic recovery of the following years. Both novels are useful as sources for social history, since each was written shortly before major changes put an end to the conditions which they describe. Neither would be useful if its date of composition could not be ascertained.

Can one find out when the Homeric poems were composed and draw from them information about the social conditions of an ascertainable period? The search for an answer to this question has been long and complex. Since 1795, when F. A. Wolf published his *Prolegomena ad Homerum* and thereby launched the Homeric question, study of the origin and transmission of the poems has decreased the area of ignorance. The present treatment can therefore be brief. It will start from late and secure things and work backwards in time. By proceeding in this way one may hope to avoid asserting guesses as certainties.[16]

The *Iliad* and the *Odyssey* are two poems preserved in numerous Byzantine manuscripts. Indeed the manuscripts are more plentiful than for any other Greek pagan work. The earliest of the extant manuscripts was written in the tenth century. Variations between the manuscripts are not great. So the critic can reconstruct the Byzantine text of the poems with a high degree of probability.

The poems were already read widely in the Hellenistic and Roman periods. Many fragments of papyri which bore copies of the *Iliad* or the *Odyssey* have been recovered. They likewise are more plentiful than for any other pagan Greek work, and they were written at dates varying between the third century B.C. and the fifth century A.D. Papyri of the first century B.C. and later yield a text which does not diverge greatly from the text found in the Byzantine manuscripts. That is, the text reconstructed from the Byzantine manuscripts can be traced back to the first century B.C. But papyrus fragments from the third and second centuries B.C. give texts markedly different from the corresponding passages in the later text. Sometimes the early papyri, which have usually been damaged so that they preserve only parts of lines, give phrases differing in wording and meaning from the Byzantine text. Occasionally they omit lines preserved in the Byzantine text. Often they include additional passages of one or several lines. The extant fragments of early papyri are relatively short. But they suffice to show that in the third and second centuries B.C. there were *Iliads* and *Odysseys* which were a good deal longer than the Byzantine *Iliad* and *Odyssey*; the long texts may well have exceeded the later text by a quarter of its length or even more.

Evidently the text of the two poems became standardized in the first century B.C. and the long texts passed out of currency. An old theory to explain this change ran on the following lines. In the third and second centuries leading scholars at Alexandria, including Zenodotos, Aristophanes, and Aristarchos, studied the *Iliad* and the *Odyssey*. The Byzantine scholia record many of their judgments, especially on the authenticity of particular lines. The old theory supposed that by collecting and comparing earlier manuscripts the Alexandrian scholars composed an edition of the *Iliad* and of the *Odyssey* and this edition had the effect of standardizing the text. The public learned to value the Alexandrian edition and reject longer texts of the poems.

This theory was refuted by the late T. W. Allen. He studied the recorded judgments of Alexandrian scholars and especially those of Aristarchos, the last of the major critics. He found that the preferences voiced by Aristarchos among variant readings have had little influence on the later standard text. Further, apart from expressing preferences among readings, the Alexandrian scholars put critical signs against lines of which they doubted the authenticity. A few papyri have such signs. But generally the standard text includes the lines athetized by Aristarchos; there are, for example, on Allen's count only six points in the *Iliad* where a line athetized by him is omitted from some later papyri or manuscripts. Indeed Alexandrian scholars wrote commentaries on the *Iliad* and the *Odyssey*, but it cannot be shown that they made an edition, that is, a model text from which copies were to be made. Allen concluded that the standardization of the text in the first century B.C. was due, not to Alexandrian scholarship, but to a successful publisher. More than one publisher of the Roman period is known. T. Pomponius Atticus, for example, employed "excellent readers and numerous scribes." One could achieve multiple production on a small scale by setting one slave to read a text aloud while many slaves sat around him and wrote down what they heard.[17] The modern text of the *Iliad* and the *Odyssey* is one of many versions which were current in the Hellenistic period, and there is no way of telling whether it is a superior version. Yet the importance of this uncertainty is limited, for the variations in early papyri of the poems do not amount to a material difference in the stories told.

As one traces the transmission of the text further backwards, the next recognizable stage is to be found in Athens in the sixth century. The Panathenaia was a festival celebrated every year in the summer from time immemorial. Toward 566 the decision was taken to celebrate this festival on a larger scale every four years; the first celebration of the Greater Panathenaia took place in 566/65. The Greater Panathenaia included a competition in reciting Homeric verse. Sometime a rule was adopted that the competitors must keep to a standard order in reciting the episodes; that is, each successive competitor must start at the point where his predecessor had ceased. Diogenes Laertios attributes this rule to Solon;

the Pseudo-Platonic *Hipparchos* attributes it to Hipparchos, the son of Peisistratos. The attribution to Solon may spring from the Athenian habit of attributing all the laws to him. The name of Hipparchos is not easy to explain away, even though the source giving it is not early. It is credible that no rule about order of episodes was made when the competition was instituted in 566, but a generation later, in the time of the sons of Peisistratos, the need for a rule had become evident.[18]

A further tradition, first attested by Cicero, said that before the time of Peisistratos there existed only the separate lays on the different episodes of the Homeric stories; Peisistratos first arranged them in their current order.[19] This tradition is compatible with the information about adoption of "the Panathenaic rule," that is, the rule concerning order of episodes, but it is not implied by that rule. It may be a Hellenistic theory devised to explain peculiarities in the poems. In other words, the Panathenaic rule implies that a standard order of episodes was recognized from the sixth century onward, but it leaves open the question whether a standard order was recognized previously. The *Iliad* and the *Odyssey* have each impressed readers by their unity of conception. The argument presented in this and the preceding paragraph does not show whether that unity was achieved with the standard order of episodes at the Panathenaia or previously. There is no justification for the assumption that people acquainted with the family of Peisistratos were devoid of poetic talent. Again, it should be noted that standardization of the order in which the poems were to be recited does not necessarily imply that the poems in full were reduced to writing. A written text of the poems would be one way of preserving the order of the episodes, but a written list of episodes would suffice.

The forms of a few words occurring in the poems can be recognized as atticisms,[20] but not much can be inferred from them in view of the hazards of transmission in the Hellenistic period. A more substantial atticism is to be found in the sixth book of the *Iliad*. There, on instructions given by Hektor, Hekabe leads the women of Troy to a temple of Athena on high ground in the city and offers a robe to the goddess; Theano, the priestess of Athena, receives the robe and puts it on the knees of the seated statue. It is surprising that the *Iliad* assigns a cult and temple of Athena to the Trojans, for in the story she is their enemy. Surely the incident is modeled on the Panathenaic festival, where the Athenians offered a robe at a seated statue of Athena in a temple on the Akropolis. That is, in Athens the *Iliad* has acquired, not merely isolated forms of individual words, but a whole incident.[21] It follows that the poems were in a highly fluid and vulnerable condition in the sixth century or later.

To trace the development of the poems before they were recited at the Panathenaia one must take note of their origin in oral composition. By studying repeated phrases in the *Iliad* and the *Odyssey*, M. Parry showed that the poems originated from an oral, formulaic and traditional technique.[22] Oral composition of verse at the speed of singing on the one hand and composition of verse with the aid of writing on the other are different arts, differing as much as verse from prose. Where oral composition is usual, the public recognizes merit, not in a particular poem, but in a performance by a skilled singer. Comparative studies, especially of Serbian oral poets, have found that the singer retains freedom to alter his song radically at each recitation, even though he may speak of it as the same song. It has also been found that a Serbian oral poet, if taught to write and encouraged to employ writing as an aid to composition, produces poor verse; he abandons the oral technique, in which he was skillful, but he has not learned a new way of composing.[23]

A poem as long as the *Iliad* or the *Odyssey* could not be preserved as recognizably the same poem by purely oral transmission.[24] So it is important to ask when the two poems were first reduced to writing. On this question relatively recent studies have achieved some progress. It has been observed that when Greeks acquired the alphabet in the later part of the eighth century, an oral poet did not face the same predicament as the modern oral poet who is encouraged to write. The latter confronts an elaborate literary culture, which is new to him and has to be learned. The Greek oral poet merely acquired a technical skill of specialized application.[25] So the possibility arises that the reduction of the poems to writing was not a single act but came about in a long and complex process; oral poets may have employed writing piecemeal as an aid to memory and occasionally to composition.

Study of recurrent phrases in the *Iliad* has found two passages of moderate length, the beguiling of Zeus at 14.153–351 and the *aristeia* of Aineias at 20.79–352, where formulaic words are used in a nonformulaic way; for example, epithets applied to Aineias in his *aristeia* are used elsewhere not of him but of other heroes, whereas within the traditional technique of composition epithets adhered as closely to their bearers as names did. The eccentricities of the two passages can best be explained by supposing that writing was used as an aid in composing them.[26] Therefore, when the *Iliad* and the *Odyssey* as whole poems attained written and therefore relatively stable form, it is likely that the authors drew on sources which had already been reduced, in whole or in part, to writing. So an attempt can be made to discern within the two extant poems their immediate predecessors.[27]

Some light is thrown on early stages in the development of Greek epic by artifacts discovered in excavation. A helmet decorated with boar's tusks is described in *Iliad* 10.261–65. Finds of boar's tusks in graves and of ivory figurines show that helmets of this design were worn in the early part of the Late Helladic period. As protection the headdress cannot have been very effective; possibly it was not a helmet but a ceremonial crown. For a long time archaeologists supposed that this headdress passed out of fashion well before the end of the Bronze Age. But in 1981 excavation of a tholos tomb of the period called Late Minoan III A at Phylaki Apokoronou in West Crete discovered "the ivory embellishments of a wooden box, including heads of warriors wearing boar's tusk helmets." About a year later study of cremated bone from a cemetery of more than three hundred graves at Knossos found "remains of slices of boar's tusks with stitch-holes"; the earliest of the graves were classified as "L[ate] M[inoan] III C / Sub-Minoan." Apparently the boar's tusk helmet remained in use until the very end of the Bronze Age, but several centuries intervene between its last attestation and the acquisition of the alphabet by the Greeks. Again, the cup of Nestor, described in *Iliad* 11.632–37, is similar, though not closely similar, to a cup found in one of the shaft graves at Mykenai.[28] In the *Iliad* and the *Odyssey* offensive weapons are nearly always made of bronze but tools are of iron. This divergence does not reflect any historical stage discovered by excavation in Greece.[29] The poetic convention which required bronze as the material of heroic weapons must be a stylized reminiscence of the Bronze Age.

In recent decades many readers have supposed that the *Iliad* and the *Odyssey* reached substantially their final form between about 750 and about 650; that period of a hundred years is proposed as the date of composition.[30] Certainly some features of the poems point to that period. In its knowledge of the Phoenicians and in its distrust for them the *Odyssey* expresses an outlook which was probably current in the early stages of Greek colonization, although it may have persisted much later. The brooch of Odysseus, described in *Odyssey* 19.226–31, resembles Etruscan work of the first half of the seventh century.[31] Some readers have thought that the art of oral composition began to decline when Greek poets took to composing in writing.[32] The securest date in the early history of written verse among Greeks is provided by the solar eclipse which Archilochos saw in 648.[33] But this argument for dating a decline in oral composition has little force. Musicians did not cease to compose operas when they began to compose symphonies. Oral and written composition of verse were different arts and they may have been practiced side by side by different poets in archaic Greece.

The *Iliad* and the *Odyssey* have features which belong outside the period 750–650. That is true of the Bronze Age artifacts noted above. The design of a Gorgon on the shield of Agamemnon can scarcely be earlier than the second half of the seventh century.[34] The account of the processional offering of a robe to a seated statue of Athena in Troy is doubtless later still, perhaps much later. Accordingly it is far better to conclude that the *Iliad* and the *Odyssey* do not have a date of composition. They came into being during a long period, which began well before the end of the Bronze Age and lasted into the sixth century or later. Some of their features can be recognized from external evidence and dated. Many others cannot.

The question of the historicity of Homeric society has another dimension. Possibly some features of the poems do not reflect actual conditions of any period. The poems tell of many kings but they have hardly any concept of kingship. The kings do not differ as kings in behavior from other men. Odysseus boasts that he can excel Eurymachos, one of the lords of Ithaka, in cutting grass with a sickle and in plowing a straight furrow with oxen. There is a heap of manure near the entrance to his palace and geese wander on the floor of its hall.[35] In their knowledge, or rather ignorance, of kings the poets of the *Odyssey* were not unlike the anonymous author of the Westphalian folksong about the king's daughter who loved the son of another king from across the sea. It was a Sunday morning and the people were all so cheerful, but the king's daughter was sad. She would not go to the church but she put on her golden crown and went to the seashore.[36]

Again, in the geography of some places important to the story the poems are not realistic. In the Bronze Age the hill at modern Hisarlık bore a large and impressive settlement. It was nearer to the coast in the thirteenth century B.C. than it is now, since the Skamander has deposited silt. There is good reason for identifying it as the Troy (or Ilion) of the *Iliad*.[37] Yet when Achilles began to pursue Hektor round the walls of Troy, they passed two springs of tepid water. At the springs there were stones well suited for scrubbing clothes. There the women of Troy used to wash clothes "in the time before, at peace, before the sons of the Achaians came." The poet describes the place of the springs with care (22.147–56). It is now called Kirk Göz ("Forty Eyes") at the village of Pınarbaşı; there are many springs and "eyelets" and different travelers count them differently. The women still wash clothes there. According to a recent inquirer, "Of all the curiosities of the Troad the Kirk Göz is perhaps the most celebrated; and if we are disposed to look for a natural feature that could have inspired the poetic description, only inveterate prejudice can deny that honour to these springs."[38] But the springs are far away from Hisarlık. The hill above them is Ballı Kaya (formerly Ballı Dağ). In 1785 J. B. Lechevalier identified it as Homeric Troy, but excavation has not found traces of any occupation earlier than the archaic period. The Troy of the *Iliad* is neither Hisarlık nor Ballı Kaya. It is an imaginary place, although the poets have drawn on knowledge of memorable things from the Troad.[39]

The diligent traveler meets a similar puzzle on following Odysseus to his native island. The modern Thiaki preserves the name of Ithaka. Thiaki is rocky; several stock epithets for Homeric Ithaka say the same. Telemachos (*Od.* 4.605–8) declines Menelaos' offer of a gift of horses because Ithaka is suited only for goats. Yet when Odysseus describes Ithaka to the king of the Phaiakians, he says that it has a prominent mountain (Thiaki does not) and that it is furthest west among the islands of its neighborhood (9.21–26). That identifies it as classical and modern Leukas, which has a prominent mountain. Elsewhere (21.346–47) Telemachos confirms the identification of Ithaka with Leukas by distinguishing it from the islands which lie towards Elis. Sometime during the lengthy development of the poems the name Ithaka moved from Leukas to Thiaki. It was probably borne by migratory inhabitants.[40]

There is no way of escaping the conclusion. The *Iliad* and the *Odyssey* are not history books. They are not travel guides. They are poems. Their truth is the truth of pathos, at the place where the women used to wash the clothes "in the time before, at peace, before the sons of the Achaians came."

Women and Goddesses

In the previous section it became apparent that for a long time the *Iliad* and the *Odyssey* were transmitted as popular poems; that is, their appeal was directed to the whole community, not to an educated section of it. This is certainly true of the many centuries when the main context of transmission was the Panathenaia, and it is probably true for the preceding period, even though the conditions for performing epic verse before 566 are still more difficult to discern. On the other hand since the Alexandrian period much, though by no means all, literature has been directed not to a whole community but to an educated elite, that is, to people trained to appreciate the literature. The expectations of the public to which work of these two kinds is addressed are different, and so the composers behave differently. A reader accustomed to the literature of an elite, and in particular a reader of the type most likely to approach the Homeric poems today, has learned to value the originality of the individual poet and therefore he demands that a fixed text be preserved with accuracy. But a poem subject to popular transmission admits constantly of modification, accretion, and improvisation. The poem has a life of its own. The merits which a listener discerns in the poem at any one time in its life are not the reflection of the single mind of one talented poet; they have accrued from the contributions of many performers during many generations.

It follows that the marriage customs presented in the *Iliad* and the *Odyssey* may draw features from any of many times and places. In their entirety they need not reflect the actual practice of any historical society; the combination of features may be fictitious. The present section will furnish reason for believing that there is a large element of fiction in Homeric portrayal of women and that the poems can be better understood when that element is recognized.

In approaching the subject one may start from Helen, for the Trojan War was fought about her. The poet of the *Iliad* introduces her first when she comes to the wall of Troy and talks with the elderly men who sit at the Skaian Gate and watch the fighting outside (3.121–244). They remark on her beauty; they say that it is not unfitting that the Trojans and the Achaians should fight long and bitterly for such a woman. Priam asks her to sit beside him and says:

> Thou art not in my eyes guilty; the gods are guilty for me,
> since they brought Achaian warfare of many tears against me.
> (3.164–65)

So Helen sits down beside Priam and at his request she identifies several of the Achaians.

In this scene Helen is presented as a dignified figure, and her dignity is maintained a little later in the story, when Hektor goes in search of Alexander (6.313–68). He reaches Alexander's dwelling and finds him there with Helen. He upbraids Alexander for staying away from the fighting. Alexander accepts the rebuke and says that he will put on his armor and go out to the war. While he makes his preparations, Helen addresses a brief speech to Hektor and he replies with courtesy. In her speech Helen expresses two wishes, which could not be realized:

> Would that, on the day when my mother first bore me, a cruel storm of wind had carried me away to a mountain or to a wave of the noisy sea, where the wave would have overwhelmed me before these deeds could have happened! But since the gods ordained these evils thus, would that I were the wife of a better man, one who recognized the censure and plentiful reproaches of public opinion! (6.345–51)

She does not wish that she had not followed Alexander to Troy. For the taking of Helen to Troy is regarded in the Homeric poems as a deed that Alexander committed with Helen as its passive object.

After conversing with Helen, Hektor goes in search of his wife, Andromache. He finds her with their small child, Astyanax, at the Skaian Gate. He talks with her and takes his leave (6.369–502). There is a complex contrast between the happy domesticity of Hektor's family and the morally untenable position of Alexander and Helen. Andromache has a son and a husband who is above reproach, but she will be destroyed when Troy is captured. Helen will survive. The contrast is aesthetically effective because Helen is presented as respected and worthy of respect. Even so, her condition is indefensible; addressing Hektor, she calls herself "a baneful dog who contrives evil" (6.344; cf. 356).

The poets present Helen again near the end of the *Iliad*. After Priam has ransomed the corpse of Hektor and brought it back to Troy, the women gather round the bier. Three of them lead the lament in turn. They are Andromache, Hekabe, and lastly Helen (24.761–75). She says that Hektor never spoke to her in an unkind manner; on the contrary he protected her when other people of the palace spoke harsh words to her. These two ways in which she was treated express the ambiguity of her condition. Moreover, by making her one of the leaders of the lament, the poet ensures that the audience will remember her as a figure of dignity.

Priam said that Helen was not "guilty" (*aitiē*, 3.164). The word which he uttered is employed also by Agamemnon in his speech of reconciliation with Achilles (19.78–144). Agamemnon says:

It is not I who am guilty (*aitios*) but Zeus and *moira* and the
erinys that walks in darkness, for in the gathering place they
put savage *atē* into my mind on the day when I myself took
away his prize from Achilles. (86–89)

This utterance is not strictly a disclaimer of responsibility, for Agamemnon proceeds to offer compensation to Achilles and says that
he offers it "because I suffered *atē* and Zeus took away my wits"
(137). The utterance is rather a statement of motivation, but it
draws on concepts which are not familiar to the modern mind. *Atē*
is a condition of temporary insanity; the sufferer loses for a time
the faculty of moral discernment and acts in a manner unlike his
usual self.[41] Helen likewise suffered *atē*, as she says in the *Odyssey*. As wife of Menelaos she entertains him and his guests by relat-
ing an exploit which Odysseus carried out during the siege of Troy
(4.235–64). He entered the city in disguise. Helen recognized him
but she did not betray him. He killed many Trojans before returning
to the Achaians. Helen continues:

But my soul rejoiced, for my heart had already changed and
longed to go back home. I groaned in regret over the *atē* which
Aphrodite had put upon me when she brought me from my
dear native land, so that I turned aside from my daughter and
my bedroom and my husband, a man without blemish in mind
or in shape. (259–64)

In short Agamemnon was not guilty, he suffered *atē*, and he offered
compensation. Helen was not guilty, she suffered *atē*, but she did
not offer compensation. Homeric women do not control property
beyond the clothes which they spin and weave.

In the *Odyssey* the figure of Helen is no longer ambiguous. She
has been restored to Menelaos and fully rehabilitated. Indeed she is
portrayed as a person of superior wisdom. When Telemachos and
Peisistratos have been welcomed by Menelaos but have not yet
identified themselves, Helen joins the party and she is the first to
guess that the stranger is Telemachos (4.138–46). When they eat,
she puts a soothing drug in the wine to make them forget their
cares (4.219–32). Later, when Telemachos with Peisistratos prepares

to take his leave, his hosts give him gifts; the gift given by Helen is a robe, which she has woven herself (15.104–8, 123–30). When Telemachos is about to depart, an eagle carrying a goose appears in the sky on the right. Telemachos asks Menelaos which of them the portent is intended for, but Menelaos is at a loss how to reply. Instead Helen explains that the eagle carrying the goose portends the return and vengeance of Odysseus (15.160–78).

Two conclusions to be drawn about Helen in the epics call for note. The first is her relative passivity. She does not take initiative. Alexander takes her as a passive object to Troy. She has wishes and sentiments, but they are ineffectual. Consequently, although as Alexander's consort she is in the wrong, in the *Iliad* she is presented not as evil but as ambivalent. She is markedly different from the wicked Helen portrayed by the Attic tragedians.[42]

The second conclusion concerns character. Modern works of imaginative literature have often presented character as the mainspring of action; they have focused on an internal condition which is manifested in action. This concept was not foreign to Greek thought, but often Greek writers, especially of the archaic period, concentrated on "external character," as it will be called here. By "external character" is meant the network of relationships linking the figure to his relatives, friends, neighbors, and enemies. A man's power and wealth and the degree of esteem in which he is held are likely to contribute to his external character. The point to note about Helen is that she derives her external character from her successive consorts. While she is in Troy, her husband, Alexander, is in the wrong but he is not an outcast; the Trojans accept him as one of themselves. So Helen is treated with courtesy, even though her position is ambiguous. Once she has been reunited to Menelaos, she is fully restored to honor. The notion that a woman takes her external character from her man will be illustrated in the portrayal of other Homeric women. It appears elsewhere in Greek thought. One may call to mind, for example, the dispute between two Athenians whose parcels of land were divided by a pathway on the slope of a hill. As long as the men were on good terms, the mothers talked together amicably (see chapter 2 above). Another illustration is provided by the story which Herodotos (9.5) tells about Lykides. When

Mardonios, the Persian commander, sent a messenger with an offer to the Athenians at Salamis, Lykides was the only member of the Athenian council who proposed bringing the messenger before the assembly. Thereupon the Athenians stoned Lykides to death. The wives of the Athenians went of their own accord to the house of Lykides and stoned his wife and children to death.

Among the mortal women prominent in the two poems the one presented in the worst light is Klytaimestra.[43] In the *Odyssey* she is the foil to Penelope. When Odysseus came home, his faithful wife was waiting for him. When Agamemnon came home, his wife's lover killed him. Several passages in the epic mention the return of Agamemnon, and the contrast between the two women is made explicit in the last book. Yet the allusions to Klytaimestra are curiously reticent. The passages telling of the death of Agamemnon call for review.

The *Odyssey* begins by stating its subject (1.1–10) and saying that Odysseus was detained by Kalypso in her island (1.11–21). Then it tells how the gods gathered in the palace of Zeus. Calling to mind the misdeed and consequent death of Aigisthos, Zeus addressed them:

Alas! How mortals now cast blame on the gods! They say that evils are from us. But they themselves incur misfortunes beyond their share on account of their own crimes. Thus even now Aigisthos, exceeding his share, married the wedded wife of Agamemnon and killed him on his return. Aigisthos embarked wittingly on a deed of sheer disaster. For previously we had sent Hermes, of keen sight and swift in appearing, and bade him neither to kill Agamemnon nor to woo his consort; for there would be vengeance for Agamemnon at the hands of Orestes, as soon as he grew up and conceived desire for his native land. That was the message which Hermes gave, but he did not persuade the mind of Aigisthos with good counsel. Now Aigisthos has paid the whole penalty at once. (1.32–43)

Spoken by the most powerful god, this is a brief but full account of the murder of Agamemnon and of its consequence. The moral aspect of the crime and its punishment is made clear. Klytaimestra is mentioned, though not by name, as the wife of Agamemnon, but she is presented as a purely passive object. The crime of taking her and killing her husband was wholly the deed of Aigisthos.

The same story is told at characteristically greater length by Nestor, when Telemachos visits him in Pylos (3.254–312). As Nestor explains, while the siege of Troy was in progress, Aigisthos stayed behind and wooed the wife of Agamemnon.

> At first illustrious Klytaimestra refused to commit the iniquitous deed. For she had a virtuous disposition. Besides there was with her a bard, whom Agamemnon on leaving for Troy had instructed repeatedly to keep watch over his wife. But when the portion assigned by the gods bound her to be subdued, Aigisthos took the bard to a desert island and left him there to be the prey and fodder of birds, but he led away the woman with her consent to his own dwelling. (265–72)

Nestor proceeds to tell how after the fall of Troy Menelaos set off to return home but was driven off his course to Egypt. Aigisthos killed Agamemnon and ruled Mykenai for seven years. But in the eighth year Orestes came back from Athens and killed Aigisthos, thus punishing the murderer of his father. Orestes held a funeral feast for the Argives "on account of his hateful mother and cowardly Aigisthos" (310); Menelaos arrived on the very same day.

Nestor here says more about Klytaimestra and her motivation than Zeus had done. Her sentiments are noted and they change. At first she resisted the advances of Aigisthos, because of her own disposition and because there was a bard to take care of her. But when Aigisthos sent the bard away and persisted in his approaches to Klytaimestra, she ceased to resist him. In telling the story of Klytaimestra through the mouth of Nestor the poet takes note of her sentiments but finds them ineffectual. His mode of treating her can be clarified by a grotesque comparison. When Agamemnon set off for Troy, he left behind a horse of good quality. In his absence Aigisthos approached the horse. At first the animal spurned his advances. For it was loyal to its true master, and Agamemnon had left a groom to care for it. Later Aigisthos sent the groom away and took the horse, which no longer resisted him, to his own stables.

If Nestor's allusions to Klytaimestra's sentiments are understood in the light of this caricature, his silence about the manner of her death becomes easy to understand. When Menelaos came back from Egypt, Orestes had killed Aigisthos and was holding a funeral feast on account of him and Klytaimestra. The audience are left to guess how she had been killed. This poetic treatment of Klytaimestra belongs to a different world of thought than the harrowing presentation of the deed of matricide in Attic tragedies.

The return and death of Agamemnon are mentioned again when Telemachos and Peisistratos are welcomed in Lakedaimon. Telemachos admires the rich decoration of the palace. So Menelaos tells of his travels during his return from Troy and remarks:

> While I was wandering in those lands and collecting much wealth, another man killed my brother in a secret and unforeseen manner by the treachery of his accursed wife. (4.90–92)

Here for the first time in the *Odyssey* some responsibility for the death of Agamemnon is attributed to Klytaimestra, but her share in the deed is much inferior to that of Aigisthos.

On the next day Menelaos tells Telemachos about his wanderings at greater length. He includes in his account the speech made to him by Proteus, the old man of the sea, on the island of Pharos off the coast of Egypt. The death of Agamemnon was among the many things narrated by Proteus to Menelaos (4.512–47). According to Proteus, Aigisthos had set a watchman to wait for the return of Agamemnon. He watched for a year and then told his master that Agamemnon had landed. Aigisthos invited Agamemnon to a meal and set twenty men in ambush. In the ensuing fight Agamemnon and all the followers of both principals were killed. Having related so much about the past, Proteus goes on to prophesy that Orestes would kill Aigisthos. Thus in Proteus' account of the return of Agamemnon Klytaimestra is omitted. As in the accounts given by Zeus and by Nestor, she was not a significant agent.

The death of Agamemnon is mentioned in two other passages of the *Odyssey*. In both Klytaimestra has a larger role, but in both the speaker is the ghost of Agamemnon. When Odysseus sailed to the far west and called up ghosts from Hades, one of the ghosts with whom he conversed was that of Agamemnon (11.387–439). The latter tells the story of his own death and begins by naming Aigisthos:

> I was not subdued on board ship by Poseidon, after he raised a dire gale of bitter winds, nor was I destroyed by hostile men on land, but Aigisthos planned my death and end. He killed me with the help of my accursed wife, after he had invited me to his house and feasted me, as one kills an ox at the manger. (406–11)

The ghost of Agamemnon says how all his companions were killed. He describes the death cry of Kassandra and says that Klytaimestra killed her beside him. He says that Klytaimestra turned away from his corpse and did not close his eyes or his mouth. He adds that there is nothing more terrible or more despicable than a woman who would undertake such a thing (427–28) and he makes the comment:

> By devising the extreme of bane she has brought disgrace upon herself and upon women of the future, even upon any woman of virtuous conduct. (432–34)

Agamemnon expresses a similar judgment, without repeating his narrative, in the last book of the *Odyssey*, when Hermes has conducted the ghosts of the suitors to Hades and their spokesman, Amphimedon, has told him how they were killed. In response Agamemnon expresses admiration for the good fortune of Odysseus, who has such a loyal wife, and continues:

> The report of her merits will never perish. The gods will create for mortals a song of grace in honor of Penelope the temperate. Not so did the daughter of Tyndareus conceive evil deeds, killing her lawful husband. There will be a hateful song about her among mankind. She will bring evil repute upon womenfolk, even upon any woman of virtuous conduct. (24.196–202)

The references in the *Odyssey* to the death of Agamemnon and in particular to Klytaimestra can be read in more than one way. On the one hand the speech of Zeus at the beginning of the poem prepares the hearer for a contrast between the unhappy return of Agamemnon and the eventually victorious return of Odysseus. The contrast in their fortunes carries with it the contrast between Klytaimestra and Penelope, and although in much of the poem the contrast between the two women is merely latent, it is made explicit in the final utterance of Agamemnon. On the other hand, that utterance is more emotional than memorable. Both in that last speech and in addressing Odysseus in book 11, Agamemnon says that the evil deed of Klytaimestra brings disgrace on women in general, including virtuous women. As a judgment this remark does not make good sense; it serves more to characterize Agamemnon than to deepen the hearer's understanding of Klytaimestra. Even Agamemnon in telling Odysseus his story recognizes that his death was primarily the work of Aigisthos.

Other narrators attribute a still greater proportion of the responsibility to Aigisthos. Admittedly Menelaos says that Aigisthos killed Agamemnon "in a secret and unforeseen manner by the treachery of his accursed wife," but Menelaos as the brother of Agamemnon may incline to his somewhat partial point of view. When Menelaos reports the story of Agamemnon's death as told him by Proteus, nothing is said about Klytaimestra. Similarly, when Zeus tells the story, the crime is committed solely by Aigisthos, Klytaimestra being the passive object of his wooing. Likewise when the loquacious Nestor gives his account of the disaster, he notes the changing sentiments of Klytaimestra, but he attributes the whole responsibility to Aigisthos. The disinterested witnesses—Zeus, the greatest of the gods, Nestor, the oldest of the heroes, and Proteus, the sea creature gifted with second sight—portray Aigisthos as the sole murderer of Agamemnon. Although Agamemnon and Menelaos attribute a share in the responsibility to Klytaimestra, it is a subordinate share, consequent upon the external character which she acquires as consort of Aigisthos. Klytaimestra, like Helen, does not take initiative.

Penelope, the loyal woman, is also relatively passive. Her appearance in the first book of the *Odyssey* is programmatic. She comes down from the upper story of the palace and asks Phemios to sing a different song, but Telemachos corrects her and tells her to go back to her proper tasks; she does as he tells her (1.328–64). There is a hint that she had played a more active part before the poem began. On leaving for Troy, Odysseus had instructed her to take care of all that he left behind, to be mindful of his father and mother, and to wait until Telemachos grew up but then to marry the man of her choice (18.266–70). Again, Eurykleia says that Penelope did not let Telemachos give orders to the maidservants while he was a growing child (22.426–27). So one presumes that she had taken an active role in the upbringing of Telemachos. But within the action of the poem her behavior is not self-assertive. She does not dismiss the suitors with a refusal but postpones her decision. When she dreams of the eagle who kills the geese, she is sorry for the geese (19.535–50). For the suspense of the story requires a real possibility that she should accept one of the suitors.

A Homeric wife derives her external character from her husband. Penelope's similarity to Odysseus is revealed fully at the time of their reunion. After Odysseus has slain the suitors, Penelope is slow to admit that the stranger is indeed Odysseus. She is not satisfied of his identity until she has tested his knowledge of the secret about the construction of their bed (23.173–230). Like Odysseus, Penelope is cautious to the point of distrusting strangers. Her similarity to her husband is displayed by the poet in an occurrence of the previous day, when she showed herself to the suitors and reminded them successfully that they ought to offer her gifts (18.274–303). The proper comment on this much-discussed scene is made by the narrator:

> The illustrious and much-enduring Odysseus rejoiced, because
> she solicited gifts from them and moved their spirit with words
> of charm but her mind was set on other things. (18.281–83)

Much has been written about the character of Penelope.[44] In soliciting gifts from the suitors she took an initiative which did not determine the development of the story but clarified personal relationships to the disguised Odysseus and to the audience. The initiative which she took on setting the contest with the bow was crucial and essential to the course of the action. The poets adopted two devices to diminish the impact of this female initiative on the audience. The first is poetic delay. Toward the end of book 19 Penelope tells the disguised Odysseus that she will set the contest (19.571–81). She sets it at the beginning of book 21. Book 20 intervenes between book 19 and book 21, and book 20 moves slowly; in it a series of people do unimportant things. Thus the audience is given time to reconcile itself to the prospect of female initiative.

The other device is presented in book 24, when the ghost of Amphimedon, speaking for the suitors, tells Agamemnon their story. Amphimedon says that Odysseus, disguised as a beggar, came to the palace and told Penelope to set the contest (24.167–69). This version of the story is not true. Indeed it is impossible, for as long as Odysseus had not made himself known to Penelope, he lacked authority to give her instructions. By suppressing Penelope's initiative Amphimedon's version enabled the Panathenaic audience who listened to the Odyssey to go away without feeling shocked.

Two other mortal women are prominent in the Odyssey. The island of Phaiakia is free from the imperfections of everyday life. So in its queen, Arete, and in her daughter, Nausikaa, one may expect to find the Homeric ideal of womanhood. Nausikaa has charm and high principles. Unlike her handmaidens, she is not afraid of Odysseus when he emerges, naked and besmirched with brine, from the undergrowth (6.127–40). She helps him. She knows that all strangers and beggars are from Zeus (6.207–8). She respects public opinion and so she bids Odysseus make his own way to the palace when they reach the city. She would disapprove of a woman who took the initiative of mixing with men against the will of her parents before public marriage took place (6.262–88).

The behavior of Arete is more revealing. Nausikaa advised Odysseus to go straight to Arete on reaching the palace. He should go past Alkinoos and appeal as a suppliant to Arete (6.303–12). Nausikaa added:

> For if she conceives sympathy for thee in her mind, thou canst hope to see thy friends and return to thy well-built house and thy native land. (6.313–15)

As Odysseus makes his way through the town of the Phaiakians, Athena joins him and praises Arete to him highly. Arete, she says, is esteemed by her husband more than any other woman by hers.

The people respect her like a god when she goes through the city. She has a *noos esthlos*, a term implying a just and kind disposition as well as a capable intellect.⁴⁵ She is able to resolve disputes among men. Athena concludes by reiterating Nausikaa's assurance that Odysseus can hope to return home if Arete conceives sympathy for him (7.66–77). Odysseus and the audience are thus led to expect in Arete a figure wielding personal authority.

Odysseus enters the palace. He goes straight to Arete and addresses his appeal to her. When he has spoken, he sits down in the ashes of the hearth. For a time the people in the hall are silent. Then Echeneos advises Alkinoos to lead the stranger to a seat. Alkinoos does so. Servants bring Odysseus water and food. Alkinoos tells a herald to pour wine for the whole company. Addressing the Phaiakians, Alkinoos says that they will entertain the stranger and escort him the next day on his way to his native land. Odysseus thanks him (7.133–227). After this lengthy exchange, the other Phaiakians go home for the night. Alkinoos, Arete, and Odysseus are left alone. Now at last Arete speaks. She has recognized the clothes which Nausikaa gave Odysseus. She asks him who he is, where he comes from, and how he has come by his clothes (7.228–39). In short, the ideal woman of the *Odyssey* may be described as a figure of wisdom and authority when she is offstage, but she does not speak until long after her husband has spoken, even though she has been spoken to first.

So far it has been maintained that the mortal women who play major parts in the *Iliad* and the *Odyssey* are markedly, though not totally, passive; they hardly ever take initiative. They have sentiments but these are ineffectual. The portrayal of goddesses is utterly different. They take initiative, they are recalcitrant, and their deeds have harmful or beneficial effects. Thetis intercedes with Zeus for Achilles successfully when Agamemnon has deprived him of his prize (*Il.* 1.495–530). Athena protects and assists Odysseus constantly. At the beginning of the *Odyssey* she sets the action in motion by complaining to Zeus because her protégé is impeded from reaching his home (1.48–62). Kirke turns men into animals until Odysseus subdues her with the stronger magic which Hermes gave him. Once Odysseus has demonstrated his superiority, she helps him with good advice about the further stages of his journey (10.487–574, 12.21–141), and when he and his companions leave her, she provides a favorable wind (12.148–50). Later in his wanderings Odysseus is detained by Kalypso on her island, since she wishes to have him for her husband (1.13–15). When Hermes brings her the order from Zeus to let Odysseus go, she rails against the high gods, because they will not let goddesses take mortal men as their consorts, and she cites several examples (5.118–28). Goddesses do not hesitate to quarrel with gods. Hera upbraids Zeus for talking with Thetis apart. Zeus responds with a threat of violence, and Hephaistos induces his mother to yield, reminding her what he had suffered at the hands of Zeus (*Il.* 1.536–94). Later Hera distracts her husband's attention so that Poseidon can intervene in the war against his prohibition (14.153–360, 15.1–33). The poets who described these scenes between Zeus and Hera had seen marriages less harmonious than that of Alkinoos and Arete.

Epic poetry created the imaginary world of the heroes and presented it as real. But it was superior to the actual world of the audiences, since the heroes were mightier men and belonged to the past. In a word, the world of the heroes was not real but Real. The world of the gods, distinct from that of the heroes, was real to the poets and their audiences. The gods, though much like the heroes in many ways, differed in a crucial respect; they were immortal. But this superiority was at the same time an inferiority. Because they could not die, the gods could not suffer unmitigated disaster. Their misfortunes could not be strictly pathetic.[46] So the circle of the gods could admit the imperfections which the poets had seen in the real world of everyday life and excluded from the Real world of the heroes. One of those imperfections was female initiative. Epic poetry relegated female independence and female recalcitrance to the distant realm of Olympos.

Rather similar considerations account for most of the rare occasions in the poems when mortal women take initiative. Usually these occurrences are distant in time or place or both from the immediate action of the story. Anteia calumniated Bellerophon to her husband, Proitos, and so Proitos sent Bellerophon to the king of Lykia with a secret message, intended to bring about his destruction (*Il.* 6.156–70). In fact Bellerophon survived and had descendants; the story is told by his grandson, Glaukos, on meeting Diomedes in battle (6.196–206). Thus the evil deed of Anteia is set at a distance of two generations from the present of the *Iliad*. Again, when Eumaios the swineherd tells the story of his origin (*Od.* 15.403–84), Odysseus learns that a Phoenician woman took effective initiative. She was a slave owned by a king of the island of Syrie. A Phoenician ship came there to trade and stayed for a year. When the crew were ready to leave, the woman kidnapped the king's son, Eumaios, and sailed away in the ship. This incident occurred in the generation previous to that of Odysseus; Eumaios as a child was bought by Laertes. Moreover, it occurred at a place far distant from Ithaka, where Eumaios tells his story. The island of Syrie is said to be where the sun turns in its course, that is, in the extreme east or the extreme west.[47] The Amazons, the dangerous women par excellence, are mentioned twice in the *Iliad*, but both contexts are distant in time from the present of the story. Priam as a young man went to help the Phrygians in battle when they were attacked by the Amazons (3.184–90), and at a still earlier date Bellerophon killed the Amazons (6.186). It is to be noted that these incidents put an end to the female threat long before the time of the siege of Troy.

In the Real world of the heroes women do not deflect the plans or fortunes of men. Consequently they have little responsibility. Twelve of the maidservants in the palace of Odysseus accepted Penelope's suitors as lovers. After the suitors had been overcome, Telemachos killed the twelve women on instructions from Odysseus; indeed although Odysseus had told him to kill them with swords, he hanged them in order to inflict a less honorable death (*Od.* 22.413–73). Their ignominious death would perhaps be an excessive punishment if it were due to their own guilt. It can be better explained from the external character which they had acquired from the suitors. The Homeric perspective on women is illustrated well by the catalogue of heroic women included among the shades whom Odysseus sees in Hades (*Od.* 11.225–330). Each of the women in the list was famous in legend, but she was remembered solely because of the men she dealt with and usually because of the sons whom she bore. Just so, when Briseis was taken from Achilles, she was reluctant to go (*Il.* 1.348), but her wish made no difference.

When Priam addressed Helen at the Skaian Gate, he told her that in his eyes she was not guilty (*Il.* 3.164). Generally mortal women in the poems are not called to account as if they themselves were responsible. But Priam's remark has an implication. To say that Helen is not guilty denies an intelligible possibility that she might be guilty. To say that she was guilty would not be nonsensical, although in Priam's opinion it would not be true. Women in the Homeric poems are not presented as congenitally incapable of responsible action. Rather, in the imaginary world of the heroes, the poems present a consistent view of female behavior. This view has several mutually coherent characteristics: women do not control property, beyond the clothes which they have woven, and so they do not offer compensation; women are not held responsible for things that turn out ill; women hardly ever take initiative; women have sentiments, but these are ineffectual; women take their external character from their men, even to the extent of being punished with them. The Homeric poets have achieved this view of the women of heroic legend by relegating other features of female behavior to a distance and usually to the world of the gods. The poems recognize mortal ladies and divine viragoes but no women. It follows that the portrayal is unrealistic. Therefore one should hesitate to suppose that Homeric institutions concerning women, notably marriage, reflect accurately those of any historical society. No doubt each particular feature of the Homeric institutions is drawn ultimately from some actual condition, but in the imaginative transfiguration which produced the world of heroic poetry those features may have been refashioned, distorted, and recombined beyond any point from which their original nature might still be recognized.

SEVEN

Women and the Unity of Greek Law

· · · · · · · · · ·

Frauen dürfen nicht zu einer Dienstleistung im Verband der Streitkräfte durch
Gesetz verpflichtet werden. Zu einem Dienst mit der Waffe dürfen sie in
keinem Fall verwendet werden.

(Women cannot be obliged by law to undertake service within the framework of
the armed forces. They cannot in any case be used for service with a weapon.)
—Fundamental Law of the Federal Republic of Germany, 12.3
(as amended 1956)

Two Athenian questions have still to be answered. First, why did
Athenian law impose disabilities on women? Second, why do Athenian women not appear in inscriptions as owners of land or partners
in major property transactions before the time of Hadrian, even
though Hellenistic inscriptions attest women exercising these capacities in other Greek cities?

Aristotle thought that women were children who never grew up.
If that was the common belief of the Athenians, it might explain
the disabilities. But objections have been offered to this explanation. Women could be tried in court for offenses, including homicide; a woman alleged to be an alien could be prosecuted for living
with a citizen as his wife. Women could serve as witnesses to transactions. Women could inherit property. They were said to own property, although their authority as owners was restricted, since they
could not alienate property or dispose of it by will.

A woman's property was managed for her by her *kyrios*. Although
his power was extensive, it was supposedly the power of an administrator. This relationship between the woman and her *kyrios* is

compatible with the hypothesis of women as perpetual children. But a better explanation of the disabilities starts from the administrative tasks of the *kyrios*. Those tasks included representing the woman in court. Judicial litigation among the Greeks had originated from self-help. Public authority intervened to interrupt the pursuer's act of self-help and entrust the issue to a court for decision. Fossilized relics of self-help persisted, for example in the designation of the plaintiff as "the pursuer."[1] People who have recourse to self-help usually bear arms. Greek women, including Athenian women, were excluded from armed and organized fighting. That exclusion may explain why an Athenian woman could not protect property by self-help or later by litigation, and that in turn would explain why a woman could not carry out transactions in property, beyond the trivialities of petty trade and dedications to gods, but had to be represented by a *kyrios*.

If this explanation is right, one would expect to find somewhat similar disabilities, though not necessarily in such extreme form, imposed on women in other Greek cities. Isolated exceptions, such as Kyniska at Sparta, do not suffice to invalidate the principle. At Gortyn, where the evidence for law is relatively good, the rights of women to property were better protected than at Athens, but women probably had far less property than men; a daughter's share in an inheritance was half of a son's share. It is likely that in Greek cities generally women were subject to disabilities in some degree and these disabilities sprang from their incapacity to bear arms. More will be said shortly about relative homogeneity in Greek law of the family.

Meanwhile it will not be amiss to illustrate what Greeks thought about women in relation to armed fighting. A woman who wielded a lethal weapon was a creature of nightmare; tragedies of the fifth century aroused pity and terror when they portrayed Klytaimestra killing her husband. The creatures of nightmare par excellence were the Amazons. As Greeks enlarged their knowledge of geography, they placed the Amazons further and further afield, always beyond the limits of the known world.[2]

More interest attaches to the story of Telesilla of Argos. About 494 the Spartan king Kleomenes defeated the Argives in battle and killed many of them. When he advanced on the city, Telesilla led the women to take up arms and man the walls. In the ensuing conflict Kleomenes lost many men and was repulsed. Demaretos, the other Spartan king, forced his way into the city but was driven out. The citizens buried the dead women by the Argive road, and the survivors set up a statue of Enyalios. The date of the battle was remembered variously as the seventh of the month Hermaios and as the first. So on the first day of that month each year the Argives continued to celebrate a festival called the Hybristika, where women wore men's clothes and men wore women's clothes. Such is the story told by Plutarch about six centuries after the event. One cannot tell how much is legendary accretion. The association of the prowess of Telesilla with a transvestite ritual should arouse suspicion. Rituals are older than the aetiological myths which explain them. But Telesilla, who is said to have composed poetry, may be a historical figure, and there may be some truth in the tale of her martial exploit. What matters is that it was remembered as extraordinary.[3]

The report of an incident which occurred at Sinope in the first half of the fourth century reveals still more about Greek attitudes toward women. The story is told by a contemporary and it is probably true.[4] Datames, an officer of the Persian king, advanced with an army against Sinope. The city was short of men to defend it. So the citizens dressed their women to look like men and gave them jars and bronze utensils in place of shields and helmets. The women marched to and fro behind the battlements, so that the enemy could see the glint of the sunlight on their armor and hear the clank of their weapons. But the citizens did not let the women throw any missiles.

The other outstanding question arises from the absence of Athenian women from epigraphic records of major transactions in property. The explanation is to be sought in the fact that the Athenians were more numerous and more wealthy than the citizens of the average Greek city. Most Greek cities were mere villages, but Athens was larger and more prosperous even than such major cities as Corinth. It has lately been argued that the wife of a well-to-do Athenian was not subjected to oriental seclusion but lived in a condition of genteel withdrawal.[5] Even among the Athenians only a minority could afford the status symbol of a wife who did not go out of the house to work. Rather more could allow themselves the pretense that their wives did not go out of the house to work. The poor would have liked to do what the rich were seen to do.[6] But if that was true within Athens, men in poor cities would surely have liked to do what men in the richest city were believed to do.

Accordingly the question must be faced, whether there were similarities in the legal condition of women in different cities. Some historians have roundly denied that there was "a single Greek concept of the family and family law."[7] Any opinion on this question is limited by the geographically sporadic character of the evidence. On the law of the family there is good information from Athens, moderately good information from Gortyn, and sporadic indications from other cities; the conditions presented in the Homeric poems, if they are historical conditions, diverge. In different cities law developed in different directions and produced different rules. Yet within these limitations one should recognize four points of fundamental similarity in the legal condition of women in different Greek cities.

(1) A woman has a *kyrios*. In consequence of birth her father is her most likely *kyrios*. If he is not available, her brother, her uncle, her grandfather, or other male relative becomes her *kyrios*. In consequence of marriage her husband becomes her *kyrios*. Later her son or her son-in-law may become her *kyrios*. The authority exercised by the *kyrios*, whatever his relation to the woman, is uniform at any one period in any one city, whereas in Rome women could be subject to authority of different kinds. In Athens the *kyrios* had full authority to administer the woman's property; he carried out transactions on her behalf, represented her at law, and gave her in marriage. In other cities the authority of the *kyrios* may have been different in extent, but at least his existence is attested. A *kyrios* collaborated with Epikteta at Thera, when she made her will. When Nikareta of Thespiai agreed to a settlement with the people of Orchomenos about their debts, her *kyrios* was present. The laws of Gortyn do not contain the word *kyrios*. But they recognize that a woman may have been given in marriage by her father

or her brother, and an innovation in the laws protects a woman's property against alienation by her husband or her son. Thus the institution of *kyrieia* was present in Gortyn, whatever words were used to express it. The authority exercised by a man over a woman had become less extreme at Gortyn, by the time the laws were written down, than it was in Athens, for at Gortyn the woman had acquired some voice in choosing her husband, certainly if she was a *patrōiōkos* and probably even if she was not. Thus the development of *kyrieia* had produced different rules in different cities. But in some form the institution was widespread, probably universal, among Greeks, and it must spring from a common assumption, most likely an assumption about the incapacity of women to bear arms.

(2) When a woman is given in marriage, a dowry or marriage portion is transferred with her. At Athens the promise of a dowry at an assessed value was the important and variable element in *engyēsis*. Although there was scarcely any effective restriction on the husband's authority to administer the dowry, it was intended for the woman's support, and so it went with her if the marriage ended in dissolution or in the husband's death. The laws of Gortyn do not employ a word for "dowry" but speak instead of the woman's own property. In the event of divorce the woman was to keep her own property, a rule similar to that obtaining at Athens. The coherence of the Gortynian laws implies that the bride's property was her fixed share as a daughter in the parental inheritance, whereas in Athens her original *kyrios* had discretion to determine the amount of the dowry. Again, in their laws the people of Gortyn showed more concern than the Athenians to protect the woman's property, a fact which does not necessarily imply that the people of Gortyn were successful in their efforts. There is little evidence on dowry from other Greek cities. When Aristotle says that the Spartans gave large dowries, he implies at least that the practice was current there, whether it was regarded as dowry in the Athenian sense or as the woman's own property as at Gortyn.

If, as seems likely, dowry was general in Greek cities, the contrast with Homeric marriage is striking. Admittedly in the *Iliad* and the *Odyssey* a woman might bring gifts to her husband, but these are portrayed as informal. The salient feature of Homeric marriage is the *hedna*, the valuables given by the bridegroom to the woman's family of origin. These are unlike anything attested in the historical cities of Greece. No doubt the Homeric poets derived the notion of *hedna* from the actual practice of some place and some time, but there is no way of identifying that place or that time. Possibly the payment of *hedna*, like the worship of the powerful god of the sky, was a practice current among Indo-European wanderers before they reached the southeastern peninsula of Europe.

(3) The law takes thought for giving an heiress or female orphan in marriage. The word for her varies and reflects different etymological images; she may be "the woman upon the inheritance" (*epi-klēros*) or "the woman who has her father's property" (*patrōiōkos, patrouchos*). But under these different names the institution is remarkably similar. The heiress is to be given in marriage to the male relative who inherits the property of her deceased father. Both at Athens and at Gortyn the order of intestate succession to property is the same as the order of succession to the heiress. As time passed the two systems devised different solutions for the inconveniences of this institution; the Athenians allowed more flexibility in the testament, but the Gortynians formulated elaborate rules, which eventually granted the heiress some voice in choosing her husband. But both systems start from a common assumption, namely that the law must assign the female orphan to a husband because she has no father or brother to do this.

Both systems share a further assumption of still wider import, namely that a woman ought to bear children. At Athens the husband was required to engage in intercourse with the heiress at least three times a month, and when the children were two years beyond puberty, they took the property of their maternal grandfather with an obligation to support their mother. At Gortyn a widowed *pa-trōiōkos* was allowed to remain single, provided that she had already borne children. At Thera the will of Epikteta shows, not merely that the institution of the *epiklēros* existed, but also that it was conceived in the same way. The reference in the will to property which Epikteta herself had acquired shows that the condition of women was different from that in Athens. Yet the people autho-

rized to participate in the cult of Phoinix and his family included
epiklaroi in perpetuity, together with their husbands and children,
but other daughters only until they were given in marriage. That is,
at Thera as at Athens an *epiklēros* continued the line of descent
which sprang from her father, but other daughters passed on marriage into other families and bore them heirs.

(4) The order of intestate succession at Gortyn, though imper-
fectly known, is similar to that at Athens. In both cities the property of a man who dies without leaving descendants passes to collaterals, that is, primarily to brothers and sisters and their descendants (and then, at least at Athens, to cousins). People related to the
deceased through women take second place after people related to
him through men but are not excluded. The Roman rule, on the
other hand, restricted succession to agnate relatives; that is, the
property was to pass through deceased male ascendants, for example, through father and paternal grandfather to uncle. The Roman
and Greek rules reflect different concepts of kinship. In Rome the
furthest male ancestor in the male line retains his authority over
his descendants until he dies (unless he parts with it explicitly, for
example, by emancipating a son or giving a daughter in marriage
with *manus*); his authority welds his descendants into a unit. In
Athens, on the other hand, the unit is the *anchisteis*, relatives as
far as first cousins and sons of first cousins both on the paternal and
on the maternal side. The *anchisteis* behaved as a unit not only in
succession to property but also in prosecution for homicide.[8]

It would be erroneous to say that in the different Greek cities the
law in relation to women and the family was uniform or even ho-
mogeneous. But comparison has shown that there were elements of
homogeneity. These point to uniform concepts and aims as their
origin. The degree of homogeneity acquires greater clarity when it
is contrasted with Roman law. Comparison has already been made
in the authority exercised by the father and the consequent rules of
succession. In Athens a woman was subject to authority which was
uniform in type, although it might be exercised by different men. In
Rome a woman could be subject to authority of different kinds because of different circumstances; there was no one type of authority

exercised over her simply because she was a woman. The contrast becomes even more graphic when one notes that the institution of the *epiklēros* is foreign to Rome. The Romans did not recognize a need for laws to assign a female orphan in marriage. As long as the *pater familias* lived, the child, whether male or female and whether young or old, was subject to his authority. After the death of the *pater familias*—that is, after the death of the father, the paternal grandfather, and every male ancestor in the direct male line—the child, whether male or female, became fully independent (*sui iuris*). If the child was under age or female, it had a *tutor*, but *tutela* did not diminish its status as a fully independent person.[9] *Tutela* was in origin merely the interest of the agnatic heir in property. Roman law did not care whether a female orphan married or bore children. In Rome descendants of both sexes were equally subject to the *pater familias*. Consequently his durable and extensive authority was a source of equality between the sexes.

In the law of the family, then, there are in different Greek cities elements of homogeneity sufficient to justify the expression "Greek law." It has also become apparent that Greek law of the family is a fully separate creation from Roman law. It is therefore remarkable that in procedural law there was similarity between Rome and at least some Greek cities. In both places a trial went through two stages. The first stage was a hearing before a magistrate—a praetor in Rome, an archon at Athens, a *kosmos* in Crete—and this was the occasion for joinder of the issue. At the second stage the parties appeared before a *iudex* at Rome, a *dikastas* in Gortyn, or many *dikastai* in Athens, and judgment was given. The evident convenience of procedure in two stages may explain why it was preserved but not how it came to be devised. The Roman legend which said that the authors of the Twelve Tables consulted Greek codes may be worthless as historical evidence.[10] But if it did not exist, it would have to be invented now.

Procedural law is germane to the study of women in antiquity in a way which leads to a last consideration. To the modern mind the most startling feature of Greek law of the family is that, at least in the classical period, it is free of any suspicion that female persons may be equal at law to men. Modern thought takes equality among human beings for granted. "We hold these truths to be self-evident, that all men are created equal. . . ." So far from being self-evident, the principle of equality has come into being in a recognizable way.

In a society where there are no courts people have recourse to self-help when they believe they have been wronged. Self-help has the merit of applying the efficiency of private enterprise to the task of righting wrongs. When criminal proceedings replace self-help, the rate of crime is likely to rise, because a judge does not have the personal incentive of a victim to bring about redress. But self-help has disadvantages. One of them arises from the fact that the parties to a dispute are often unequal in power. Self-help gives an advantage to the more powerful party, whatever the merits of his case. In superseding self-help, judicial litigation creates an artificial equality between the parties. It pretends that they are equal in power and it makes this pretense effective for the duration of the trial. The belief that all men are equal springs from procedural law. So far from being self-evident, equality between the parties to a transaction and eventually a dispute has been brought about by thought and effort.

Equality between men and women is likewise not self-evident. In particular, it is not self-evident that bridegroom and bride enter into marriage as equal partners. The assertion of equality between man and wife springs from the doctrine stated in the *Digest* (35.1.15, 50.17): "Marriage is constituted not by corporeal union but by joint consent." In taking this view the Roman jurists made the woman's consent essential to marriage. That belief was foreign to Greek law, even though the laws of Gortyn allowed the woman some degree of freedom to choose a husband. Marriage as a partnership between equals and more generally all institutions which assert equality between the sexes are not self-evident but have been brought into being by thought and effort. They have also been achieved at a price.

Improvement in the status of women has been accomplished at the expense of the status of children. The law protects the rights of the woman if it insists that a union imposed on her without her consent is not a valid marriage and does not bind her. But in this manner the law creates the possibility that a union may be actual but invalid. Systems influenced in varying degrees by Roman law have accepted and extended this possibility. Apart from absence of the woman's consent, an actual union may in modern systems be invalid for other reasons, for example, because the parties are related within specific degrees of kinship or because one party is still bound by a previous marriage and is therefore not free to marry. The rules under which a union can be declared invalid expose the status of children to risk. If an actual union is invalid for any reason, a child of that union suffers the disabilities of bastardy. Greek law, on the other hand, based the right of children to succeed to parental status and property on the identity of the actual parents without necessarily inquiring into the nature of the union. The Greeks took thought for their children and their wives.

The Size of the Liturgical Class in Athens

. . . .

It is reasonable to suppose that in Athens poor people longed to imitate the way they saw rich people behave, and in Greece people of poor cities would have liked to imitate people of rich cities. That is, the behavior or presumed behavior of the rich set norms for the poor to follow, from however great a distance. Within Athens the liturgical class, the men who undertook major expenditures for public activities, constituted a minority easy to recognize, since those expenditures were occasions for display. It could therefore be important to discover the approximate size of that class. The problem can be outlined as follows.

When the Perikles of Thucydides reviewed Athenian resources in 431, he said that there were 300 triremes in seaworthy condition (Thuc. 2.13.8). This figure of 300 triremes as the total available in the Archidamian War is confirmed by remarks of Aristophanes (*Ach.* 545), Xenophon (*Anab.* 7.1.27), and Aischines (2.175, in a confused review of the history of fifth-century warfare). But referring approximately to the same period, Pseudo-Xenophon (*AP* 3.4) says that 400 trierarchs are established each year, and for what it is worth Andokides (3.9) gives a review of fifth-century history much like that of Aischines but says that there were more than 400 triremes. The discrepancy between 300 and 400 as the total of trierarchs (or triremes) in the age of the Archidamian War can be explained by supposing that someone performing a festival liturgy could claim exemption from a trierarchy of that year. This ground of exemption is attested for the fourth century: Demosthenes (20.19, 21.155) says that people performing the trierarchy are exempt from other liturgies; Pseudo-Demosthenes (50.9) says the same, with reference to the trierarchy and the *proeisphora*, and adds that the laws do not allow that one person be required to perform two liturgies at once. When the *proeisphora* was introduced in 378/77, a body of 300 men was constituted to bear this burden (Isai. 6.60; Dem. 2.29, 21.153; [Dem.] 42.3–5, 25; cf. Dem. 37.37; [Dem.] 50.9; Ste. Croix 1953). In 340 the naval law of Demosthenes restricted the burden of the trierarchy to 300 men (Hyper. fr. 134 K; cf. Aischin. 3.222), and these were the same as the 300 who paid the *proeisphora* (Dem. 18.102–3; cf. [Dem.] 42.3–5, 25).

The data given above indicate that the total liable for military liturgies in any one year was 300 to 400. In times of economic hardship it may have dropped somewhat lower. The number of triremes sent out to sea was always lower than 300 and often much lower. For example, in 431, when Perikles said that the Athenians had 300 triremes in a seaworthy condition, rather more than 130 were sent to sea: 100 round the Peloponnese (Thuc. 2.23.2), 30 to Lokris and Euboia (2.26.1), an unknown number to Aigina (2.27). The largest number known to have been sent out on expeditions simultaneously is about 218 in the spring of 413: the 30 ships sent to Argos and Lakonia under Pythodoros and others (Thuc. 6.105.1–2, 7.18.3) had doubtless returned before 30 were sent under Charikles to Argos and the Peloponnese (7.20.1); 10 were dispatched under Euthydemos (7.16.2) and 60 under Demosthenes (7.20.2) for Sicily; there were 18 at Naupaktos (7.31.4); 100 triremes had been sent to Sicily two years before (6.31.3), and even if some of them had been lost in action, that does not diminish the number of trierarchs employed. Since the total of triremes in service at any one time was lower than the number of men liable for the trierarchy, it follows that the latter figure was determined, not by the actual need for naval expeditions, but by the number of men wealthy enough to bear the financial burden. In times of economic hardship the total of the liturgical class may have dropped below 300. So far one may estimate it at 200 to 400 in the fifth and fourth centuries.

A complication arises because in the fourth century performance of a liturgy entitled the performer to a period of exemption. Performance of a festival liturgy brought exemption for one year (Dem. 20.8) and performance of a trierarchy brought exemption for two years (Isai. 7.38). Did the law offer these exemptions already in the fifth century? The answer depends on understanding two texts.

(1) Lysias 21.1–5. The speaker says that he came of age in 411/10 and he lists the liturgies which he performed, starting in that year and continuing through 403/2. The list includes 11 festival liturgies. The speaker also says that he served for seven years as trierarch and made two payments of *eisphora*, all within the same period. He concludes by saying:

> If I had preferred to perform liturgies in accordance with the terms written in the law, I would not have spent a quarter of the sums which I have just listed.

(2) Isaios 7.38. The speaker, Thrasyllos II, had been adopted by Apollodoros and claimed his estate in a lawsuit where he delivered this speech. Apollodoros was the son of Thrasyllos I, who died while serving in the expedition of 415–413 to Sicily (7.5). At 7.38 the speaker boasts of the services of Thrasyllos I:

> His father performed all the other liturgies. He continued serving as a trierarch the whole time, not as a member of a contribution group as people do now but by spending from his own resources, nor as one of two colleagues but on his own, nor after an interval of two years but continuously, nor acquitting himself perfunctorily but providing the best equipment.

These texts have been interpreted in two ways.

(1) From Isaios 7.38 one view notes that toward the middle of the fourth century, when the speech was delivered, the law offered an interval of two years between successive trierarchies, but Thrasyllos I had performed trierarchies in successive years. Likewise the speaker of Lysias 21 had performed trierarchies and other liturgies in successive years. The conclusion is drawn that in the fifth century the law did not offer exemption for one or two years after the performance of a liturgy. On this view, which is expounded by Davies (1981, 15–28), a liturgical class of about 200 to 400 sufficed to

perform public burdens even in the years of the Peloponnesian War, when comparatively large fleets were kept at sea.

(2) The other view draws attention to the last sentence, quoted above, of the boast in Lysias 21.5. The speaker insists that he spent much more than the law required. His words imply that there was a restriction, although he chose not to take advantage of it. Similarly the speaker of Isaios 7.38 says that Thrasyllos I had not had an exemption of two years between trierarchies but does not say that he could not have claimed that exemption, had he wished. The conclusion drawn is that already in the fifth century the law offered an exemption of one year after a festival liturgy and of two years after a trierarchy. If so, the liturgical class must have numbered about 800 to 1,200, if it was to supply 300 to 400 trierarchs at the beginning of the Peloponnesian War. It is to be noted that in 358/57 the law of Periander established a panel of 1,200 men to be liable for the trierarchy ([Dem.] 47.21; Dem. 14.16, 21.155; Isok. 15.145). This view is propounded by Rhodes (1982, 2–5).

There does not seem to be any good ground at present for choosing between the two views.

APPENDIX B

Some Predecessors

. . . .

Inquiries into the condition of women in classical Greece have appeared intermittently since the critical study of ancient history began early in the nineteenth century. Indeed as a great deal of classical literature portrays women, it tells the reader, not necessarily anything about women, but something about what men thought about women. This is true even of works, like that of Thucydides, which reduce the role of women to a minimum. Consequently many of the inquiries which have been made into Greek literature have some bearing on the subject of women in antiquity. To trace the way scholarly treatment of this subject has developed in the nineteenth and twentieth centuries would be a long and laborious task, and it might throw more light on modern thought than on ancient society. It will not be attempted here. But some debts call for acknowledgment and some lines of disagreement need to be made explicit.

On the legal condition of Athenian women the study by A. Ledl, "Das attische Bürgerrecht und die Frauen," *Wiener Studien* 29 (1907) 173–227, 30 (1908) 1–46, 173–230, superseded earlier inquiries and some of its theses have stood the test of time. Ledl concerned himself primarily with the relation of women to citizenship and to the public or quasi-public institutions of the deme and the phratry. A significant advance was accomplished by H. J. Wolff in "Marriage Law and Family Organization in Ancient Athens: A Study in the Interrelation of Public and Private Law in the Greek

City," *Traditio* 2 (1944) 43–95. This article does justice to its subtitle and has rightly won wide recognition. Two years later, in the inquiry called "The Origin of Judicial Litigation among the Greeks," *Traditio* 4 (1946) 31–87, Wolff revolutionized the study of Greek law. The effects of his ideas are still being absorbed.

A new epoch in the study of Greek women began with the publication of W. K. Lacey's *The Family in Classical Greece* in 1968. It appeared at a time when beliefs about the proper behavior of women were changing. In consequence of the changes contemporary assumptions, with which historical findings invite comparison, are no longer the same. It would be audacious to say whether the new beliefs are better than those which they seek to replace. They have prompted a good deal of writing on women in Greek literature and society. Much enlightenment can be gained from J. P. Gould's article of 1980 and from the writings of M. R. Lefkowitz (see Bibliography). On the other hand utterances about the legal condition of Greek women have sometimes been remarkably defective. To avoid polemics elsewhere a sample will be presented and criticized here.

(1) "In legal matters the Athenian gynophobia is best evidenced by a peculiar quirk of Attic law. Under a statute attributed to Solon and perhaps really initiated by him, virtually any legal action undertaken by a man was invalid if it could be shown to have been conceived 'under the influence of a woman' or 'through the persuasion of a woman'" (Keuls 1985, 322). In fact the statute attributed to Solon concerned the last will or testament only. Persuasion by a woman was one of many grounds on which a will could be declared invalid ([Dem.] 46.14; Ar. *AP* 35.2; Plut. *Sol.* 21.3). About 341 a pleader in a lawsuit alleged that by a law of Solon any transaction carried out under the influence of a woman was invalid ([Dem.] 48.56), but an advocate's trick is not a statement of law.

(2) "In the last decades of the seventh century, Draco gave the Athenians their first laws. The most important and the only one to have come down to us forbade private revenge and established that anyone who killed another man would be punished with a penalty (death or exile) to be inflicted by a tribunal specially constituted for the purpose. The penalty would be determined according to

whether the homicide was willful or involuntary. But there was one exception. In violation of the new fundamental principles that signaled the birth of a genuine penal law, he established that a citizen who had killed a *moichos*, a man caught in the act of sexual relations with the former's wife, concubine (*pallake*), mother, daughter, or sister, could not be punished because he had committed a legitimate—or *dikaios*—homicide, provided that, as in the Homeric period, the *moichos* did not pay his debt to society by offering a *poine*, acceptance of which was left to the discretion of the offended party" (Cantarella 1987, 40). In fact the law recognized homicide as legitimate, not only if one killed the sexual intruder, but in several other cases, namely:

> If anyone kills involuntarily in the course of athletics, or on taking a man in the road, or on mistaking his identity in warfare, or on taking him with one's wife or mother or sister or daughter or with the concubine whom one keeps for begetting free children. (Dem. 23.53)

(3) "For the possible coexistence of wife and concubine under the same roof, see Antiph. *de Venef.* 17ff." (Cantarella 1987, 198 n. 48). Admittedly the speech of Antiphon tells of a wife and a concubine under the same roof, but that roof also sheltered two men, the householder and a lodger. The wife was the wife of the householder. The concubine was the concubine of the lodger, who rented the upper part of the house. The lodger is not known to have had a wife, and the householder is not known to have had a concubine. Certainly two different women bore the householder sons, and some readers of the speech (Heitsch 1984, 22; Gagarin 1987, 59) have supposed that the one son was illegitimate, his mother being a concubine. This view rests on an assumption, challenged in chapter 2 above, about an Athenian concept of legitimacy. There is in any case no reason to suppose that both women lived under the same roof at the same time.

(4) "The law of the city concerned itself with prostitutes for only two reasons: to set a ceiling on their prices and to collect a tax on their income.[52]" Note 52: "For the limit on prices see Arist. *Ath. Pol.* 52.2, and Hypereid. *pro Euxen.* 3. For the tax, see Aeschin. *In*

Tim. 110ff." (Cantarella 1987, 50, 198.) In fact the law set a limit, not to the prices charged by prostitutes, but to those at which female musicians could be hired. Aristotle (*AP* 50.2) says that flautists and other female musicians could be hired at 2 drachmas. Hypereides (*Eux.* 3) mentions two men who were prosecuted for leasing flute-girls above the legal rate. There were vocational schools for training flute-girls. A slaveowner who sent one of his young women to such a school undertook considerable expense, since the training lasted six months. He expected a corresponding return. Two drachmas (= 12 obols) may have been a reasonable fee for a flautist's services for an evening; public control of the price and the prosecution mentioned by Hypereides imply that higher prices were charged on the black market. The price for a prostitute's services varied but was nearer to 1 obol (see Starr 1978).

A catalogue of errors soon becomes tedious, especially when they spring from a single root. Let it suffice to say that feminist indignation is out of place in the study of ancient Greece. The Greeks may have been at fault in their treatment of women. For that matter the Athenians may have been at fault before the battle of Aigospotamoi, when they voted to cut off the right hands of captives if they should win (Xen. *Hell.* 2.1.31). But it is too late to correct those faults.

NOTES

Chapter 1

1. The passages have been collected and important inferences have been drawn by Wiedemann (1983). He offers the observation about Dionysios.

2. *Wanderers Sturmlied*; see the comments of von Wilamowitz-Moellendorff (1922, 4–5).

3. These two positions are approximately those of Gomme (1925) and Shaw (1975). See also Lefkowitz (1986, 80–94 = Cameron and Kuhrt 1983, 49–64). Lefkowitz argues successfully that in Graeco-Roman antiquity women did not take political action independently but acted through men; on the rare occasions when they attempted independence, they suffered disaster.

4. On the difficulty of interpreting the vases see Williams (1983).

5. Earlier skepticism began to recede in 1867, when the inscribed text of the law on homicide (now *IG* I³, 104 = Meiggs and Lewis 1969, no. 86) was first published. The question was studied comprehensively by Drerup (1898).

6. On the settlement of 322 see Diod. 18.18.4–5, with the figure from the manuscripts corrected from Plut. *Phok.* 28.4. On the census of Demetrios see Athen. 6.272c. Ruschenbusch (1984b) concludes a series of articles on the total population. A different view and a higher total are defended by Rhodes (1980). Hansen (1985, esp. 18–20, 33–36) argues that the figure of 21,000 ascertained by Demetrios was the total of citizens available for service in the armed forces and omits those who were physically unfit; he estimates the latter as at least 20 percent of the adult male citizens, and so he reaches a much higher figure for the total population than Ruschenbusch. Hansen bases his estimate of the proportion of citizens unfit for service on records of European societies of the nineteenth and twentieth centuries. But modern medicine prolongs the life of the physically unfit. At any one time in the fourth century B.C. the proportion of citizens who were both unfit and alive is likely to have been far lower. Even so, Hansen's study is a valuable reminder that estimates of Athenian population must be highly approximate.

7. [Lys.] 20.13. For the plan see Thuc. 8.65.3; 8.97.1.

8. Ruschenbusch (1979, 133–52, esp. 149).

9. Ruschenbusch (1985, 258): "eine Dorfmark, bei der die Felder in der Reichweite der Siedlung liegen" (a village with its land, where the fields lie within reach of the settlement). See also Merkelbach and Varinlioğlu (1985); Ruschenbusch (1984a, 1983a, 1983b).

10. Jones (1957, 76–79) (20,000); Beloch (1886, 84–99) (75,000); cf. Sealey (1987, 8–9).

11. Harpok. s.v. *metoikion*; Poll. 3.55.

12. Harpok. s.v. *metoikion*; cf. Hesych. s.v. *isotelēs*; Whitehead (1986, 16–17).

13. Dem. 45.30.

14. Xen. *Hieron* 6.10; Dem. 18.51. Much of the material of this and the next paragraph is taken from Davies (1981, 9–37).

15. At Artemision in 480 Kleinias commanded his own trireme, which he maintained at his own expense (Hdt. 8.17); this illustrates the practice from which the trierarchy developed. On the introduction of the *proeisphora* see Ste. Croix (1953). A contrary view has been presented by MacDowell (1986a), but Ste. Croix seems to have the stronger arguments. See further Appendix A.

16. Men liable for liturgies are called *plousiōtatoi* and contrasted with *penētes* at Dem. 20.18; they are contrasted with *aporoi* at Dem. 18.104.

17. Dem. 21.151, 208; Isok. 8.128; Lys. 27.9–10; cf. [Xen.] *AP* 1.13; Dem. 18.102 (where "those owning moderate or little property" are equated with the *penētes* and contrasted with the *plousioi*).

18. Davies (1971, xxiii–xxiv).

Chapter 2

1. Ar. *AP* 26.5; cf. Patterson (1981).

2. For example, *astē* at Aristoph. *Thesm.* 541; *politis* at Dem. 57.30; Ar. *Pol.* 3.1275b33. I have not been able to detect any difference in the legal meaning of the words.

3. Ar. *AP* 55.3.

4. Megakles (Hdt. 6.130–31), Peisistratos (one of his successive wives was an Argive: Hdt. 5.94.1; Ar. *AP* 17.3–4), Miltiades (Hdt. 6.39.2; Plut. *Kim.* 4.1). The mother of Themistokles was probably an alien (Davies 1971, 213–14).

5. Ar. *AP* 42.1. On the question, much discussed, of the age for candidature see Golden (1979).

6. Harrison (1968, 237).

7. Cf. Pomeroy (1982, 128–29).

8. Cf. Ruschenbusch (1979, 83–87).

9. [Dem.] 59.122, delivered toward 340; see note 17 below.

10. Dem. 57.30. The mother of Timotheos was a Thracian: Athen. 13.577a. The condition of Hermogenes (Plat. *Krat.* 384c, 391b–c) is obscure; see Davies (1971, 269). Late stories of a law permitting bigamy should be dismissed as fanciful; see Sealey (1984a, 130).

11. The decree of Nikomenes: schol. Aischin. 1.39; cf. Isai. 8.43; Dem. 57.30. The decree of Aristophon: Athen. 13.577c; cf. Isai. 6.47.

12. Inheritance: Isai. 11.1–3. Homicide: *IG* I³, 104 = Meiggs and Lewis 1969, no. 86, ll. 15, 21–22; [Dem.] 43.57.

13. Isai. 6.47; [Dem.] 43.51.

14. Cf. Wolff (1944, 85–91). Like all students of Athenian marriage, I am much indebted to Wolff's work.

15. Aristoph. *Birds* 1655–56 with schol.; Harpok. s.v. *notheia;* Suda s.v. *epiklēros.*

16. Dem. 23.213; Plut. *Them.* 1.3; Polemon fr. 78 (Preller) apud Athen. 6.234d–e; cf. Humphreys (1974).

17. [Dem.] 59.16 and 52. On the date of the speech see Blass (1887–93, 3.1:536).

18. "Loss of civic rights" is an intentionally vague translation of *atimia.* I have discussed the nature of *atimia* elsewhere (1983, 98–110), but a further study may be needed.

19. For a full study with references see Davies (1971, 427–42). That Pasion was manumitted is implied by Dem. 36.48. The grant of citizenship to him with his sons is known from Dem. 45.78; [Dem.] 53.18, 59.2. The date of his death and the age of Apollodoros at the time are known from [Dem.] 46.13; Dem. 36.22. The provisions of Pasion's will for Archippe are given at Dem. 45.28; cf. [Dem.] 46.13. The two sons of Phormion and Archippe are known from Dem. 45.75. The date of Archippe's death is inferred from [Dem.] 50.60. The acquisition of Athenian citizenship by Phormion in 361/60 is known from [Dem.] 46.13; cf. Dem. 36.6 and 47.

20. Cf. Whitehead (1986). My solution is much like that of Whitehead; I differ from him in supposing a later date for the law penalizing mixed marriages.

21. Davies (1971, 430).

22. [Dem.] 46.23; cf. Ar. *AP* 58.3.

23. Dem. 57; Aischin. 1.77–78, 86, 182; Androt. *FGrHist* 3B:324 F52; Philoch. *FGrHist* 3B:328 F52. Historicity of earlier alleged revisions of the list has been doubted by Jacoby, *FGrHist* 3b (Supplement) 1:158–61; he is followed by Day and Chambers (1962, 118); cf. Sealey (1983, 117–18).

24. See Lloyd-Jones (1983a, 92–93).

25. Isai. 8.19, 3.80. Readers of the Aristophanic passage (for example,

Cantarella 1987, 22–23 with n. 18) have seen in the ceremonies steps of initiation and have speculated about their origin. That may be legitimate, but it is scarcely enlightening.

26. Cf. Gould (1980, 49).

27. Andrewes (1961a, 1961b). Roussel (1976) and Bourriot (1976) offer properly skeptical treatment of earlier views.

28. *IG* II², 1237; Isai. 7.15; Aischin. 2.147; [Dem.] 59.59–61.

29. Some illustrative texts: the *gamēlia* is mentioned in Isai. 3.76; the *dekatē* for a boy in Dem. 39.22, [Dem.] 40.28 and 59; and the *dekatē* for a girl in Isai. 3.30–34. On the significance of these rituals see Rudhardt (1962). Probably only a few relatives and closest associates were invited to the *amphidromia*, celebrated a few days after the birth; see Golden (1986).

30. The introduction and the *koureion* are simultaneous at Isai. 6.21–22; cf. [Dem.] 43.11–14 and 82. An interval of a year is prescribed in *IG* II², 1237, ll. 26–29. Other texts illustrating the introduction of the son by the father to the phratry or to the phratry and the *genos* include Isai. 8.19; Dem. 57.54; [Dem.] 59.59–61 (phratry and *genos*); Andok. 1.127 (*genos* alone).

31. At Isai. 8.19 the formal introduction of the son to the phratry appears to take place promptly after his birth.

32. Dem. 39 and [Dem.] 40, passim. The two *phylai* are named at 39.23–24. The bribe and the testimony of Plangon are recounted at 39.3–4 and 40.8–11. For reconstruction see Rudhardt (1962); cf. Davies (1971, 364–68).

33. For the admission of Boiotos to the phratry and the deme see Dem. 39.4–5. For the expedition of Mantias to the coast of Macedon see Diod. 16.2.6, 16.3.5. For the notoriety see Ar. *Rhet.* 2.1398b2–3.

34. For example, Isai. 2.14, 16, 7.15–17, 27–28, 8.19 (phratry alone); Dem. 57.23.

35. This argument was developed fully by Ledl (1907). I have summarized it elsewhere (1987, 16–18). For recent and cautious discussion see Golden (1985). "Donatus," commenting on Ter. *Ad.* 350–52, says that "Sostratae frater" was mentioned in the second *Adelphoi* of Menander. Golden plausibly explains "frater" as a transliteration of Greek *phratēr*; he infers that Athenian women were associated with members of the phratry and could appeal to them for help in emergencies. That conclusion is compatible with my view. Golden admits that women were not included in phratry lists.

36. Hdt. 6.130; Menand. *Dys.* 842–43; parts of the form of words are cited at Menand. *Mis.* 444–45; *Perikeir.* 1013–14; *Sam.* 726–27.

37. Cf. Wolff (1944, 51–53).

38. Isai. 3.35. On dowry in general see Wolff (1944, 53–65; 1957).

39. Isai. 5.26–37.

40. Isai. 3.39.

41. [Dem.] 59.52; Isai. 3.9. There was also a *dikē proikos* (Ar. *AP* 52.2) available as a remedy; on its relation to the *dikē sitou* see Lipsius (1905–15, 496–98).

42. [Dem.] 47.57.

43. The dowry is distinguished from the paraphernalia at Isai. 2.9, 8.8. The speaker of Dem. 41 asserts that the paraphernalia of his wife's sister were assessed as part of her dowry (41.27–28); the assertion was an attempt to lead the judges behind the light.

44. [Dem.] 46.13; Dem. 36.22. Pasikles was probably declared of age at the beginning of 362/61, for he gave evidence early in that year: [Dem.] 49.42–43.

45. For the date see Blass (1887–93, 3.1:468).

46. Dem. 45.75; cf. 36.32.

47. Dem. 36.14.

48. [Dem.] 50.60.

49. Dem. 36.14–15, 32.

50. Dem. 45.3–4; [Dem.] 46.18–23.

51. [Dem.] 40.2–3, 6–7, 20, 22, 60.

52. The law preserved in Dem. 23.53 says what kinds of homicide were justified; they included killing the man whom one took with one's wife, mother, sister, daughter, or with the concubine whom one kept for begetting free children. Starting from this text, Paoli (1950, 125–39; followed, for example by Cantarella 1987, 40) maintained that *moicheia* included not only adultery, that is, corruption of the wife, but also corruption of the other specified women of the household. But the law preserved in Dem. 23.53 does not employ the word *moichos* or *moicheia*. It does not profess to be the Athenian law of adultery but an exception in the Athenian law of homicide (cf. Cohen 1984). No occurrence has been found where *moichos* or *moicheia* necessarily refers to corruption of a woman other than the wife. The question will arise again in relation to the Gortynian law of adultery.

53. There were probably at least two remedies. A husband who found a strange man in his house could tie him up on suspicion of adultery and a third party could initiate the *graphē adikōs heirchthēnai hōs moichon*, so that the issue was brought into court: [Dem.] 59.66; Ruschenbusch (1982, 5–7). Alternatively a husband could have recourse to the procedure called *apagōgē* against an adulterer; see Cohen (1984).

54. [Dem.] 59.87; cf. Harrison (1968, 36).

55. The order of the relatives is given at [Dem.] 43.51; cf. Isai. 3.72–73, 10.4–5. It is the same as for intestate succession to property (Isai. 11.1–3).

56. Dem. 57.41.

57. Ar. *AP* 56.6–7; cf. 43.4. The polemarch performed the same function for metics: [Dem.] 46.22.

58. Isai. 6.14.

59. [Dem.] 46.20; Isai. 8.31, 10.12; Harpok. s.v. *epi dietes hēbēsai*.

60. Plut. *Sol.* 20.4; *Mor.* 769a.

61. The law governing bequest and adoption is given at [Dem.] 46.14. Parts of it are cited at [Dem.] 44.68; Dem. 20.102; Ar. *AP* 35.2; Plut. *Sol.* 21.3. Opinions differ on the question whether it was designed for *adoptio inter vivos* and applied to bequest (Gernet 1955, 121–49) or designed for bequest and applied to *adoptio inter vivos* (Ruschenbusch 1962).

62. Isai. 3.42, 68, 10.13.

63. This refutes the thesis of Wolff (1944, 65–75), that the woman usually entered this condition on her own initiative and enjoyed greater freedom than in engyetic marriage. In addition to the two texts discussed here *pallakai* are mentioned at [Dem.] 59.122 (quoted in chapter 1), but the remark is colloquial, not legal, and uninformative.

64. [Dem.] 40.8–9.

65. The content of Plangon's testimony: Dem. 39.4; cf. [Dem.] 40.10–11. Pamphilos' third of the inheritance: 39.6, 40.2, 40.48. Boiotos is said to have gained citizenship through the testimony of Plangon: 39.31, 34, 40.42; the same should be inferred for Pamphilos.

66. Nicholas (1962, 83); cf. Watson (1967, 27–29). The later principle, which modern systems follow, is stated in the *Digest* 35.1.15, 35.50.17: "nuptias enim non concubitus sed consensus facit" (marriage is constituted not by corporeal union but by joint consent). I have presented my theory previously (1984a), and as will be recognized, I have since made a small modification in the view taken of *nothoi* and of [Plut.] *Mor.* 834a–b.

67. Isai. 8.19; Dem. 57.54; [Dem.] 59.59–60.

68. Andok. 1.127; *IG* II², 1237, ll. 109–11. The word *gamos* with the verb *gamein* was used of marriage in the *Iliad* and the *Odyssey*. In the prose of the orators it had been displaced by forms of *engyan*. It survived in poetry, but it could be used of nonmarital unions; see, for example, Aisch. fr. 13 (Nauck and Radt).

69. [Plut.] *Mor.* 834a–b. On loss of civic rights see note 18 above.

70. The decree against Arthmios of Zeleia (Dem. 9.42–44) would be a counter-example, if it were genuine. But it is probably a forgery or, at best, a distortion; see Habicht (1961).

71. Dem. 30.15, 17, 26, 31. The share of Onetor in recording the divorce with the archon is mentioned at 30.17. Since a woman initiating divorce was said to "depart" (*apoleipein, apoleipsis*) from her husband, the expression uttered at 30.31 is noteworthy; Demosthenes says there that Onetor "carried out the departure." The procedure followed when divorce was initiated by a woman is also illustrated, though less clearly, by the argument of Isai. 3.8 and 78 and by the scandalous story of Alkibiades and his wife ([Andok.] 4.14; Plut. *Alk.* 8).

72. *IG* II², 776.

73. *IG* II², 1514–31.

74. *IG* II², 1532–39.

75. *IG* II², 2776. The objection was made by Ste. Croix (1970). On Hellenistic cities see chapter 4.

76. Cf. Blass (1887–93, 3.1:249–53). Speech 41 does not avoid uninterrupted sequences of short syllables with the rigor characteristic of Demosthenes in his maturity; see Adams (1917) and Vogel (1923).

77. Ste. Croix (1970, 276).

78. Dem. 27.53–57; cf. 29.46–49.

79. Isai. 11.1–3; cf. [Dem.] 43.51; Isai. 7.20,22. Isaios 11.3 says that relatives in the stated degree were the *anchisteis* recognized by the law. If there were no relatives surviving within these degrees, the estate passed to the nearest relative on the father's side: [Dem.] 43.51.

80. Kränzlein (1963, 31–37). Aristotle (*Rhet.* 1.1361a19–22) recognized the power to alienate as the test of ownership.

81. [Dem.] 35.24: *kratein tōn chrēmatōn*. Other speeches dealing with loans made for maritime ventures are Dem. 32 and [Dem.] 56.

82. *Kyrios*: [Dem.] 56.24. For examples of expressions of ownership see Dem. 32.9, 12, 18, 30; [Dem.] 35.4, 22, 25, 26, 37, 38, 40, 52; 56.1, 4, 17, 18, 34, 44, 50.

83. Dem. 45.72, 80.

84. Dem. 36.3, 22.

85. Dem. 27.15.

86. Cf. Wittfogel (1981, 228).

87. Wolff (1944, 53–65) argued against importing the Roman notion of *ius in re aliena* to explain the relation of the *kyrios* to the dowry. Accepting the validity of his objection, I prefer to introduce a negative definition of ownership.

88. [Antiphon] 3 presents a *meirakion* who is tried in court and defended by his father on a charge of homicide. But it is not clear how far the *Tetralogies* reflect Athenian practice; see Sealey (1984b). It is to be presumed that a slave who committed homicide was to be punished by his master (and the treatment of the *pelatēs* in Plat. *Euthyph.* 4c–d may follow this principle); if the master did not punish the homicidal slave, the master could doubtless be prosecuted for "instigation" (*bouleusis*: Ar. *AP* 57.3; cf. Andok. 1.94).

Chapter 3

1. References will be given to the code by Roman numeral for the column and Arabic numeral for the line. Guarducci in *IC* IV, 72, provides the text, a Latin translation, and a commentary. Willetts (1967) provides an

introduction, the text, an English translation, and commentary. Although many of Willetts's explanations are useful, some are flawed by a priori belief in a transition from matriarchy to patriarchy and by importation of extraneous customs; see Meyer-Laurin (1969). Willetts's hypothesis of a compact for continuous intermarriage between two groups of kinsmen (cf. 1964–65) rests on the dubious assertion of Strabo, that all men married collectively on leaving the *agela*. On the date of the inscription see Guarducci (1938, 268–73); she inclines to a date ca. 480–460. Another inscription, *IC* IV, 41, is sometimes called "the second code." It consists of seven columns. It has provisions about damage inflicted by farm animals, about the slave who takes refuge in a sanctuary, and about the man who has pledged his person as security for a loan, but none about women.

2. Cf. Jacoby, *FGrHist* 2C: p. 80 ("nicht ausgeschlossen").

3. 1592.57–58, on *Od.* 8.247. The information is doubtless taken from Aristophanes of Byzantium; cf. Nauck (1848, 91).

4. For discussion see Willetts (1967, 12–13).

5. The fundamental study is Dittenberger (1863). See also Pélékidis (1962). Aristotle (*AP* 42) tells how a young Athenian came of age and consequently served for two years as *ephēbos*. On the age see Golden (1979).

6. This discussion of ages is intended as an answer to Willetts (1955, 7–17). He holds that a boy became *ēbiōn* at the age of twelve, since that was the age when a girl became *ēbionsa*. But it is difficult to see force in this argument. He draws also on Strabo's statement, that men completing their training in the *agela* were required to marry at the same time; understanding *apodromos* as "a minor," he supposes that the provision in the code about the *apodromos* (VII 35–40) was an innovation, which departed from Strabo's rule by permitting the *apodromos* to marry. But that is highly speculative. The view defended here agrees with that adopted by Guarducci, *IC* IV, p. 150.

7. Thus Meyer-Laurin (1969, 163): "*Kadestai* heisst es an allen Stellen stets dann, wenn die Sorge und die Verpflichtung zur Vornahme einer Handlung für jemanden in Rede steht, und *epiballontes*, wenn es um eine Berechtigung geht" (the word used is *kadestai* in all passages, when care for someone or the obligation to carry out a deed for him is mentioned, but *epiballontes* in reference to an entitlement). Reference may be made to Meyer-Laurin for criticism of Willetts's views on Cretan kinship.

8. The outlines of Roman and Athenian procedure are well known and one may consult standard handbooks, for example, Nicholas (1962, 19–27, on the praetor's edict and the formulary procedure; 126–27, on the *actio Publiciana*, which includes an *exceptio* and a *replicatio*); cf. Wolff (1951, 76–79). On Athenian procedure in two stages see Sealey (1987, 53–54, 68–69, 79–81, 135). There is a full study of *paragraphē* by Wolff (1966).

9. Meiggs and Lewis 1969, no. 2; cf. Gagarin (1986, 84–85).

10. For the oath of Athenian *dikastai* see Fränkel (1878). On the notion of "gaps" between the laws see Ruschenbusch (1957, 263–65).

11. This hypothesis about Crete was propounded and defended by Wolff (1946, 62–67). Cf. Meyer-Laurin (1969, 164).

12. This is the theory of Wolff (1946). Additional grounds for holding it have been presented by Ruschenbusch (1982). In early Athenian procedure for homicide a finding of the court for the defendant probably had the consequence that the state gave him a safe-conduct to the border, since it was not powerful enough to protect him indefinitely: Dem. 23.72; Ruschenbusch (1960).

13. Guarducci (*IC* IV, p. 160) suggests that these residual heirs were neighbors. Willetts (1967, 66) suggests that they were serfs belonging to the land which the deceased owned.

14. The Athenian law preserved in [Dem.] 46.14 served both for testamentary bequest and for *adoptio inter vivos*; see note 61 to chapter 2.

15. One may compare *adrogatio* before the *comitia curiata* in Rome; see Nicholas (1962, 77).

16. Isai. 10.10.

17. Dem. 27.4–5. The flexibility of the Athenian will can also be illustrated from the testaments of Konon (Lys. 19.39), of Epikouros (Diog. L. 10.16–21), of Pasion (Dem. 36.33–35, 45.27–28), and of Aristotle (Diog. L. 5.11–16). Cf. Sealey (1987, 27–28).

18. For the classification of Athenian laws see Dem. 24.20. On Athenian procedures for adultery see chapter 2 at notes 52–53; for the share of the *thesmothetai* see Ar. *AP* 59.3. On the law concerning the male prostitute see Dover (1978, 19–31).

19. The words chosen in translation and paraphrase try to reproduce the distinctions of the original. In delicts 1 and 3 the verb is *oipen*, "to copulate (with)." In delict 2 it is *daman* or *damnan*, presumably "to deflower," from a root sense "to subdue." In delict 4 the crucial word is the participle *moikion*, "committing adultery with." This is etymologically akin to *moichos*, *moicheia*, attested in Attic and other Greek. It is assumed here that words of the root *moich-*, *moik-* refer to adultery, that is, to intercourse with a married woman by a man other than her husband. A different view, extending the concept to other women of the household, might perhaps be maintained, but no passage is known where *moicheia* certainly has a wider sense than adultery (cf. note 52 to chapter 2), and to attribute the wider sense to *moikion* in the code of Gortyn would make parts at least of the rules about delicts 1 and 2 otiose.

20. Crime in modern law is an offense against the monarch or, in countries which have no monarch, against an abstraction, the state or the people, which has replaced him. Crime defies the monarch's authority by disturbing the peace which he maintains. Delict is an offense against a private

person and defies his authority. An adulterer, for example, intrudes into the sphere of authority of the husband. A payment for delict should not be confused with compensation for loss or damage; see Nicholas (1962, 207–9).

21. Gernet (1955, 57–59).

22. Gagarin (1984, 347–49); cf. Gernet (1955, 51–55); Willetts (1964–65). If *kadestai* has the wider sense, to include the father and the brother, it does not include the husband. If it is right to understand the word in this wider sense, the four delicts constitute a system which is easy to understand: the primary distinction is between the married woman (delict 4) and other women (delicts 1, 2, 3); if the woman is not married, a further distinction is drawn between offenses where force is employed (delicts 1, 2) and those where it is not (delict 3).

23. See note 66 to chapter 2.

24. The provisions on disposal of property at termination of the marriage continue by setting a limit to *komistra* (III 37–40); these are explained well by Willetts (1967, 62) as "payments for porterage," that is, fees paid to a bearer for carrying the property of the divorced or bereft person to another dwelling.

25. "By pledge" (*epispensai*): probably a promise in connection with marriage, as suggested by Willetts (1967, 21).

26. Schaps (1979, 58–59).

27. [Hdt.] 6.122: among the memorable deeds of the wealthy Kallias, he gave each of his three daughters to the Athenian whom she herself chose.

28. Dem. 27.4; cf. [Dem.] 40.24; Theophr. *Char.* 22.10.

Chapter 4

1. MacDowell (1986b, 1–22) offers a serviceable introduction to the sources on Spartan institutions but does not allow for this inherent weakness.

2. Plutarch (*Lyk.* 10–12, 14–25) gives a detailed account, but it may have been influenced by the Spartan movement for reform in the third century B.C. Xenophon (*Lak. Pol.* 2–4) describes the system of education in less detail; he offers the crucial information that there was a *paidonomos*, a public officer in charge of education. It follows that education was not private, as in Athens, but controlled by the state.

3. Xen. *Lak. Pol.* 1.4; Plut. *Lyk.* 14.3, *Mor.* 227d.

4. Redfield (1977–78, 158–61).

5. Paus. 3.8.1, o.1.6; *IG* V, 1, 1564a (at the front of the volume). By the middle of the third century some women controlled plentiful property; Agis IV, attempting reform, asked some rich women to give up their property (Plut. *Agis* 4.1, 7.1–7, 9.6; cf. 6.7). This information concerns actual

control of wealth and does not say what legal institutions had enabled the women to gain that control.

6. [Dem.] 43.54.

7. MacDowell (1986b, 107–9); Cartledge (1981, 99).

8. Xen. *Lak. Pol.* 1.7–9. Plutarch (*Lyk.* 15.12–13) states the same two practices without the explanations; he may draw on Xenophon as his source.

9. Isai. 2.3–9. Two further cases deserve note. (1) The sister of Onetor was taken from her first husband, Timokrates, and given in marriage promptly to Aphobos (Dem. 30.7–8, 33). Demosthenes represents this as an incident in a conspiracy in which the three men took part. (2) From Plut. *Per.* 24.8 it appears that a woman was at different times wife of Perikles and of Hipponikos. It is disputed whether Perikles gave her to Hipponikos (Davies 1971, 262–63) or Hipponikos gave her to Perikles (Bicknell 1982, 248–49).

10. Herodotos (6.57.4, 6.71.2) speaks of Spartan fathers who gave their daughters in marriage. Other passages (Plut. *Lyk.* 15.4–9; Athen. 13.555b–c; cf. Hdt. 6.65.2) tell of a mode of contracting marriage which consisted in a ritualized seizure of the bride by the bridegroom. If the latter mode (discussed by MacDowell 1986b, 77–82) is more than a traveler's tale, the two customs are difficult to reconcile; for the ritualized seizure treats the woman as an asset, which the bridegroom wishes to take, but if the father gives her in marriage with a dowry, custom focuses on the burden of supporting her. But the two customs are alike in that they treat the woman as an object and allow her no voice in selecting her husband.

11. See especially Schaps (1979) and Schuller (1985, 106–26).

12. "Poseidonios" is perhaps most easily explained as a by-form of the name of the god Poseidon; cf. Soph. *OC* 1494. The alternative would be to take it as the name of a man in the inscription, but divine honors for a private person would be surprising at so early a date.

13. By Van Bremen (1983).

14. Lefkowitz (1983, 88).

15. Cf. Beasley (1906).

16. See Wolff (1973).

17. From Saint Matthew 1:18–19, 24, Nörr (1961, 110–15) detects two stages in the conclusion of marriage in Palestine; he finds them comparable to Greek *engyēsis* and *ekdosis* but he attributes them to independent development.

Chapter 5

1. Riccobono (1941, 21–75, the Twelve Tables; 335–89, the edict of the urban praetor).

2. Wolff (1951, 63–65, interpretation; 111, *advocati*; 160, the Law of Ci-

tations). The professions of jurist and advocate were fully separate in Rome, unlike many modern states, where judges, advocates, and professors of law are often embraced by the same professional organization.

3. Gaius 1.55. The Galatians were of Celtic origin and had settled in Asia Minor in the third century B.C.

4. Nicholas (1962, 65–69).

5. Plut. *Sol.* 22.1.

6. Cf. Maine (1894, 182–88).

7. Gaius 1.119: "hunc ego hominem ex iure Quiritium meum esse aio isque mihi emptus esto hoc aere aeneaque libra." Cf. Nicholas (1962, 63).

8. For *res mancipi* see Gaius 2.14a; cf. Nicholas (1962, 105–6). The explanation was offered by Maine (1894, 277).

9. Gaius 2.102–8; cf. Nicholas (1962, 253–54); Maine (1894, 203–14).

10. Twelve Tables IV 26: "si pater filium ter venum duuit, filius a patre liber esto." Cf. Nicholas (1962, 80). The implications are not understood by Cantarella (1987, 116).

11. Nicholas (1962, 122–25) expounds the conditions.

12. Nicholas (1962, 82). Gaius (1.49) distinguishes three mutually exclusive kinds of authority to which free persons who are not *sui iuris* are subject; they are *potestas, manus,* and *mancipium.* It has been conjectured that the distinctions between these kinds of authority are secondary and that originally there was only one undifferentiated type of authority, the word for it being *manus;* when the other kinds of authority split off from it, this word was kept for the authority of husband over wife (Maine 1894, 316–17).

13. One of the rights constituting Roman citizenship was *conubium,* the capacity to contract a marriage recognized by Roman law as *iustae nuptiae,* so that the relation of the children to the father's authority and property would be upheld. As time passed, the Roman Republic granted *conubium* and other rights to some communities in Italy (see, for example, Scullard 1935, 34, 89–90, 127–29). Complications arise over the children of a Roman woman and a male alien who had *conubium;* see Nicholas (1962, 83).

14. It can, however, be argued that in the Republic a woman could not herself initiate divorce but depended on her *pater familias;* see McDonnell (1983).

15. Watson (1967, 11–18); the evidence for actionable *sponsalia* at the early stage is Gell. 4.4.1–4.

16. Cic. *Flacc.* 84; Gell. 3.2.12–13; cf. Watson (1967, 19–31). Two related men of the name Q. Mucius Scaevola were active about the end of the second century; see Wolff (1951, 102).

17. Twelve Tables V 4; cf. Nicholas (1962, 66). It is convenient to recall, with Nicholas, that the transmission of family names in English is agnatic, except when a woman takes her husband's name on marriage.

18. Twelve Tables V 1 = Gaius 1.144–45; Gaius points to the better explanation at 1.192.

19. Cf. Nicholas (1962, 90–91).

20. Twelve Tables V 2 = Gaius 2.47; cf. Cic. *ad Att.* 1.5.6.

21. This is the theory of Watson (1967, 19–31). Cicero indicates at *Flacc.* 84 that the consent of all the *tutores* was required for marriage with *manus*, whether concluded by *usus* or *coemptio*.

22. Liv. 39.19.3–7 ("tutoris optio . . . quasi ei vir testamento dedisset," 5).

23. Liv. 39.9.7.

24. Cic. *Cael.* 68, *Caec.* 72.

25. The consequent capacity of women to carry out transactions in property helps to explain why conventional Roman thought portrayed mothers as respected and indeed authoritarian figures (this is the thesis of Dixon 1988).

26. Watson (1967, 41–47).

27. See note 66 to chapter 2.

28. It is illustrated still more strikingly by the recognition that in some circumstances possession, as distinct from ownership, deserved to be protected; see Nicholas (1962, 107–15). That need not be considered here, except to note that Greek law cannot be shown to have taken that important step; see Wolff (1964).

29. In a thorough inquiry Gardner has maintained (1986, 263–64): "Women's major personal and financial freedoms had already been conferred upon them by a very early date in Roman history, and for reasons which had more to do with the necessity of maintenance of the social status of the *familia* and co-operation with other *familiae* in a city-based civilisation than with any concern to 'liberate' the female members. Subsequent changes were by no means all in the direction of greater independence for women." Gardner presents strong arguments for these conclusions. There is no reason to deny that the germs from which the legal capacities of women grew were present at the earliest discernible stage of the Republic. But Gardner's attempt (pp. 13–14) to explain the decline of marriage with *manus* from concern for the property of the *familia* remains speculative, and it is admitted (pp. 20–22) that the restrictive force of *tutela* over women decreased. Surely it is reasonable to associate such developments, in however vague a way, with the general trend of Roman law from status to contract.

30. See Roussel (1976) and Bourriot (1976).

Chapter 6

1. Of a wife: *Il.* 1.114, 7.392, 11.243, 13.626, 19.298; *Od.* 13.45, 14.245, 15.356. Of a husband: *Il.* 5.414; *Od.* 11.430, 15.22, 19.266, 23.150, 24.196, 200. Of their bed: *Il.* 15.40. Of their house: *Od.* 19.580 = 21.78.

2. *Od.* 4.10–14; cf. 15.100–104, 122, 141.

3. For example, *Il.* 18.491–96; *Od.* 1.226.

4. I have learned much from Finley (1955), Lacey (1966), Snodgrass (1974), and Morris (1986). I am convinced by Morris's argument against the occurrence of dowry in any strict sense in the poems.

5. Thus Morris (1986, 105–10).

6. *Il.* 9.146, 288, 13.366.

7. This conclusion was established by Finley (1955). Trade in Lemnian wine is indicated at *Il.* 7.467–75 and in Phoenician jewelry at *Od.* 15.415–16 (cf. 459–63).

8. The suggestion is made, not only by the rascally Antinoos (*Od.* 2.113–14), but also by the better-behaved Eurymachos (2.194–97) and by Athena (1.275–78), and it is implied by Telemachos (2.50–58).

9. For example, *Il.* 22.51. At 9.147–48 Agamemnon implies that a bride's father often gives gifts to the bridegroom.

10. *Od.* 4.735–36, 23.227–28.

11. *Od.* 1.277, 2.196, 11.117, 13.378, 15.18, 16.391–92, 19.529, 21.161–62.

12. *Od.* 8.581–83. Pindar (*O.* 7.1–6) draws on the love of father-in-law for son-in-law in a memorable simile.

13. This institution is well known. For references and discussion see, for example, Sealey (1987, 74).

14. *Thebais* fr. 6 (Allen) = Apollod. *Bibl.* 1.74.

15. *Od.* 2.332–36, 16.383–86; cf. 2.367–68, 17.79–80. The view taken in this paragraph owes much to Lacey (1966). If the poets say relatively little about disposal of the kingdom, that is because they have only a vague notion of kingship; see Geddes (1984, 28–36).

16. The bibliography which could be cited for this section is enormous. (For a less skeptical introduction to problems of composition and transmission one may consult Heubeck, West, and Hainsworth 1988, 3–48). Since I do not wish to engage in polemics, I have restricted myself to references necessary for my arguments. Moreover, I have tried to restrict my inferences to the minimum which current knowledge compels. There is plentiful room left for legitimate speculation, for example on the possibility that the poems reached in some sense a final form in the period 750–650, but speculation would be out of place here. My aim has been, not to show that the poems were not composed between 750 and 650, but to show that one cannot know at present that they were.

17. The quotation is from Nep. *Att.* 13.3 ("anagnostae optimi et plurimi librarii"). See Allen (1924, 302–27). A theory of the type challenged by Allen was presented by Murray (1924, 282–95). General knowledge of the transmission of classical texts in the Hellenistic period depends largely on the cases of the *Iliad* and the *Odyssey*, since the scholia to these are far richer than the scholia to most other works. Yet the ghosts of Alexandrian editions continue to haunt textual critics; see, for example, Page (1938, xxxix–xli); Reynolds and Wilson (1968, 8).

18. Diog. L. 1.57; [Plat.] *Hipparch.* 228b; see Davison (1958).

19. Cic. *De Orat.* 3.137. I have learned much from Merkelbach (1952).

20. Chantraine (1948, 12, 15–16, 37, 72, 476).

21. *Il.* 6.87–98, 242–311. It is amazing that a reader can assert "the absence of any hint of the sixth century itself in the poems" (Morris 1986, 92).

22. M. Parry (1928). Parry enlarged on his discovery in a series of articles (collected in Parry 1971). His method of argument has been challenged by Austin (1975, 11–80). Austin argues that some major figures of the poems are designated in a nonformulaic manner. But it is not clear what he professes to demonstrate, since he recognizes (p. 181) that the tradition on which Homer drew was oral. Thus it is agreed that the poems arose from a tradition of oral composition but are now available in writing; the task is to discover how this change came about.

23. Lord (1953).

24. This point has been defended adequately by A. Parry (1966).

25. Thus A. Parry (1966).

26. Dihle (1970, 65–93). Lloyd-Jones (1981) offers a general hypothesis of composition with the aid of writing.

27. An attempt of this kind has been made recently by van Thiel (1982; cf. 1977, 1979).

28. Lorimer (1950, 212–19, 328–35). *Archaeological Reports for 1981–82* (published by the Council of the Society for the Promotion of Hellenic Studies and The Managing Committee of the British School at Athens), 58; *Archaeological Reports for 1982–83*, 53; cf. *Archaeological Reports for 1978–79*, 45–46 (for the date of the graves).

29. Gray (1954).

30. As far as I know, the current popularity of this suggested date of composition began from the study by Lorimer (1950, 462–528). More precise dates have been defended, for example by Janko (1982, 228–31). Lorimer drew one of her main arguments from the absence of hoplite tactics from the *Iliad* ("a poem so largely martial cannot possibly have been composed in an obsolete idiom and first addressed to the generation which first practised the new and revolutionary method of warfare," pp. 462–63). But the poems resisted the adoption of iron as the material of offensive

weapons for many centuries successfully. Besides, battles fought by massed hoplites may not lend themselves to poetic composition as readily as duels between Homeric heroes. No account in verse of a hoplite battle springs to mind.

31. Lorimer (1950, 511–15).

32. For example, the supposition of changes in the art of music under oriental influence is crucial to Dihle's reconstruction of the beginnings of written epic (1970, 120–43).

33. Jacoby (1941).

34. *Il.* 11.36–37; Lorimer (1950, 190–91).

35. Geddes (1984); *Od.* 18.366–75 (the boast of Odysseus), 17.297–99 (the manure), 19.552–53 (the geese). By comparing oral poetry and other anthropological data from other cultures Morris (1986) maintains that the institutions presented in the poems belonged to their time of composition (which he puts in the eighth century), although recollections of things capable of being seen or visualized might be preserved from an earlier period. This hypothesis cannot be tested, since there is no external evidence for the institutions of most of the period when the poems were developing. The surest conclusion from the comparative material is that there is no limit to the variety of human behavior. Toward the view taken here I have learned much from Long (1970, 122–23, 137 n. 58).

36. "Et wassen twee Künigeskinner," first taken down by Annette von Droste-Hülshoff, and accessible (for example) in F. Martini, ed. *Klassische deutsche Dichtung*, vol. 19, *Balladen* (Freiburg, Basel, and Vienna 1967), 36–38.

37. Korfmann (1986).

38. Cook (1973, 145).

39. As Cook remarks (1973, 91–92), since Schliemann's excavations it has often been assumed that there is a single solution to all the problems of locating Homeric Troy; but "the question that is not asked is whether there ever was such a solution." Cf. Carpenter (1946, 45–67).

40. Lorimer (1950, 494–97).

41. Dodds (1951, 2–8); cf. Fraenkel (1950, 3:545, on l. 1192). Among subsequent discussions the remarks of Lloyd-Jones (1983b, 10, 17, 22–23, 240) are noteworthy, as are those also of Adkins (1982) for a rather different view.

42. Helen is notably wanton and unscrupulous in the *Orestes* of Euripides (note especially ll. 128–29, 1110–14, 1528), also in *The Trojan Women* 895–965. The *Encomium of Helen* by Gorgias attests to the contemporary assessment, with which it took issue.

43. But the poets did Klytaimestra the courtesy of uttering her name aright. It was left to scholars of the Middle Byzantine period to insert an -*n*-; see Fraenkel (1950, 52–53).

44. I have been stimulated by the discussions of Devereux (1957), Amory (1966), and Van Nortwick (1979). On the general role of mortal women in the *Iliad* and the *Odyssey* much can be learned from Lefkowitz (1987).

45. Cf. von Fritz (1943).

46. Deities can even provide comic relief, as when Aphrodite intervenes in the fighting at Troy and gets her arm scratched (*Il.* 5.311–430). Beye (1974) stresses the anthropomorphic character of Homeric gods and therefore declines to draw a distinction between goddesses and mortal women. A better course is followed by Farron (1979), who studies four mortal women (Helen, Andromache, Hekabe, and Briseis) and finds that the poet attributes intense but ineffectual sentiments to them with tragic effect. My thinking in this paragraph has been stimulated by Vermeule (1979, 122–23) and by Kästner (1969, chap. 7).

47. Syrie is probably a romanticized recollection of a place at the mouth of the Orontes; see Lorimer (1950, 80–83).

Chapter 7

1. Wolff (1946).

2. Lefkowitz (1986, 17–23).

3. Plut. *Mor.* 245c–f; cf. Lefkowitz (1986, 141–42).

4. Ain. Tact. 40.4; the incident probably took place about 370; cf. *RE* 4:2225 (Judeich).

5. Schuller (1985, 44–77, at 51): "vornehme Zurückgezogenheit." I thank my colleague G. Barth for suggesting "genteel withdrawal" as a translation of this phrase.

6. Cf. Schuller (1985, 51): "Die normale Athenerin führte den Haushalt, ging natürlich aus (wenn wir auch zahlreiche Belege einkaufender Männer haben) und war, wenn sie es nötig hatte, am aushäusigen Erwerbsleben beteiligt. Das Ideal freilich war das der vornehm zurückgezogen lebenden Dame, und dieses Ideal wurde natürlich auch gegenüber dem athenischen Durchschnittsbürger verkündet, selbst wenn dieser Biedermann so eine Vornehmtuerei bei sich zu Hause scheusslich gefunden hätte—der Bauer Strepsiades in Aristophanes' 'Wolken' litt entsprechend unter der Vornehmheit seiner Frau" (The normal Athenian woman conducted the housekeeping, went out naturally—even though we have plentiful attestation of men who went shopping—and when she had the need, she took part in earning a livelihood outside the house. Admittedly the ideal was that of the lady living in genteel withdrawal, and naturally this ideal was also proclaimed to the average Athenian citizen, even if that worthy would have found such display of gentility abominable in his own house—the farmer Strepsiades in the *Clouds* of Aristophanes suffered accordingly under the gentility of his wife).

7. Finley (1985, 93, with n. 19 on p. 123). Finley remarks that standard works on Greek family law accept such a concept and he asserts that there is "overwhelming evidence to the contrary." He had propounded and defended his view in the chapter "The Problem of the Unity of Greek Law" (1975). But that chapter is focused on particular rules; it does not try to penetrate to the assumptions and aims which gave rise to the rules. The view proposed here agrees with that of Wolff (1974, 6–7): the Greek cities differed in political organization, in laws and in their systems of courts, but there were "gemeinsame juristische Grundanschauungen" (common juristic basic outlooks).

8. *IG* I³, 104 = Meiggs and Lewis 1969, no. 86, ll. 13–16, 20–21; [Dem.] 43.57.

9. Gaius 1.48–49, 142–43: all persons are either *sui iuris* or *alieno iuri subiectae*. If they are *alieno iuri subiectae*, they are either *in potestate* or *in manu* or *in mancipio*. If they are neither *in potestate* nor *in manu* nor *in mancipio*, they are either under *tutela* or under *curatio* or under neither.

10. Liv. 3.31.8–3.33.5; Dion. Hal. *Antiq. Rom.* 10.51.5–10.52.4, 10.54.3, 10.55.5, 10.57.5. A point of similarity between Rome and Gortyn may deserve notice. The laws of Gortyn begin with a rule about procedure, that one must not seize a person before trial. The Twelve Tables probably began also with a rule about procedure: "si in ius vocat, ito" (if he summons him to court, let him go). Both rules discourage an aggrieved person from having recourse to self-help and encourage him to take his complaint to court; the Gortynian rule does this directly, the Roman rule pursues the same aim by requiring the defendant to respond to the aggrieved person's summons.

GLOSSARY

Athenian Legal Terms

anchisteis: kinsmen. Athenian law recognized kinship as far as cousins and children of cousins.

archon: The nine archons were annual officers. Their entry into office about the middle of summer marked the beginning of the year. One of them had the generic term "archon" as his sole title; he is sometimes called "the eponymous archon," since his name was used to specify the year. Another had the title of *basileus* ("king") and a third had that of polemarch. The other six were called *thesmothetai*. A tenth officer, called "the secretary of the *thesmothetai*," was associated as a colleague with the other nine, probably in consequence of the reforms of Kleisthenes shortly before 500; but the collective designation continued to be "the nine archons." From 487 they were chosen by sortition. Each of them received lawsuits of a defined type and conducted a preliminary hearing; then he brought the parties before a panel of *dikastai* (q.v.).

atimia: loss of civic rights. This was imposed on Athenian citizens as a penalty for some offenses. Originally it amounted to outlawry. Its effect in the classical period is obscure and disputed; in some cases it was formidable enough to make the convicted man withdraw into exile.

deme: The reforms of Kleisthenes divided Attica into 139 territorial units, called "demes" (*dēmoi*). Some of these may have originated as natural villages; the reforms extended the division through the whole territory, including the town of Athens. At the time of the reforms each adult male citizen was registered in the deme where he resided; for the future membership was hereditary in the male line. Each deme kept a list of its members, and these constituted an assembly of the demesmen.

dikastēs: judge. The Athenians kept and revised annually a list of 6,000 male citizens available to serve as *dikastai*; they had to be at least thirty years old and they had to swear an oath. Each court (*dikastērion*) consisted of a panel of *dikastai*. The standard sizes of the panels were 201, 401, and 501; the size of the panel depended on the importance of the case. The panel heard the speeches of the two parties and decided the issue by vote of a majority without deliberating. The translation "juror," "jury" is often favored but can mislead, since Athenian procedure did not distinguish between question of law and question of fact.

eisphora: the tax on property, levied for military and naval expeditions. In 378/77 the property of the citizens was assessed and the total was found to be 5,750 talents. Henceforth, when the assembly ordered a levy of the tax, it stated the desired amount as a proportion of the total. Probably in 378/77 those liable to pay the tax, that is, owners of property, were organized into one hundred *symmoriai* or "contribution groups." Probably at the same time the richest members of each symmory were made liable for the *proeisphora*; that is, they had to pay in advance the sum due from their symmory and could then recoup themselves from its other members.

ekdosis: transfer of a bride from her original family to the house of the bridegroom. This normally followed after *engyēsis* (q.v.).

Eleven, the: officers in charge of the prison and of execution.

engyēsis: "pledge," an oral contract, whereby a woman's father or brother or the other male head of her original family promised her in marriage to a prospective husband.

epidikasia: adjudication by the archon, assigning an *epiklēros* (q.v.) in marriage.

epiklēros: "heiress" or female orphan. A woman whose father and brothers had died was said to be *epiklēros* and was assigned in marriage with the inheritance to her nearest male relative, so that she could bear heirs to the property of her deceased father.

genos: "clan," a group of people who claimed descent from a common ancestor, real or fictitious, and practiced a common cult.

gnēsios: "legitimate," of children. See *nothos*.

himatia kai chrysia: literally "clothes and gold objects." This is the stock phrase for the personal possessions (paraphernalia) of a married woman as distinct from her dowry; they could include things other than clothes and gold jewelry.

kyrios: guardian, master, administrator. A woman required a male *kyrios* at all times. Before marriage her *kyrios* was her father, brother, or other relative; during marriage her husband was her *kyrios*; after his death her adult son or son-in-law could be her *kyrios*. The same word could be used for the administrator of property lent to him under a contract and for the guardian of an orphaned minor.

liturgy: a fiscal burden. From the earliest times rich citizens had paid the expenses of public activities out of their private fortunes and had thereby earned popularity. By the fourth century *leitourgiai* were of two kinds. (1) The military liturgies. These were the trierarchy (q.v.) and the *proeisphora* (see *eisphora*). These were expensive and men often had to be compelled to undertake them. (2) The agonistic liturgies. These were the expenses of equipping choruses or teams to compete in festivals. They were less expensive, and volunteers may often have sufficed.

metic: *metoikos*, an alien resident in Athens. Metics were free but did not have Athenian citizenship. They were of two kinds: (1) people of foreign descent who settled in Attica, and (2) former slaves manumitted by Athenian owners.

moichos, moicheia: adulterer, adultery. Probably the offense consisted in intercourse with a married woman by a man other than her husband. An alternative theory would extend the offense to intercourse with any free and female member of a citizen's household, but this theory cannot be substantiated.

nothos: "illegitimate," of children. The criterion of (il)legitimacy in Athens is not fully clear.

pallakē: concubine.

phratry: The *phratria* may have originated as a group of dependents who attached themselves to a powerful family (*genos*, q.v.) for protection. In classical Athens phratries were numerous, although their number cannot be estimated. Probably every male citizen belonged to a phratry. The religious activities of the phratry had social significance for the marriages of its members and for recognizing their children.

phylē: From the earliest times Athenian citizens were divided into four *phylai* with hereditary membership. The reforms of Kleisthenes divided them afresh into ten *phylai*, assigning some demes to each on a complex pattern. The *phylē* in a Greek city played much the same part as the *tribus* in Rome, and therefore the word is often translated as "tribe," but the associations of the English word are different.

polemarch: See "archon."

proeisphora: See *eisphora*.

proix: dowry. This was an amount of money or of valuables on which a monetary value was stated. At marriage it was transferred from the original family of the bride to her husband. It was intended for her support.

symmory: contribution group. Probably in 378/77 owners of property were grouped in one hundred *symmoriai* for the purpose of paying the *eisphora* (q.v.). In 357 the burden of the trierarchy (q.v.) was assigned to the 1,200 richest men, and these were grouped in twenty *symmoriai* for that purpose. The contribution groups for the trierarchy were probably a separate system, distinct from the contribution groups for the *eisphora*.

thesmothetai: See "archon."

trierarchy: one of the military liturgies (see "liturgy"). Originally the trierarch equipped a trireme and served as its captain. In the fourth century the trierarch still sailed with his ship, but his essential tasks were the financial ones of getting together a crew, making the ship ready for sailing, and providing for its maintenance and repair.

Monetary Units

In Greek cities the units were the following:

> 1 talent = 60 minai = 6,000 drachmas
> 1 mina = 100 drachmas
> 1 drachma = 6 obols.

A Note on Translations

For the information provided by the Athenian orators on private law attention is drawn to the following volumes in the series called The Loeb Classical Library:

Lysias, translated by W. R. M. Lamb.
Isaeus, translated by E. S. Forster.
Demosthenes, 7 vols., translated by J. H. Vince, A. T. Murray, and others.
Minor Attic Orators, vol. 1, translated by K. J. Maidment, consists of the speeches of Antiphon and Andokides.

Law often employs concepts peculiar to the society where it operates. There can be no satisfactory translation, for example, of *epiklēros* or even *dikastēs*. Translators may have recourse to words which are makeshifts, and different translators choose different words for the same term. *Phratria*, for example, appears sometimes as "ward" (Forster) and sometimes as "clan" (Murray). The Loeb volumes, providing text and translation on opposite pages, give the reader a chance to make sure what the translator means.

BIBLIOGRAPHY

The abbreviations employed for the names and works of ancient authors are customary or easy to recognize. The same applies to standard works of reference, including the *Realencyclopädie der klassischen Altertumswissenschaft*, begun by Pauly, and Jacoby's *Fragmente der griechischen Historiker*. The abbreviations employed for titles of journals conform to *L'Année Philologique*.

Adams, C. D. 1917. "Demosthenes' Avoidance of Breves." *CP* 12:271–94.

Adkins, A. W. H. 1982. "Values, Goals, and Emotions." *CP* 77:292–326.

Allen, T. W. 1924. *Homer: The Origins and the Transmission*. Oxford.

Amory, A. 1966. "The Gates of Horn and Ivory. *YCS* 20:1–57.

Andrewes, A. 1961a. "Philochoros on Phratries." *JHS* 81:1–15.

———. 1961b. "Phratries in Homer." *Hermes* 89:129–40.

Austin, N. 1975. *Archery at the Dark of the Moon: Poetic Problems in Homer's Odyssey*. Berkeley and Los Angeles.

Beasley, T. W. 1906. "The *kyrios* in Greek States Other than Athens." *CR* 20:249–53.

Beloch, K. J. 1886. *Die Bevölkerung der griechisch-römishen Welt*. Leipzig.

Beye, C. R. 1974. "Male and Female in the Homeric Poems." *Ramus* 3(2):87–101.

Bicknell, P. J. 1982. "Axiochos Alkibiadou, Aspasia and Aspasios." *AC* 51:240–50.

Blass, F. 1887–93. *Die attische Beredsamkeit*. 3 vols. Leipzig.

Bourriot, F. 1976. *Recherches sur la nature du génos: étude d'histoire sociale athénienne—périodes archaïque et classique*. Lille.

Cameron, A., and A. Kuhrt. 1983. *Images of Women in Antiquity*. London and Canberra.

Cantarella, E. 1987. *Pandora's Daughters: The Role and Status of Women in Greek and Roman Antiquity*. Baltimore.

Carpenter, R. 1946. *Folk Tale, Fiction and Saga in the Homeric Epics*. Berkeley and Los Angeles.

Cartledge, P. 1981. "Spartan Women: Liberation or Licence." *CQ*, n.s. 31:84–105.

Chambers, M. *See* Day, J.

Chantraine, P. 1948. *Grammaire homérique*. Vol. 1, *Phonétique et morphologie*. Paris.

Cohen, D. 1984. "The Athenian Law of Adultery." *RIDA*, ser. 3, 31:147–65.

Cook, J. M. 1973. *The Troad*. Oxford.

Davies, J. K. 1971. *Athenian Propertied Families*. Oxford.

————. 1981. *Wealth and the Power of Wealth in Classical Athens*. New York.

Davison, J. A. 1958. "Notes on the Panathenaea." *JHS* 78:23–42.

Day, J., and M. Chambers. 1962. *Aristotle's History of Athenian Democracy*. Berkeley and Los Angeles.

de Ste. Croix, G. E. M. *See* Ste. Croix, G. E. M. de.

Devereux, G. 1957. "Penelope's Character." *Psychoanalytic Quarterly* 26:378–86.

Dihle, A. 1970. *Homer-Probleme*. Opladen.

Dittenberger, W. 1863. *De ephebis atticis*. Göttingen.

Dixon, S. 1988. *The Roman Mother*. Norman, Okla.

Dodds, E. R. 1951. *The Greeks and the Irrational*. Berkeley and Los Angeles.

Dover, K. J. 1978. *Greek Homosexuality*. London.

Drerup, E. 1898. "Über die bei den attischen Rednern eingelegten Urkunden." *Jahrbücher für classische Philologie*, Supplementband 24:221–366.

Farron, S. 1979. "The Portrayal of Women in the *Iliad*." *Acta Classica* 22:15–31.

Finley, M. I. 1955. "Marriage, Sale and Gift in the Homeric World." *RIDA*, ser. 3, 2:167–94. Reprinted in Finley, *Economy and Society in Ancient Greece*, edited by R. P. Saller and B. D. Shaw, 233–45. London 1981.

————. 1975. *The Use and Abuse of History*. London.

————. 1985. *Ancient History: Evidence and Models*. London.

Fraenkel, E. 1950. *Aeschylus: Agamemnon*. 3 vols. Oxford.

Fränkel, M. 1878. "Der attische Heliasteneid." *Hermes* 13:452–66.

Gagarin, M. 1984. "The Testimony of Witnesses in the Gortyn Laws." *GRBS* 25:345–49.

————. 1986. *Early Greek Law*. Berkeley and Los Angeles.

————. 1987. Review of Heitsch 1984. *Göttingische Gelehrte Anzeigen* 239:56–66.

Gardner, J. F. 1986. *Women in Roman Law and Society*. Bloomington, Ind.

Geddes, A. G. 1984. "Who's Who in Homeric Society?" *CQ*, n.s. 34:17–36.

Gernet, L. 1955. *Droit et société dans la Grèce ancienne*. Paris.

Golden, M. 1979. "Demosthenes and the Age of Majority at Athens." *Phoenix* 33:25–38.

———. 1985. " 'Donatus' and Athenian Phratries." *CQ*, n.s. 35:9–13.

———. 1986. "Names and Naming at Athens: Three Studies." *EMC*, n.s. 5:245–69.

Gomme, A. W. 1925. "The Position of Women in Athens in the Fifth and Fourth Centuries B.C." *CP* 20:1–25. Reprinted in Gomme, *Essays in Greek History and Literature*, 89–115. Oxford 1937.

Gould, J. P. 1980. "Law, Custom and Myth: Aspects of the Social Position of Women in Classical Athens." *JHS* 100:38–59.

Gray, D. H. F. 1954. "Metal-Working in Homer." *JHS* 74:1–15.

Guarducci, M. 1938. "Intorno alle vicende e all'età della grande iscrizione di Gortina." *RFIC*, n.s. 16:264–73.

Habicht, C. 1961. "Falsche Urkunden zur Geschichte Athens im Zeitalter der Perserkriege." *Hermes* 89:1–35.

Hainsworth, J. B. *See* Heubeck, A.

Hansen, M. H. 1985. *Demography and Democracy: The Number of Athenian Citizens in the Fourth Century B.C.* Gjellerup.

Harrison, A. R. W. 1968. *The Law of Athens*. Vol. 1, *The Family and Property*. Oxford.

Heitsch, E. 1984. *Antiphon aus Rhamnus*. Akademie der Wissenschaften und der Literatur, Mainz, Abhandlungen der Geistes- und Sozialwissenschaftlichen Klasse, 3.

Heubeck, A., S. West, and J. B. Hainsworth. 1988. *A Commentary on Homer's Odyssey*. Vol. 1. Oxford.

Humphreys, S. C. 1974. "The *nothoi* of Kynosarges." *JHS* 94:88–95.

Jacoby, F. 1941. "The Date of Archilochos." *CQ* 35:97–109.

Janko, R. 1982. *Homer, Hesiod and the Hymns*. Cambridge.

Jones, A. H. M. 1957. *Athenian Democracy*. Oxford.

Kästner, E. 1969. *Der Zauberlehrling*. Zurich.

Keuls, E. C. 1985. *The Reign of the Phallus: Sexual Politics in Ancient Athens*. New York.

Korfmann, M. 1986. "Troy: Topography and Navigation." In *Troy and the Trojan War*, edited by M. J. Mellink, 1–16. Bryn Mawr.

Kränzlein, A. 1963. *Eigentum und Besitz im griechischen Recht des fünften und vierten Jahrhunderts v. Chr.* Berlin.

Lacey, W. K. 1966. "Homeric *hedna* and Penelope's *kyrios*." *JHS* 86:55–68.

———. 1968. *The Family in Classical Greece*. London.

Ledl, A. 1907. "Das attische Bürgerrecht und die Frauen, I." *WS* 29:173–96.

Lefkowitz, M. R. 1983. "Influential Women." In Cameron and Kuhrt 1983, 49–64. Reprinted in Lefkowitz 1986, 80–94.

———. 1986. *Women in Greek Myth.* Baltimore.

———. 1987. "The Heroic Women of Greek Epic." *American Scholar* 56:503–18.

Lewis, D. *See* Meiggs, R.

Lipsius, J. H. 1905–15. *Das attische Recht und Rechtsverfahren.* 3 vols. Leipzig.

Lloyd-Jones, H. 1981. "Remarks on the Homeric Question." In *History and Imagination: Essays in Honour of H. R. Trevor-Roper,* edited by H. Lloyd-Jones, V. Pearl, and B. Worden, 15–29. London.

———. 1983a. "Artemis and Iphigeneia." *JHS* 103:87–102.

———. 1983b. *The Justice of Zeus.* 2d ed. Berkeley and Los Angeles.

Long, A. A. 1970. "Morals and Values in Homer." *JHS* 90:121–39.

Lord, A. B. 1953. "Homer's Originality: Oral Dictated Texts." *TAPhA* 84:124–34.

Lorimer, H. L. 1950. *Homer and the Monuments.* London.

McDonnell, M. 1983. "Divorce Initiated by Women in Rome: The Evidence of Plautus." *AJAH* 8:54–80.

MacDowell, D. M. 1986a. "The Law of Periandros about Symmories." *CQ,* n.s. 36:438–49.

———. 1986b. *Spartan Law.* Edinburgh.

Maine, H. S. 1894. *Ancient Law.* 15th ed. London.

Meiggs, R., and D. Lewis. 1969. *A Selection of Greek Historical Inscriptions.* Oxford.

Merkelbach, R. 1952. "Die pisistratische Redaktion der homerischen Gedichte." *RM,* n.s. 95:23–47.

———, and E. Varinlioğlu. 1985. "Die Einwohnerzahl von Keramos." *ZPE* 59:264.

Meyer-Laurin, H. 1969. Review of Willetts 1967. *Gnomon* 41:160–65.

Morris, I. 1986. "The Use and Abuse of Homer." *CA* 5:81–138.

Murray, G. 1924. *The Rise of the Greek Epic.* 2d ed. Oxford.

Nauck, A. 1848. *Aristophanis Byzantii grammatici Alexandrini fragmenta.* Halle.

Nicholas, B. 1962. *An Introduction to Roman Law.* Oxford.

Nörr, D. 1961. "Die Evangelien des Neuen Testaments und die sogenannte hellenistische Rechtskoine." *ZSR* 78:92–141.

Page, D. L. 1938. *Euripides' Medea.* Oxford.

Paoli, M. E. 1950. "Il reato di adulterio (*moicheia*) in diritto attica." *Studia et documenta historiae et iuris* 16:123–82.

Parry, A. 1966. "Have We Homer's *Iliad*?" *YCS* 20:175–216.

Parry, M. 1928. *L'épithète traditionnelle dans Homère.* Paris.

———. 1971. *The Making of Homeric Verse.* Oxford.

Patterson, C. 1981. *Pericles' Citizenship Law of 451–50 B.C.* New York.

Pélékidis, C. 1962. *Histoire de l'éphébie attique des origines à 31 avant Jésus-Christ.* Paris.

Pomeroy, S. B. 1982. "Charities for Greek Women." *Mnemosyne* 35:115–35.

Redfield, J. 1977–78. "The Women of Sparta." *CJ* 73:146–61.

Reynolds, L. D., and N. G. Wilson. 1968. *Scribes and Scholars.* Oxford.

Rhodes, P. J. 1980. "Ephebi, Bouleutae and the Population of Athens." *ZPE* 38:191–202.

———. 1982. "Problems in Athenian *eisphora* and Liturgies." *AJAH* 7:1–19.

Riccobono, S. 1941. *Fontes iuris Romani antejustiniani.* Vol. 1. Florence.

Roussel, D. 1976. *Tribu et cité.* Paris.

Rudhardt, J. 1962. "La reconnaissance de la paternité, sa nature et sa portée dans la société athénienne." *MH* 19:39–64.

Ruschenbusch, E. 1957. "*Dikastērion pantōn kyrion.*" *Historia* 6:257–74.

———. 1960. "*Phonos:* zum Recht Drakons und seiner Bedeutung für das Werden des athenischen Staats." *Historia* 9:129–54.

———. 1962. "*Diatithesthai ta heautou:* ein Beitrag zum sogenannten Testamentsgesetz des Solon." *ZSR* 79:307–11.

———. 1979. *Athenische Innenpolitik im 5. Jahrhundert v. Chr.* Bamberg.

———. 1982. "Der Ursprung des gerichtlichen Rechtsstreits bei den Griechen." In *Symposion 1977,* edited by J. Modrzejewski and D. Leibs, 1–8. Cologne and Vienna.

———. 1983a. "Das Machtpotential der Bündner im ersten athenischen Seebund." *ZPE* 53:144–48.

———. 1983b. "Tribut und Bürgerzahl im ersten athenischen Seebund." *ZPE* 53:125–43.

———. 1984a. "Modell Amorgos." In *Aux origines de l'hellénisme: la Crète et la Grèce: hommage à H. van Effenterre,* 265–69. Paris.

———. 1984b. "Zum letzten Mal: die Bürgerzahl Athens im 4. Jh. v. Chr." *ZPE* 54:253–69.

———. 1985. "Die Zahl der griechischen Staaten und Arealgrösse und Bürgerzahl der 'Normalpolis.'" *ZPE* 59:253–63.

Ste. Croix, G. E. M. de. 1953. "Demosthenes' *TIMHMA* and the Athenian *eisphora.*" *C et M* 14:30–70.

———. 1970. "Some Observations on the Property Rights of Athenian Women." *CR,* n.s. 20:273–78.

Schaps, D. M. 1979. *Economic Rights of Women in Ancient Greece.* Edinburgh.

Schuller, W. 1985. *Frauen in der griechischen Geschichte.* Constance.

Scullard, H. H. 1935. *A History of the Roman World from 753 to 146 B.C.* London.

Sealey, R. 1983. "How Citizenship and the City Began in Athens." *AJAH* 8:97–129.
———. 1984a. "On Lawful Concubinage in Athens." *CA* 3:111–33.
———. 1984b. "The *Tetralogies* Ascribed to Antiphon." *TAPhA* 114:71–85.
———. 1987. *The Athenian Republic*. University Park, Pa., and London.
Shaw, M. 1975. "The Female Intruder: Women in Fifth-Century Drama." *CP* 70:255–66.
Snodgrass, A. M. 1974. "An Historical Homeric Society?" *JHS* 94:114–25.
Starr, C. G. 1978. "An Evening with the Flute-Girls." *PP* 183:401–10.
Van Bremen, R. 1983. "Women and Wealth." In Cameron and Kuhrt 1983, 223–42.
Van Nortwick, T. 1979. "Penelope and Nausicaa." *TAPhA* 109:269–76.
van Thiel, H. 1977. "Konkurrierende Varianten in der Ilias." *MH* 34:81–98.
———. 1979. "Telemachie und Odyssee." *MH* 36:65–89.
———. 1982. *Iliaden und Ilias*. Basel and Stuttgart.
Varinlioğlu, E. *See* Merkelbach, R.
Vermeule, E. 1979. *Aspects of Death in Early Greek Art and Poetry.* Berkeley and Los Angeles.
Vogel, F. 1923. "Die Kürzenmeidung in der griechischen Prosa." *Hermes* 58:77–108.
von Fritz, K. 1943. "*Noos* and *noein* in the Homeric Poems." *CP* 38:79–93.
von Wilamowitz-Moellendorff, U. 1922. *Pindaros*. Berlin.
Watson, A. 1967. *The Law of Persons in the Later Roman Republic.* Oxford.
West, S. *See* Heubeck, A.
Whitehead, D. 1977. *The Ideology of the Athenian Metic.* Cambridge Philological Society, Supplementary volume 4.
———. 1986. "Women and Naturalisation in Fourth-Century Athens: The Case of Archippe." *CQ*, n.s. 36:109–14.
Wiedemann, T. E. J. 1983. "*Elachiston . . . en tois arsesi kleos*: Thucydides, Women, and the Limits of Rational Analysis." *G&R*, ser. 2, 30:163–70.
Willetts, R. F. 1955. *Aristocratic Society in Ancient Crete.* London.
———. 1964–65. "Observations on Leg. Gort. II.16–20." *Kadmos* 3:170–76.
———. 1967. *The Law Code of Gortyn*. Kadmos Supplement 1. Berlin.
Williams, D. 1983. "Women on Athenian Vases: Problems of Interpretation." In Cameron and Kuhrt 1983, 92–106.
Wilson, N. G. *See* Reynolds, L. D.
Wittfogel, K. A. 1981. *Oriental Despotism*. New ed. New York.
Wolff, H. J. 1944. "Marriage Law and Family Organization in Ancient Athens: A Study in the Interrelation of Public and Private Law in the Greek City." *Traditio* 2:43–95.

———. 1946. "The Origin of Judicial Litigation among the Greeks." *Traditio* 4:31–87.

———. 1951. *Roman Law: An Historical Introduction*. Norman, Okla.

———. 1957. "Proix." *RE* 23(1):133–70.

———. 1964. Review of Kränzlein 1963. *ZSR* 81:333–40.

———. 1966. *Die attische Paragraphe*. Weimar.

———. 1973. "Hellenistisches Privatrecht." *ZSR* 90:63–90.

———. 1974. *Opuscula dispersa*. Amsterdam.

INDEX